THE INDIAN MUTINY AND THE BRITISH IMAGINATION

Gautam Chakravarty explores representations of the event which has become known in the British imagination as the 'Indian Mutiny' of 1857 in British popular fiction and historiography. Drawing on a wide range of primary sources including diaries, autobiographies and state papers, Chakravarty shows how narratives of the rebellion were inflected by the concerns of colonial policy and by the demands of imperial self-image. He goes on to discuss the wider context of British involvement in India from 1765 to the 1940s, and engages with constitutional debates, administrative measures and the early nineteenth-century Anglo-Indian novel. Chakravarty approaches the Mutiny from the perspectives of postcolonial theory as well as from historical and literary perspectives to show the extent to which the insurrection took hold of the popular imagination in both Britain and India. The book has a broad interdisciplinary appeal and will be of interest to scholars of English literature, British imperial history, modern Indian history and cultural studies.

GAUTAM CHAKRAVARTY is Reader in the Department of English at the University of Delhi. He is the translator of *Jibananananda Das, Short Fiction, 1931–1933* (2001), and has recently translated *Kapalakundala* by Bankim Chandra Chatterjee (2003).

CAMBRIDGE STUDIES IN NINETEENTH-CENTURY LITERATURE AND CULTURE

General editor
Gillian Beer, *University of Cambridge*

Editorial board
Isobel Armstrong, *Birkbeck College, London*
Leonore Davidoff, *University of Essex*
Terry Eagleton, *University of Manchester*
Catherine Gallagher, *University of California, Berkeley*
D. A. Miller, *Columbia University*
J. Hillis Miller, *University of California, Irvine*
Mary Poovey, *New York University*
Elaine Showalter, *Princeton University*

Nineteenth-century British literature and culture have been rich fields for interdisciplinary studies. Since the turn of the twentieth century, scholars and critics have tracked the intersections and tensions between Victorian literature and the visual arts, social organisation, economic life, technical innovations, scientific thought – in short, culture in its broadest sense. In recent years, theoretical challenges and historiographical shifts have unsettled the assumptions of previous scholarly synthesis and called into question the terms of older debates. Whereas the tendency in much past literary critical interpretation was to use the metaphor of culture as 'background', feminist, Foucauldian and other analyses have employed more dynamic models that raise questions of power and of circulation. Such developments and have reanimated the field.

This series aims to accommodate and promote the most interesting work being undertaken on the frontiers of the field of nineteenth-century literary studies: work which intersects fruitfully with other fields of study such as history, or literary theory, or the history of science. Comparative as well as interdisciplinary approaches are welcomed.

A complete list of titles published will be found at the end of the book.

THE INDIAN MUTINY AND
THE BRITISH IMAGINATION

GAUTAM CHAKRAVARTY

CAMBRIDGE
UNIVERSITY PRESS

CAMBRIDGE UNIVERSITY PRESS
Cambridge, New York, Melbourne, Madrid, Cape Town, Singapore, São Paulo

Cambridge University Press
The Edinburgh Building, Cambridge CB2 8RU, UK

Published in the United States of America by Cambridge University Press, New York

www.cambridge.org
Information on this title: www.cambridge.org/9780521832748

First published 2005
Reprinted 2005

A catalogue record for this publication is available from the British Library

ISBN 978-0-521-83274-8 hardback

Transferred to digital printing 2007

Contents

Acknowledgements

This book began as a Ph.D. thesis, and I should start by thanking the Trustees of the Inlaks Foundation for a generous scholarship, Kirori Mal College, University of Delhi for granting a timely study leave, and Churchill College, Cambridge for funding my third year in residence, and for a handsome Arts Bursary in the tenth term.

I should also thank G. K. Das of the University of Delhi, who provided the first nudge into an area that took clearer shape as I worked with my supervisors, John Lennard of Trinity Hall, Cambridge, and Nigel Leask of Queen's College, Cambridge. I am especially grateful to John for closely reading the chapters at several stages, and for pointing out errors of style and substance. Chris Bayly of St. Catharine's College read parts of the work while it was still a thesis, and I have profited as much from his fine books as from his conversation, his knowledge of modern Indian history, and his familiarity with sources. Tim Cribb, Basudev Chatterjee, Douglas Peers, Tom Metcalf, Michael Fisher, and my Ph.D. examiner, Bart Moore-Gilbert, read parts of the book at later stages, and their comments and insights were most useful. I must also thank the two anonymous readers for encouragement and suggestions, and the editors and staff at Cambridge University Press for their patience.

Neil, Jaydeep, Anne, Maria, Desmond, Paul, Naoko, Isabel, Suman, Cheng, Gordon, and Mrs. Baxter will know why their names are here, as will Charles and his wife at the Devonshire Arms. My parents were as ever a source of quiet support and inspiration, and Nikita, who went over this many times with her careful eye, is now waiting to see the book in print.

GAUTAM CHAKRAVARTY
New Delhi
2003

Glossary

baboo/babu: a Hindu gentleman; but a disparaging Anglo-Indian term for English-educated Indians, especially Bengali clerks

banjara: a nomadic tribe of artisans, peddlers and performers

bahadur: lit., brave

begum: a lady of rank, or wife

Benares: the British spelling for Banaras or Varanasi

bhang: a variety of cannabis

bibi: Persian-Urdu term for lady; but Anglo-Indian argot for the Indian wife or mistress of a British male in India

budmashees or, budmash: a criminal or one with a criminal record

Camdeo or, Kamadeva: the god of love in Hindu mythology

Cawnpore: the British spelling for Kanpur

Collector: the chief administrator of a district under British rule

Company Bahadur: popular Indian name for the East India Company

dacaiti/dacoity/dacoitee: armed robbery by a gang of five or more men

Delhi Ridge: a wooded spur north of the city wall; the British were camped on the Ridge during the siege of Delhi

diwani: here, the post of minister, or steward; but also, council chamber and reception hall; also, the collected works of a poet

durbar: the royal or imperial court

fakir: a Muslim mendicant

farman/firman: an order, edict, royal charter

Feringhee/Firangi: a Hindustani term for Europeans

Futtehghur: the British spelling for Fatehgarh

ghat: landing stage, wharf or riverbank

gosain: a Hindu mendicant order; also a Brahmin sub-caste

Governor-General: the chief administrator of the East India Company's Indian territories; renamed Viceroy after the Crown takeover in 1858

griffin: the Anglo-Indian argot for a newly arrived British subaltern in India

haveli: an Indian-style house, usually single-storeyed with rooms arranged around a central courtyard

Hindostanis/Hindustanis: the people of Hindustan, including Hindus and Muslims

jehad/jihad: the religious duty to defend and proselytise Islam

Jahanpanah: lit., 'shelter of the world': a honorific for the Mughal Emperor

khansaman: lit., the keeper of stores: chief steward or butler

khidmatgar: a waiter; male domestic servant under the *khansaman* (q.v.)

khufia: of or pertaining to secret or criminal intelligence; an intelligence agent or police informer

Lal Quila: lit., 'the red fortress'; the popular name for the red sandstone Mughal city-palace at Delhi

Mahatma: 'great soul'; the honorific of M. K. Gandhi

Mahratta: another spelling for Maratha

memsahib: an Indian word for a white woman

moffusil: the district and other provincial towns as distinct from the presidency towns

mujahid: an Islamic religious warrior

munshi: a clerk or administrative officer

Mullah/Maulavi/Maulvi: Islamic clergyman

nabob: the Anglo-Indian argot for an East India Company clerk, official or private trader who had made a fortune in India

nawab: the pl. of *Naib* or deputy; the title of provincial governors in the late Mughal administration, though under British rule it came sometimes to mean independent rulers

newab wazir/nawab wazir: the governor and minister of finance, or principal minister

Oude/Oudh: the British spelling for Awadh

Plassey: the British spelling for Palasi or Palashi, where the East India Company defeated the Nawab of Bengal in 1757

peshwa/peishwa: the chief minister of the Maratha kingdom; later the ruler of an independent Maratha state.

pindari: the roving bands of plunderers in central and western India in the late eighteenth and early nineteenth centuries. The *pindaris* were unemployed soldiers and mercenaries hired by Indian states against each other.

Raj: the term for the British government of India after 1858

Resident: the British agent stationed in an Indian court, and the instrument of 'indirect rule'

Rohilcund: British spelling for Rohilkhand, a region near Delhi

sadar adalat: the chief civil court of a province or presidency

sarai: inn

sati: the Hindu practice of cremating widows with their dead husbands; also, a virtuous wife

sawar/sowar: a cavalryman

seth: Hindu banker or merchant

sipahi or sepoy: a trooper, usually an infantryman

sharif: pl. of *ashraf* or the Mughal service class; the culture of this class

swadeshi: lit., produced in one's own country; a nationalist agitation that began in 1905, calling for the boycott of British imports to India

subah: a province; political or administrative subdivision of the Mughal empire

subedar: sergeant major, or the senior most Indian officer in the army; also the governor of a *subah* (q.v.) in the Mughal administration

talukdar: a superior *zamindar* (q.v.) with proprietary rights in land who collected rent on behalf of the government from other landlords; after the rebellion, the *talukdars* of Awadh were given proprietary rights over the land whose rent they had earlier collected

thag/thug: a fraudster or highway robber; see *thagi* (q.v.)

thagi: a form of highway robbery in which victims were ritually murdered. Unlike *dacoits* (q.v.), *thags* usually disguised themselves as travellers to befriend the genuine travellers whom they robbed and murdered on the way; also known as *phansigar*, or strangler

tulwar: sword

vaishya: an intermediate Hindu trading caste

wahabi: a follower of Abu Wahab, the eighteenth-century Arab reformer

zamindar: under British rule, a holder of property rights in land who collected rent from tenants and paid revenue to the government

zenana: the women's quarter in a Muslim household

Introduction

In 'The Indian Mutiny in Fiction', a review article that appeared in *Blackwood's Edinburgh Magazine* in 1897, Hilda Gregg made an observation that bears recall. At the start of her survey of recent novels on the subject Gregg noted that: 'Of all the great events of this century, as they are reflected in fiction, the Indian Mutiny has taken the firmest hold on the popular imagination.'[1] Gregg does not quite explain her meaning, but as this book hopes to show, the imagination that seized on the rebellion of 1857–9 was the vulgate of late-nineteenth century British expansionism. The literary yield of the rebellion, as indeed the event itself, loses much of its meaning when not read alongside the many foreign and colonial conflicts of the century which provided material for fiction: from the momentous Napoleonic wars through the cycle of warfare in India as in other colonial and para-colonial possessions from the mid-eighteenth century to the Crimean and the Boer Wars. Militarily, the nineteenth century was perhaps the busiest period in British history, laying the basic groundwork for the geo-political configurations which some have called the 'world-system', and for the legal and constitutional bases of sovereignty and intervention. The need to open markets, protect commercial interests, enforce tariffs, contain European and coerce extra-European powers continuously provided reasons for armed conflict. These recurring motives make it possible to reduce the many military engagements of nineteenth-century Britain into one Long War; prefiguring the next Long War – from the Berlin Conference of 1884 to the end of the Cold War – fought over a set of constitutional issues, a single conflict suppurating at different times and places, and driven, ultimately, by the aggrandising impulses of the classic nation state.[2]

But it would be impossible for a nation to engage in warfare for a century without a public culture that sanctioned war as the legitimate arm of state and commercial policy, and that viewed expansion as the expression of an inevitable national and racial urge with very real material dividends. This culture took distinct and successive forms through the century, with exponents ranging from liberals, conservatives, imperial federationists, free traders, evangelicals, the gentlemanly muscular Christians of Rugby–Oxford, the National Volunteer League, social Darwinists, Victorian race theorists, the Society for Propagation of Christian Knowledge, and even popular periodicals like the *Boys' Own Paper*. These together gave purpose to British-led colonial globalisation, and brought legitimacy to a vast, thriving military–industrial machinery, which policed the global beat and kept markets and frontiers in order. The machinery and its operation anticipates on most counts US-led neo-colonial globalisation of the twentieth century, where gaudy malls of goods and opportunity provide the façade for arsenals, deterrent deployments and the crony capitalism of client-states. But where nineteenth-century globalisation justified multiform violence through self-serving, self-congratulatory high talk about civilising and racial missions while expropriating subject peoples and denying them agency, the second wave, which began with the Cold War, has modified the ideological schema, using the heraldic devices of democracy and freedom to prop up the despotisms of the South. Humbug has been thumpingly profitable for two centuries now: the civilising mission created jobs and funnelled wealth home along with ornamental freebies like Indian diamonds and the Elgin marbles, while State Department platitudes on democracy fuel the squadrons that bomb ancient civilisations for oil and gas.

To be sure, the imperial idea had its enemies, and for much longer than A. P. Thornton's selection of dissenters suggests.[3] From the late eighteenth century, individuals, factions, loose bodies of intellectuals, and labour groups questioned the drive for territorial and commercial expansion, the wisdom of over-extending national resources and the morality of violating other forms of life and polities, even as they warned of the consequences of colonial expansion and militarism on British society and politics. But the history of dissent that dogged at nearly every step the Long War was, like the career of Edmund Burke, the Rockingham oligarch and early dissenter, that of a minority in perennial opposition. India, where it all began after the loss of America, was far too lucrative for Cabinets and MPs of all stripes, for East India Company directors, merchant lobbies, shareholders, as an unfailing source of private wealth, corporate profit, sinecures and preferment. The revival of party in the early nineteenth century, and the arrival of party government after 1832, changed British politics, government and civil society in some fundamental ways. But the Parliamentary Reform Act of 1832, which created a middle-class electorate, and the Reform and Redistribution Acts of 1867 and 1884–5, which extended the vote to working men, successively introduced new and large constituencies to the heady pleasures of national expansion. Significantly, the Reform of 1832 coincided with the arrival of a rationalised liberal-administrative state in India following the Charter Act of 1833, headed by a peer but run by a middle-class British bureaucracy: pious, hard-working, reformist and generally parochial and xenophobic. No less significantly, the franchise of 1884–5 coincided neatly with the Berlin Conference of 1884, which set off the European 'scramble for Africa', inaugurating a new phase of international avarice, with more urgent need for popular endorsement and participation than ever before. This reforged an imperial–national identity that rose above intra-British ethnicity, and that was sometimes stretched to include the settler colonies and America in an imagined 'greater Britain': militarist, philathletic, Christian, certain of a superiority that could be proved as much by social and anthropological applications of the Darwinian model of evolution as by their intellectual precursor, the hundred-year-old 'stage-theory' of the Scottish Enlightenment. The 'New' or 'High' imperialism of the 1880s and after was buoyed by the newly enfranchised working men, who quickly became the shock troops of national expansion and competitive imperialism. The pathology of jingoism that John Hobson diagnosed at the end of the century grew out of these developments, and part of the pathology was the 'popular imagination' that settled around the Indian rebellion as among the exemplary episodes of the Long War.[4]

If the literary yield of the rebellion surpasses in volume the literary representation of the other conflicts during the long nineteenth century of expansion, it is no less prominent in the history of Anglo-Indian letters. Measured against British writing on India from the late eighteenth century to decolonisation and after, the seventy-odd novels on the rebellion from 1859 to the present day show how more than any other event in the British career in India the rebellion was the single favourite subject for metropolitan and Anglo-Indian novelists. Initially circulated by the periodical press in India and in Britain, and soon the subject of histories, first-person accounts, official reports, polemical pamphlets, sermons, lectures, parliamentary debates, poetry and the stage, the rebellion acquired form, meaning and mythography that was most fully elaborated in a spate of popular adventure novels between the 1890s and the First War. The magnitude of the event and its consequences were often occasions for a good deal of astonished apostrophising by the earliest chroniclers and publicists, and by novelists, poets and reviewers. The reasons then adduced to explain the fascination with the rebellion, and faithfully reiterated through the first few decades of the twentieth century by a class of British writings, literary and historical, form an interesting constellation. The rebellion had threatened a territorial and commercial stake that grew into the centre-piece of British expansion following the loss of America. But unlike the American War of Independence, the rebellion and its much-debated causes underscored a model of radical conflict between cultures, civilisations and races; a conflict that at once justified conquest and dominion and proved the impossibility of assimilating and acculturating subject peoples. No less significant were the several thousand British casualties in the war the rebel militias launched. For, not only did the fatalities reveal the precariousness of British power, and the inherent difficulty of knowing and controlling the motions of the communities and polities of India, they were also a serious interruption of the habitual hierarchy of status and authority that structured British relations with India.

Yet, the many revivals of pre-British authority and government in north and central India did not converge into an organised resistance, nor did the rebel leaders in Delhi, Awadh, Kanpur, Jhansi or the numerous rebel garrisons in scattered towns have a plan for the future. By the start of the summer of 1858 the resistance grew attenuated, even as the restoration of the administrative machinery gave a moral annotation to the event in the British imagination. The suppression of the rebellion brought new legitimacy and sonority to the British in India, for the event was quickly configured in the idiom of Victorian medievalism and Christian heroism, while the fateful demonstration of superior technology was read as the unmistakable sign of an essential racial superiority. And to that extent, the Mutiny, as the rebellion came to be known, required a continuous commemoration from the faithful, an imperial thanksgiving never entirely without a trace of incredulity, and signifying always a caesural moment in the history of the Indian empire – replete with signs and wonders, as the pious Punjab evangelical Herbert Edwardes would have it – when all was nearly lost only to be regained once more, and when, more prosaically perhaps, the formal imperialism of the Crown and Parliament replaced a hundred years of the East India Company's expansion and rule.

At the end of her article, Hilda Gregg noted that '*the* novel of the Mutiny is still to be written'.[5] What she meant by that emphatic article is left unclear, but it is likely that in her view – and she too wrote a Mutiny novel, *The Keepers of the Gate* (1911), under the pseudonym 'S. C. Grier' – such a novel must retail the mythography of the victors, perhaps more tastefully than its predecessors had done. At any rate, a hundred years after Gregg it seems unlikely that such a novel will ever be written. Occasional novels on the subject have appeared in each decade after the political independence of

India, but with the end of empire and its inner circuitry of myths, memories and meanings, its statuary of heroes and villains, such novels amount to little more than ironic coda or naive nostalgia.

Precisely for that reason the present study begins with a short novel by Charles Dickens and Wilkie Collins, which appeared in the Christmas 1857 issue of *Household Words*, and ends in 1947, when the transfer of power was the immediate provocation of C. Lestock Reid's bellicose novel, *Masque of the Mutiny*. While Dickens and Collins wrote an allegory of the rebellion set in Central America, the first novel to treat the subject directly was *The Wife and the Ward; or, a Life's Error* (1859) by Edward Money. In the following ten years there were only two novels, of which H. P. Malet's *Lost Links in the Indian Mutiny* (1867), a diffuse romance with a large cast of Indian characters, meanders from the Company's military campaigns against the Afghans and the Sikhs to the rebellion. *First Love and Last Love* (1868) by James Grant was the first three-decker Mutiny novel by an author who, before turning his hand to India, had written military-historical novels such as *The Romance of War; or, the Highlanders in Spain* (1846–7).[6] Set in Delhi, the resurgent Mughal capital, the novel represents life in the rebel-held city, and in the British encampment beyond the city walls. Unlike *The Wife and the Ward*, which was confined to the Anglo-Indian life, these are the first novels to represent the rebel world in some detail; a development possibly encouraged by the forensic investigations of the colonial state in the years after the rebellion, and which adumbrates the future interests of the Mutiny novel.

The number goes up to four in the next decade, and of these the most significant novels were the three-deckers: *Seeta* (1872) by Phillip Meadows Taylor, *The Afghan Knife* (1879) by Robert A. Sterndale and *The Dilemma* (1876) by George Chesney. Taylor, who began as a police officer in the kingdom of Hyderabad, was the author of the *Confessions of a Thug* (1839), and his Mutiny novel was the third of a historical trilogy based on centenary episodes from Indian history.[7] In *Seeta*, Taylor brought his interest in Indian criminology to bear upon the rebellion, and the villain of the piece, Azrael Pande, is a former *thag* and robber turned rebel leader. The plot of the rebellion is, however, subordinate to another interest, the love and marriage of a British civil servant with the Brahmin widow, Seeta.

Echoing a current debate between W. W. Hunter and Sir Syed Ahmad Khan on the religious duty or otherwise of Muslims to revolt against a non-Islamic government, over the wahabi movement of Islamic reform, and the Frontier conflicts on the north-west in the early 1870s, Sterndale's novel, *The Afghan Knife*, represents Islam as the prime mover of the rebellion and, with a nod to the Great Game, suggests the involvement of Czarist Russia in the rebel plot. George Chesney, formerly of the Bengal Engineers regiment and wounded during the assault on Delhi in 1857, returned to England in 1867, and turned his attention to warcraft and army reform. His first novel was *The Battle of Dorking* (1871), a sensational fantasy of a German invasion of Britain that was perhaps a model for H. G. Wells's invasion fantasy, *The War of the Worlds* (1896). Chesney's first Indian novel was *The True Reformer* (1874), set in Shimla and London, where the hero, after making a fortune in India, leaves for England to become an MP and a champion of army reform. *The Dilemma*, first serialised in *Blackwood's*, was based on the rebel siege of the Lucknow Residency in 1857, and the rebellion served mainly as an exotic background to a romance plot hinged around love, adultery, scandals and mysterious jewels. Two of the three Mutiny novels published in the 1880s were *Douglas Achdale* (1885) by Katherine C. M. Phipps, a novel about the siege of the Lucknow Residency, and *The Touchstone of Peril* (1887) by D. M. Thomas. The latter was based in the fictional north Indian town of Hajipur where rebels led by the dispossessed Muslim landed gentry besieged a party of Europeans.

The most productive period in the history of the Mutiny novel was the 1890s, when nineteen novels appeared. Despite Gregg's possibly aesthetic dissatisfaction, the novels of the nineties say a good deal about the British self-image in India, as they are among the indices of a high imperial culture. The novels include G. A. Henty's first novel on the subject, *Rujjub the Juggler* (1893), Flora Annie Steel's *On the Face of the Waters* (1896), *A Man of Honour* (1896) by H. C. Irwin and A. F. P. Harcourt's *Jenetha's Venture* (1899). Among the novels that will be examined in detail in this study, their most obvious difference from earlier writing is that the rebellion now turns into a site of heroic imperial adventure, and an occasion for conspicuous demonstrations of racial superiority. Also, while Sterndale or Grant represented the indigenous rebel world alongside the Anglo-Indian world, in Steel and Harcourt a white hero or heroine mediates between the two and functions as a crucial instrument of surveillance, sabotage and counter-insurgency.

These altered emphases mesh well with emerging trends in late nineteenth-century popular fiction. The majority of the Mutiny novels of this period are aimed primarily at a juvenile readership, and in which character-building, empire, military exploits, and state security and espionage are among the commonest themes. Moreover, for contemporary novelists such as Henty, his closest rival and follower, George Manville Fenn, and Gordon Stables, the Mutiny was but one topic from a history of national expansion serially exploited in hundreds of immensely popular novels about Canada, Australia, Africa and South and Central America. This geographical range was also evident in other, less popular, novelists such as J. E. P. Muddock and Hugh Stowell Scott. Born and partly raised in Calcutta, Muddock, who was in India during the rebellion and later was the Swiss correspondent of the *Daily News*, wrote two Mutiny novels, *The Star of Fortune* (1895) and *The Great White Hand* (1896). But his fictional territory was not only India and, under the pseudonym 'Dick Donovan', Muddock published some twenty-four novels of crime detection, besides novels on espionage and the Russian secret service such as the *Chronicles of Daniel Danevitch* (1897) and for *God and the Czar* (1892). Hugh Stowell Scott, who used the pseudonym 'H. S. Merriman', visited India as a tourist in 1877–8, and was possibly employed by the British secret services in later life. His only Mutiny novel was *Flotsam* (1896), in which intrepid British heroes easily slip in and out of rebel Delhi and Lucknow disguised as Hindu 'sepoys' or fakirs. While in this novel Scott treated colonial resistance and counter-insurgency, his *Prisoners and Captives* (1891) and *The Sowers* (1896) were about Russian nihilist conspiracies, while *With Edged Tools* (1894) was a violently pro-imperialist tale of slave and ivory trade in West Africa.

The precursors of Joseph Conrad's ironic reversal of the themes of colonial adventure and espionage in *The Heart of Darkness* (1899), *The Secret Agent* (1907) and *Under Western Eyes* (1911), these novels were alive to the problems of 'pacifying' and administering foreign territory. There is a double significance to the *fin de siècle* colonial adventure hero in disguise who penetrates into rebel conclaves to thwart rebel plans or to gather intelligence. Imagined in the 1890s and extrapolated into the 1850s, such insertions suggest at once a fantasy of mastery that sutures actual intelligence failures during the rebellion; a fantasy made possible and rendered credible by British dominance in India during the 1890s, and acquiring another urgency from the great games of British foreign and diplomatic policy in India, and in Central and West Asia. But these fantasies also suggest the underlying anxieties of a colonial regime and a garrison state, in the midst of, yet usually exiled – for a complex of reasons – from the forms of life and the lived everydayness of the indigenous world. Through the historical prism of the rebellion, the novels of the nineties and thereafter represent the recurring obsessions of the colonial state: surveillance, knowledge and co-optation, which, hardly a surprise, are also the salient concerns of those two canonical Anglo-Indian novels, Taylor's *Confessions of a Thug* and Rudyard Kipling's *Kim* (1901).

In the first decade of the twentieth century the number of Mutiny novels drops sharply to eight, though imperial adventure and the culture of heroism persist in boys' novels like *A Hero of Lucknow* (1905) by F. S. Brereton, *The Disputed VC* (1909) by Frederick P. Gibson and *The Red Year* (1907) by Louis Tracy, who, incidentally, started the tabloid *Sun* in 1894. The decline continues in the second decade when only six novels appeared, including C. E. Pearce's *Red Revenge* (*c.* 1911), *The Devil's Wind* (1912) by Patricia Wentworth and *Rung Ho! A Novel of India* (1914) by 'Talbott Mundy' (Sylvia Anne Matheson). Between 1914 and 1947 there seem to be only two novels on the rebellion, J. C. Wood's *When Nicholson Kept the Border* (1922) and *Masque of the Mutiny* by C. L. Reid, which appeared in 1947, the year of Indian independence. The last novel is interesting for several reasons, not the least of which is that a Gandhi-like 'Mahatma' is the imagined leader and chief ideologue of the rebellion. *Masque* interpolates a coherent centre that the rebellion, by all accounts, did not possess, though happily enough the novel's English hero and his Indian collaborator assassinate the 'Mahatma', a deed that helps to put out the 'Brahmin conspiracy' to free India from British rule.

After independence, the rebellion has figured as the subject of occasional novels such as *The Nightrunners of Bengal* (1955) by John Masters, *The Siege of Krishnapur* (1973) by J. G. Farrell, Norman Partington's *And Red Flows the Ganges* (1972), *Flashman in the Great Game* (1975) by George Macdonald Fraser and *Blood-Seed* (1985) by Andrew Ward, the historian of the rebellion in Kanpur. As suggested at the beginning of this rough guide to the history of the Mutiny novel, these novels are of no interest here. Though post-1947 novels continued to employ the themes and representational emphases of the main body of the Mutiny novel with various degrees of criticism, irony or fidelity, they are vestigial to a project that came to an end in 1947 not only with the transfer of power but also, 'poetically', with the assassination of the 'Mahatma' in a novel that draws the curtain upon a ninety-year old 'masque'.

Between the two moments of Dickens–Collins and Reid's *Masque*, the main body of British fiction on the rebellion bears the impress of formative intersections such as those between the historical novel and the history of empire, between popular culture in Britain and the British self-image in India, between colonial knowledge and its transcription in fiction, between the metropolis and the Anglo-Indian periphery and, not least, between the history of Anglo-Indian literature and its substantial subset, the Mutiny novel. Despite an appearance of unimaginative repetitiveness, an appearance that is not allayed, moreover, by the usually pedestrian writing and the often flat-footed ventures into history interwoven with febrile romance-plots, the novels of the rebellion were responsive to contemporary events in the colony and in the metropolis. While the general perspective from which the rebellion was represented in British fiction between 1857 and 1947 shows little change, there are significant modulations of theme, emphasis and register between the earliest novels and the novels of the 1890s. Some of these shifts have to do with imperial propaganda, or a Samuel Smiles-like character-building exercise where the hero represents the exemplary 'empire boy'; others derive from metropolitan gender-politics; and still others respond to an increasingly combative Indian nationalism and the exigencies of administration. The regularities governing the representation of the rebellion in ninety years of novel-writing suggest a fundamental resistance in the popular imagination to anti-colonial resistance, though there were often networks of historical, political and literary-stylistic contingencies inflecting and revising the imaginings of resistance.

Given these intersections and the presence of politically significant inflections, it is curious that there has not been more historical and literary critical engagement with the Mutiny novel. There is a longish history tucked behind the present study, a history no less responsive to political and cultural mutability than its subject matter. The study of Anglo-Indian letters in general and fiction in particular began in the late 1840s with J. W. Kaye's review articles in the *North British Review* and the *Calcutta Review*. These early formulations were followed by 'high imperial' assessments from the 1890s through to the 1930s: review articles by Alfred C. Lyall and Hilda Gregg among others, and studies such as E. F. Oaten's *A Sketch of Anglo-Indian Literature* (1907), P. Sheshadri's *An Anglo-Indian Poet: John Leyden* (1912), *India in English Literature* (1923) by Robert Sencourt and *A Survey of Anglo-Indian Fiction* (1934) by Bhupal Singh.

It often goes unnoticed that early Anglo-Indian literary criticism too had theorised the relation between national expansion and literary writing, and on the characteristics and habits of culture of an expatriate community, stratified by administrative and military rank, and ruling over vastly different peoples. In the reviews by J. W. Kaye – author of the Punjab war novel *Peregrine Pultuney* (1844) – there was already the sense that Anglo-Indian literary culture was intimately responsive to the British project in India, with its militarism, its drive towards centralisation and the sense of a reformist mission, and to everyday life in a garrison society surrounded by but self-consciously distant from the subject indigenous society. It was specifically the conquest of Punjab and Sind over the 1840s, and the ensuing work of colonial 'settlement', which prompted Kaye's own review article 'The Romance of Indian Warfare'.[8] These events helped to design a potent and fashionable Anglo-Indian sub-culture of the frontier hero or Punjab administrator over the next hundred years or so: a gloomy 'berserker' spirit leading irregular corps to 'pacify' Waziristan or Chitral on the Afghan border, or carrying out administrative and judicial settlements from Lahore with a mix of evangelical dourness and liberal-reformist energy. Lyall's 'Novels of Adventure and Manners' (1894) elaborates the same theme half a century on: that adventure was the most appropriate subject of the British–Indian aesthetic, built around the settlement of conquered or ceded territories, the memories of the Mutiny and the ongoing warfare at the frontier culminating in the somewhat humbling experience of the Tirah Expeditionary Force in 1897–98.[9] Unlike Kaye, however, Lyall saw a larger design in this aesthetic: adventure in India was part of a global narrative of Anglo-Saxon adventure, following the steady commercial, military and governmental penetration of four continents, and recently reinvigorated by the emergence of European competitors.

The candid correlation between expansion, warfare and novel writing grew muted in later years, and was replaced by other interests such as, for example, the oddities of Anglo-Indian life and society, and some literary-critical attention to the representation of the subject people in the novels. There was, moreover, in Sencourt, Oaten and Singh an urge to classify Anglo-Indian fiction writing into periods distinguishable by particular forms of attitudinally determined literary engagement with India as the subject, a tribute perhaps to the burgeoning corpus of metropolitan and expatriate novels about India that made classification and periodisation necessary. The classificatory impulse survived the end of empire. To take two examples, Allen Greenberger's *The British Image of India* (1969) and *Delusions of Discoveries* (1972) by Benita Parry pull out correlations between Anglo-Indian literary history and distinct periods of the British empire in India. Mutations of racial, cultural and political attitude are highlighted to explain the working of novels; and these studies venture beyond 1947 to attach the post-1947 British–Indian novel to a list that begins with the late nineteenth-century. It is a rather late starting point, for the Anglo-Indian novel had been around since the end of the eighteenth century, with a fairly rich crop that appeared between the 1820s and 1857.

Two interests stand out in these literary-historical mappings: broad-gauge periodisation, and an interest in British attitudes towards empire. The correlation of attitude with empire offered a method for reading the representation of expatriate life in Anglo-Indian letters. *Nabobs* (1932) by Percival

Spear and George Bearce's *British Attitudes to India: 1784–1858* (1961) had anticipated the method and the modelling, but the applications were now specifically geared for literary texts narrowly defined. Parry's take on these writings is more energetically anti-imperial in tone than Greenberger's, but on the whole questions of chromatism, xenophobia or cultural contact were seen in affective, humanist terms. E. M. Forster, Edward Thompson and Edmund Candler were a decent sort, liberals sympathetic to Indians and a bit embarrassed by imperial chest-thumping, and their 'attitudes' were an appropriate reflex to what Greenberger called the 'Era of Doubt', while the fictional writings of Flora Annie Steele and Rudyard Kipling were redolent with high imperial hubris.

The transformation of these practices of literary-historical mapping and judgement in the last twenty years have been influenced largely by cultural and anthropological studies of Western penetration of Africa and West Asia. Edward Said's *Orientalism* (1978) is the most celebrated instance of this transformation and justly so, but Franz Fanon, Talal Asad, K. M. Pannikar and Anwar Abdel Malik had already, and with great acuity and attention to historical specificity, acknowledged the nexus of power and discourse, the cultures of domination and subordination and consequent modifications of identity.[10] Fanon's clinical studies of colonial pathologies are particularly bilateral, where sophisticated analyses of power, knowledge and culture in colonial situations – which *Orientalism* elaborated with a sometimes unhistorical compendiousness not in itself blameworthy – are balanced by a close interest in the psychic effects and affects of colonialism and the making of national cultures following decolonisation, a subject that did not interest Said very much. The combined Fanon–Said model of nineteenth- and twentieth-century colonialism produced in time skilful analyses of the cultural anthropology of colonialism and sometimes its literature, as witness *Europe and its Others* (1985) by Francis Barker *et al.*, *'Race', Writing, Difference*, edited by Henry Louis Gates Jr (1986), Peter Hulme's *Colonial Encounters: Europe and the Native Caribbean* (1986) and *The Rule of Darkness: British Literature and Imperialism, 1830–1914* by Patrick Brantlinger (1988). These first essays into what came in time to be known as colonial discourse studies were followed in the 1990s by numerous monographs, edited volumes and articles, of which some engaged with new archival resources, or with genres and practices not expressly literary, while others turned to theorise the cultures of colonialism. *Colonialism and Culture* (1992) by Nicholas Dirks, *Imperial Eyes: Travel Writing and Transculturalism* (1992) by Marie Louise Pratt, *Orientalism and the Postcolonial Predicament* (1993) by C. A. Breckenridge and P. van der Veer, *Colonialism's*

Culture: Anthropology, Travel and Government by Nicholas Thomas (1994) and *Colonialism and the Object: Empire, Material Culture and the Museum* (1998) by Tim Bassinger and Tom Flynn are among the more general kinds of modelling, covering a wide range of colonial geographies and with a shared sense that colonialism was, as Dirks observed, 'a cultural project of control'.[11]

For studies of Anglo-Indian letters, these intervening developments have meant that correlations of period, attitude and literary writing have given way to a broadly defined interest in the semiotics of imperial represen-tation; an interest first explored by Bernard Cohn in the early 1980s.[12] This necessarily enlarged the corpus from novels to travel writing, mem-oirs, periodical literature, ethnographic accounts, popular media, visual representations, imperial pageantry and colonial architecture. Mirroring disciplinary developments elsewhere, these inflections and enlargements have brought the literature of the Indian empire into closer proximity with the history of that empire. While broad-gauge literary periodisations had leaned against the scaffolding of (a primarily political) history while keep-ing the two spheres separate, the new and intimate proximity between the literature and the history of empire – indeed, the transformation of the two into cultural anthropology – laid the conceptual groundwork for the studies of Anglo-Indian letters that followed the work of Greenberger and Parry. These include *Kipling and 'Orientalism'* (1986) by B. J. Moore-Gilbert, *The Rhetoric of English India* (1992) by Sara Suleri, *British Romantic Writers and the East* (1992) by Nigel Leask, Kate Teltscher's *India Inscribed* (1995), *The White Woman's Own Burden* (1995) by Kumari Jayawardena and the collection of essays, *Writing India* (1996), edited by Moore-Gilbert.

The Mutiny novel does not, however, figure prominently in any of this as a coherent set of nearly seventy novels, though British representation of the rebellion appears sometimes in studies of particular novelists such as Flora Annie Steel, in mapping the literary history of British India while examining colonial articulations of British gender politics, or in media studies of popular imperialism. Of the articles and monographs that have viewed the Mutiny novels as a composite whole the first is *Novels on the Indian Mutiny* (1973) by Shailendra Dhari Singh, a useful bibliographic resource that uses broad-gauge periodisation to explore the making and the modulations of the Mutiny story through the decades after the event. More recent readings include Brantlinger's essay on 'The Well at Cawnpore' in his study of the literature of nineteenth-century British imperial expansion, *The Rule of Darkness* (1988); Nancy Paxton's article, 'Mobilizing Chivalry: Rape in British Indian Novels about the Indian Uprising of 1857' (1992);

Jenny Sharpe's essay, 'The Civilising Mission Disfigured', a study of the circulation of the sign of white femininity in fictional and other accounts of the Mutiny in her book, *Allegories of Empire* (1993); and the essay by Robert Druce, 'Ideologies of Anglo-Indian Novels from 1859 to 1947' in the edited volume, *Shades of Empire in Colonial and Post-Colonial Literatures* (1993). There are, moreover, three essays on the literary interest of Charles Dickens and Wilkie Collins in the rebellion, and while these throw interesting light on contemporary metropolitan popular culture, there still remains the question of the persistence of the Mutiny novel over eighty or ninety years.[13]

These essays and studies do not quite address the historical matter of the novels: the rebellion of 1857–9. In these recent readings the rebellion appears as little more than an obscure but bloody event in nineteenth-century India that, for one reason or another, became the site for gender constructions or for a popular imperial culture. As critical windows, the studies by Brantlinger, Sharpe, Paxton, Druce and others are certainly useful. In Brantlinger's essay on British representations of the rebellion at Kanpur, the Mutiny novel serves to instantiate a moment in the cavalcade of the British colonial adventure novel. In Sharpe and in Paxton, the discursive production of white womanhood in India reveals the dynamics of a reception that structures and mobilises the rhetoric of counter-insurgency. But on the whole these studies have tended to sidestep the fact that as event and as discourse, the rebellion turns upon congeries of political, ideological, literary, cultural, ethnographic and administrative representations and decisions by means of which the British had construed their presence in the Indian subcontinent since at least 1765, the year in which the Mughal emperor granted the *diwani* of the province of Bengal, Bihar and Orissa to the East India Company. To that extent, the Mutiny novel always already drags along a considerable historical undertow; a history that cannot be ignored without depriving analysis of an area of significance that is the enabling rationale of the novels and of the events they claim to represent.

Moreover, the Mutiny novel is at the intersection of several idioms, genres and representational emphases, with some – for instance, travel and survey writing – in continuous practice from the late eighteenth century. The literary history in which these novels form a significant constituency is inseparable from those regimes and practices of knowledge, representation and colonial control that drove the British machinery in India through the nineteenth century and after. Put another way, the novels of the rebellion certainly construct and employ visions of threatened or violated white femininity just as they instantiate the popular imperialism of late Victorian and Edwardian Britain; yet these images and applications are the epiphenomenon of certain fundamental axes of surveillance, knowledge and representation that were central to, in as much as they held together, the British project in India, and that were seriously challenged in 1857.

For these reasons the present study stands between two well-established methods of approaching the history and cultures of the British in India, drawing on the resources of both without wholly belonging to either. The first of these is the literary-historical interest in Anglo-Indian letters, now transmogrified into colonial discourse studies with their rich interdisciplinary possibilities, albeit with a propensity to run aground at times in shallow channels of post-colonial speculation. There is something quite unique about Anglo-Indian literature, which has unfailingly guided critical and literary-historical engagement from the 1840s to this day. It is possible to say radical things about the mid-Victorian novel without necessarily discussing the nature of the contemporary British state; impossible to write anything about Anglo-Indian writing of the same period without addressing the political and governmental conditions under which such writing appeared. There are naturally differences between specific readings of the meshing of conquest, politics and literary culture in literary histories and in single-author studies, as there is unevenness in treating historical referents, but recognising the fact of empire is a necessary condition for reading Anglo-Indian writing. There is one other thing these studies have in common. Despite the methodological differences between the studies by Bhupal Singh and Greenberger on the one hand, and Sara Suleri or Moore-Gilbert's *Writing India* on the other hand – and more than anything else, their differences are the indices of mutations within the discipline of English studies – the textual corpus is virtually identical, and consists mainly of novels.[14] The choice of texts is inevitable since these studies have their provenance in departments of English in India, Britain and elsewhere, and there has been for nearly a century a firm Anglo-Indian canon of novels, though studies in popular imperialism have now introduced juvenile literature, the periodical press and the Anglo-Indian domestic novel.[15]

The second approach belongs to departments of history and politics, with interests in the political and intellectual history of empire. This approach too has a long history that goes back to the beginnings of British rule in the late eighteenth century, and has served many ends for nearly two hundred years: representing Company interests before home opinion and parliament, mediating party politics, theories of government and colonial transformation, and detailing the specifics of Indian administration.

Following the formal dissolution of empire, historiography of this variety has overhauled itself in the last fifty years or thereabouts to readdress the influence of metropolitan political, economic and ideological investments in administrative debates over India, their impact on war, diplomacy and state-building, on revenue systems, education and reform, and their complex interface with various Indian pressure groups.

The post-1947 renovation of this branch of history writing began with *The English Utilitarians and India* (1959) by Eric Stokes, which led the way for subsequent studies of policy, administration and intellectual history, such as *British Policy in India* (1965) by S. Gopal, *Liberalism and Indian Politics* (1966) by R. J. Moore, *A Rule of Property for Bengal* by Ranajit Guha, *Ideologies of the Raj* (1995) by Thomas R. Metcalfe, *Empire and Information* (1996) by C. A. Bayly, *Edmund Burke and India* (1996) by Frederick Whelen and *Liberalism and Empire* (1999) by Uday Singh Mehta. Some among these studies take the long view of British–Indian history, identifying types of colonial governmentality, arranging them along a historical series and focusing on the applications of metropolitan intellectual, political and religious ideas to explain these types. At the thick end of the wedge such enquiries rest on events and archives: immigration patterns, military campaigns, administrative projects, cadastral techniques, Acts, Charters, Bills, economy and trade, railways, irrigation, penal codes, gazetteer projects, census surveys, constitutional wrangles and educational projects. At the thin end of the wedge, however, these enquiries sometimes raise questions of attitude and everydayness: the bearing, habits and settlement patterns of the British 'middle-class aristocracy' in India, and the multi-media semiotics of power and cultural encounter.

But in either case the intellectual history of empire rarely ever troubles with literary writing. These histories are often by practising historians (or anthropologists, such as Cohn), and they turn instinctively to an archive that is not literary, with a method not quite that of literary studies. Conversely, recent scholarship on Anglo-Indian letters, while carrying over contemporary emphases in metropolitan literary studies on discourse, rhetoric, race and gender have usually shied away from the detailing that intellectual histories of the British empire in India routinely attempt. If this separation of spheres has left intellectual history without the resources of the literary archive, it leaves colonial discourse studies often with a rather attenuated history, embellished at times by a baroque skein of speculation. It is in search of a possible middle ground between the political and intellectual history of the British empire in India on the one hand, and its specifically literary history on the other, that this study explores the many ntexts in which the Mutiny novel and its historical referents are located. his has meant looking at the textual and generic archives and sediments that constitute these novels: historiography, first-person accounts, debates over policy and administrative measures. Foregrounding history with far greater political investment than most novels of Anglo-Indian domesticity, the Mutiny novel reworks antecedent and metropolitan literary idioms to represent indigenous resistance, and in so doing serves for a time as the potent medium of popular imperialism and jingoism.

In the first two chapters, the reading of several early British histories of the rebellion gives a sense of the public and political debates the rebellion raised, which, as chapter 2 shows, reappear with not a little irony in Indian nationalist readings of the event early in the twentieth century. The debates were of course responses to those parlous questions the rebellion raised, from military-tactical issues to the need to contain and resolve an administrative impasse, but they also show how quickly British public opinion in India and Britain drew up a version of events that was to dominate the imperial imaginary for a long time to come. Weaving these concerns with a chronological account of the progress of the rebellion over two years, the histories map the event along a gratifying parabola of success. But the deliberative apostrophes framing the narratives of events and explaining their meaning reckon with more than a sequence of military episodes. For historians such as Robert Montgomery Martin, the narrative of events needed to be buttressed by long-view disquisitions on Indian history and society; while for J. W. Kaye the transformation of the Company from a mercantile corporation to a liberal-administrative state provided the framework for the event he sets out to record.

The presence of these deliberative devices warrant the claim that it is useful to read British historiography of the rebellion as part of a mammoth discursive venture that began in the third quarter of the eighteenth century, a wide-ranging discursive project that gradually produced a historiography of India. It will take another book to explore the genealogy and the long-term consequences of this project not only for colonial knowledge of India, but also for nationalist and contemporary historiography. The programmatic aim to map Indian pasts was coeval with, for example, the Trigonometrical Survey that sought to produce cartographies, and with the many ethnographic and gazetteer projects that attempted a panoptic survey of the life-world of the subject people through the nineteenth century. That much of this knowledge served commercial and governmental interests is now common knowledge; what is perhaps less regarded is the fact that much of this knowledge continues to determine South Asian societies, polities, frontiers and, indeed, historiography in multiple ways, some obvious, some insidious.

The other advantage of looking closely at historiography is the window it opens on the ways in which the rebellion was explained, and how explanations differed. The book does not aim at a substantive explanation of the rebellion, a project that has exercised historians and demagogues, British and Indian, for a hundred and fifty years now. Its interest lies rather in reading some of these explanations, especially British imperial explanations, to understand what meanings were ascribed to the event, and how these meanings shaped narratives historical and literary, and determined post-rebellion reckonings with India. But explanation and narrative are prompted by explanandums that required these *post hoc* tasks, and, in the case of J. W. Kaye, the most Rankean of the early historians and with access to government papers, the explanans is a constellation of political and administrative theories and practices. Like George Berkeley, for whom hearing the rattling on the street was an immediate perception that yielded the mediate perception that a carriage was on its way, the immediacy of the rebellion leads Kaye to infer and trace the contours of a policy history that effected what he, and before him Marx, had described as the 'social revolution' the British had worked in north and north-western India.[16] From the Permanent Settlement of Bengal in 1783, through the 'settlement' of the conquered and ceded provinces over the first half of the nineteenth century, to the annexation of the kingdom of Awadh in February 1856, there took place what today we would call a series of 'structural readjustments', geared towards a set of economic, political and cultural goals, and highlighting the constitutional and practical problems of sovereignty, intervention and 'settlement'.

In politics and historiography as in everyday life, perspectives are relative to positions, and the positions we take at home or in the world outside bear the impress of the interests they minister. What to many British was a military aberration became a war of independence in the nationalist imaginary that took shape by the turn of the century, which stridently rejected the 'mutiny' thesis as a deliberate slur. But it would be an error to consolidate and polarise a British and an Indian interpretation; for, as the second chapter will show there were gaping differences in the British view of the matter as there were in Indian opinion. The irreconcilability of the 'prince and the pretender' is not specific to either the Jacobite or the Indian rebellion; and whether the account be nationalist or imperial, Hanoverian or Jacobite, there is at bottom a problem of historical knowledge, compounded when

not constituted by express conflicts of interest, and the vagaries of explanatory narrative.[17] Partly for the sheer obviousness of polarisation, Indian
nationalist versions of the event do not appear here, though that other
corpus – spanning Bengali, Hindi, Marathi and Urdu and represented by
popular art and government-sponsored memorials – is no less worthy of
study.

As compensation, there is, however, a brief detour into the readings of
the event by Sir Syed Ahmad Khan in 1858 and by V. D. Savarkar in 1909
in chapter 2. The two make unlikely bedfellows, for, if the former is often
regarded as the originator of Muslim separatism, the latter became one of
the leaders and organisers of the chauvinist Hindu Mahasabha from the
1920s. But the detour is useful for it shows the making of an Indian political
theory in the sixty years following the rebellion. While Sir Syed's refusal
to grant radical racial or religious significance to the rebellion was driven
by comprador loyalty, and by a recognisable Whig political theory, *The
Indian War of Independence* (1909) by Savarkar, though it quickly became a
nationalist icon, was nonetheless driven by a deep-rooted complicity with
the modular forms of European republicanism, and with the European idea
of the nation state.

From chronicle to history

Whatever brings you in contact with a greater number of states, increases, in the same proportion, those clashings of interest and pride out of which the pretexts for war are frequently created.

James Mill, 'Colonies' (1824)

War makes rattling good history.

Thomas Hardy, *The Dynasts* (1910)

CHRONICLE TO HISTORY

Well before the Queen's Proclamation read by Governor-General Canning at Allahabad on 1 November 1858 marked an official end of the rebellion, G. B. Malleson wrote the first part of *The Mutiny of the Bengal Army: A Historical Narrative*, which appeared in June 1857, only two months after the first uprising at the Meerut garrison.[1] The same year two more accounts of the war in progress appeared: J. F. Lee and Captain F. W. Radcliffe co-authored *The Indian Mutiny up to the Relief of Lucknow*, which may have preceded Malleson's anonymous pamphlet, and Thomas Frost edited the *Complete Narrative of the Mutiny in India from its Commencement to the Present Time*. More substantive accounts appeared from 1859, notably the *History of the Indian Mutiny* by Charles Ball, the *Chambers History of the Indian Revolt*, E. H. Nolan's *Illustrated History of the British Empire in India and the East* and *The Indian Empire with a Full Account of the Mutiny* by Robert Montgomery Martin.[2] Published within two or three years of the rebellion, these comprehensive accounts of events and causes some-times appended the two rebellious years to a narrative that began with the Macedonian invasion of north-west India in the third century BCE.

Accompanying and often preceding these wide-angle histories were local accounts. There was a ready rationale for such texts: the rebellion was spread over large swathes of north and central India; the many instances of mutiny, popular insurgency and British reconquest were not simultaneous;

and the presence of the British (as the besieged, in Lucknow or Kanpur, or as besiegers, in Delhi by August 1857) invested certain regions and cities with added significance. Local accounts also began appearing in 1857, and in at least two distinct modes: quasi-official accounts by civil and army officers of the Company recording the state of the region in question in the manner of government reports and military despatches, and more first-person accounts, many by women, which gave a sense of the experience of the rebellion for beleaguered garrisons, and whose popularity in Britain was immediate and immense.

Whether local or comprehensive, the first pool of writing has a mediatory function in distilling a mass of heterogeneous primary material comprising letters, diaries, memoirs, newspaper reports, telegrams, civil and military despatches, parliamentary debates and, sometimes, rumour, and so preparing the ground for history writing in subsequent decades. An example of the process of generic mutation is *The Punjab and Delhi in 1857* by the Reverend Cave-Brown, which began as a diary he wrote in camp 'for the private information of his own family', and was subsequently published in *Blackwood's Magazine* under the title 'Poorbeah Mutiny'. The venture was 'so well received in England (as well as in India, where [its] general accuracy was frequently noticed)' that Cave-Brown decided 'to amplify' the work into 'a continuous narrative'. In this project he was assisted by additional documentation (letters, memoirs, official despatches), including 'pencilled notes from the very scenes of blood' from correspondents who had witnessed the rebellion, and it led eventually to the history published in 1861.[3] Like numerous other works in the same genre, if not of the same provenance, Cave-Brown's muscular Christian account of retaliation and reconquest contributed to the popular perception of the events in India.

Additionally, the accounts written between 1857 and 1861 demonstrate growing skill in organising a large number of military engagements, massacres and sieges into narrative history, as the British forces and the rebel militias fought for nearly two years over several thousand square miles. The sophistication is primarily a result of accumulating knowledge. In their chronicles of 1857, Malleson and Frost wrote accounts of a war in progress, and for that reason lacked the manifest sense of an ending of, for instance, the *Chambers History*. Again, for all the polemical cut and thrust of *The Mutiny of the Bengal Army*, Malleson knew little or nothing about the revived Mughal court and government in Delhi between May and September 1857. Nor, indeed, could Malleson or Frost have had any knowledge of the popular and protracted insurgency in the Awadh countryside that began in earnest only upon the recapture of the capital, Lucknow, in early 1858.

In the latter case the absence of knowledge is unsurprising since neither author could have written of events that followed the moment of writing. But in the former case the lack of certain knowledge about the state of Mughal government during the summer of 1857 results from the collapse of British authority in Delhi; a collapse leading to failures of intelligence mirrored by the corresponding textual lack in Frost and Malleson.

Such deficiencies were usually rectified in histories written after the fact. By the close of 1858 the last Mughal Emperor, Bahadur Shah II, was a British prisoner, the Nana Sahib of Bithur and the Begum Hazrat Mahal, the queen of the now-annexed kingdom of Awadh, were desperate fugitives, the Queen of Jhansi, Laxmi Bai, was dead, and nearly all rebel areas once again under British rule. The recapture of rebel-held territories was soon followed by vigorous reclamation of knowledge following a government directive of 30 April 1858 instructing 'Commissioners and Collectors in the North-Western Provinces . . . to prepare narratives of the events in each district from the outbreak of the disturbances to the restoration of authority'.[4] While district-level narratives exhumed the military, forensic, fiscal, administrative, social and political aspects of the rebellion in specific localities, other exercises aimed to de-legitimise the sources of authority the rebels had invoked in their search for an alternative to Company rule. The juristic performance encoded in the *Trial of Muhammad Bahadur Shah* amassed witnesses and evidence on rebel Delhi, only to render the rebellion and its principal actors criminal, outlawing the Mughal government during the summer of 1857 and cleverly obscuring the constitutional subservience of the Company to the emperor.[5] Though these appeared in a published form much later, the records were available to some early historians, and formed the textual basis for local detail, and for explaining the causes of the rebellion.

The early histories exemplify the ways in which historiography worked in tandem with the administrative needs of the colonial state during periods of crisis, producing narratives, explaining events and enlisting opinion. There is moreover the question of the form the early histories gave to the rebellion. Notwithstanding the already voluminous and still-growing literature on the rebellion, there was, as R. M. Martin notes, the want of 'a connected statement of the view taken by the home or Indian authorities of the cause, origin, or progress of the mutiny, which has now lasted fully eighteen months'.[6] In Martin's view, historiography alone redresses the lack by wrapping discrete particulars in a coherent whole, reflecting on the significance of the rebellion, while retracing its episodic 'progress' in the manner of the early chronicles.

This development is evident from textual practices. Where Frost's *Complete Narrative* is mainly a patchwork of extended citations from primary sources, especially unascribed letters from officers and others in India, a somewhat later history such as the one by Charles Ball – a jobbing historian and journalist who wrote a history of the *Risorgimento* and of the American War of Independence – aspires to the condition of narrative history. The *History of the Indian Mutiny* certainly cites epistolary and other sources quite as liberally as Frost, but the primary material is now encased within a framework of certainties. Earlier reports are tested against later evidence and reflections on Indian history and society pepper the narrative of events, with assessments of the Company's administration and summaries of parliamentary debates, and a cautionary sense of the threat the rebellion had posed to British interests. Unlike the simple linearity of accounts driven by a chronological series that terminates but does not conclude, historiography of the rebellion assigns to itself an exegetical task. As the early chronicles based on a chronological series grow vestigial after 1858, histories premised upon British victory relocate the rebellion in a Whig version of empire, so that the discontinuous events of 1857–9 are braided into a complete whole, whose meaning lies in its synecdochic relation with the architectonic design of Indian past and present.[7] And while E. H. Nolan begins his Introduction, 'written soon after the suppression of the Mutiny and the abolition of political control of the East India Company', with the confident prediction that 'the hurricane which has passed over Hindoostan will purify the political and social atmosphere, and leave a brighter and more benign calm than has prevailed before',[8] Ball closes his mammoth history with the claim that: 'By valour and energy India had once more been fairly conquered in the field, and it was now that the triumphs of civilisation and of peace were to recommence.'[9]

FRAMES OF REFERENCE

While British advance in India from *c.* 1750 to the 1840s was marked by resistance from states such as Bengal, Mysore, the Marathas confederacy, the Nepali and Sikh kingdoms and by Afghans, besides numerous popular rebellions, and mutinies in the Company's Indian army, the events of 1857–9 were by far the most protracted and extensive resistance to colonial rule.[10] Though confined to north and central India, the Madras and Bombay presidencies remaining largely unaffected, the extent of insurgency within the region, the degree of popular participation and the number of violent attacks on British property and persons were a disturbing comment on the security of colonial possessions. As the combined resistance of Hindus and Muslims, the peasantry, the urban citizenry, the soldiers in the Company's army, the *zamindars* and *talukdars* and several dispossessed royal houses, the rebellion drew upon many accumulated fears and grievances, though the fractiousness within and amongst these groups, and chronic weakness in organisation, made British reconquest possible. As suggested earlier, one of the first responses to the crisis was enquiries into the causes and meaning of the rebellion as a means of containment; for 'any misinterpretation of the character and the causes of the revolt of the Bengal sepoys, adopted by the British Government, would inevitably lead to yet direr calamities, and finally to the overthrow of a splendid empire'.[11]

However, the interpretation of insurgency, like the conduct of counter-insurgency, was marked from the outset by disagreements among policy-makers, publicists and historians. The clearest evidence of the difficulty of interpreting the rebellion lay in the search for, and the quarrel over, a rubric that would adequately signify the event in its totality, while mirroring the constitutional relation between the state and its subjects. Malleson's claim in Part II of *The Mutiny of the Bengal Army* that what began as a 'military mutiny' had in fact all the signs of a 'national insur-rection', is among the earliest attempts to formulate a rubric. Though he did not supply enough reasons for this conclusion, nor clarified whether by 'national' he meant 'nation-wide' or national-*ist* (and therefore anti-imperial) content, the quarrel amongst British policymakers and historians prefigured, with no little irony, the often bitter debate in the early twentieth century between imperialist and Indian nationalist understanding of the event.

The debate was at first between critics and partisans of the Company, and the latter tried anxiously but unsuccessfully to contain the crisis by describing the events as a mutiny. If it were a purely military aberration all was not unwell with British India, though the town 'mob' and the 'predatory' and 'criminal tribes' had followed in the wake of the mutineers.[12] Thus, Charles Raikes, a judge at the Agra court before the outbreak, clarified in 1858 (though not without considerable terminological embarrassment) that popular 'disaffection' was only a corollary of a mutiny:

I attribute the existing disturbances in India to a *mutiny* in the Bengal army, and to that cause alone; I mean that the exciting and immediate cause of the *revolution* is to be found in the mutiny. That we have in many parts of the country drifted from mutiny into *rebellion*, is all too true; but I repeat my assertion, that we have to deal now with a *revolt* caused by a mutiny, not with a mutiny growing out of a national discontent.[13]

Similarly, the *Chambers History* argued that 'the outbreak was a military revolt rather than a national insurrection', that there was 'almost a total absence of anything like nationality in the motions of the insurgents'.[14]

Conversely, to claim that the rebellion was more than a military event was an explanatory move adducing reasons other than the professional grievances of the soldiers (and their cause, mismanagement of the army), and leading to criticism of administrative and revenue policies and of inadequate knowledge of Indian society, as well as to culturalist accusations of native ingratitude, fanaticism, irrationality and, sometimes, to a hesitant admission that the uprising may have possessed a national-*ist* content. Malleson was the Adjutant-General of the Bengal Army in Calcutta, and his Advertisement to his account claimed that though 'at first apparently a military mutiny', the disturbance 'speedily changed its character and became a national insurrection'.[15] Though at odds with the title of the chronicle, this definition is vindicated by a breathless criticism of the civil service, specifically the administration under Governor-General Dalhousie (1848–56) and his viceregal successor, Canning (1856–62), and an implied acquittal of the Bengal Army. Instead of heeding the signs of an imminent revolt: 'All was confidence, superciliousness, and self-congratulation on the part of the Government officials', whose 'pattern statesman was Lord Dalhousie (the real author of the mutiny)'. More serious still was Malleson's charge that in jealously guarding 'their own domination, extending over a hundred years', the civil arm of the administration 'had completely failed in attaching even one section of the population to British rule'.[16]

But Malleson's argument neither proceeds from nor is accompanied by the assessment of Indian history and an imperial future that Nolan and Ball constructed along the lines cited earlier. Signalled by the prefaces, introductions and epilogues to the early histories, this expansive framing has several impulses. Of these, a declaration of the magnitude of the event – 'which has by its extent and duration, astonished the whole civilised world . . . and threatened seriously to affect the *prestige* of a flag that during the past century and a half has waved in proud supremacy over the fortresses and cities of India'[17] – locates the rebellion in the context of the Company's advance in India, and serves to remind metropolitan readers that at stake was the survival of the 'Anglo-Indian Empire', the 'dominion over a far-distant sunny land, rich in barbaric gold, precious stones, and architectural beauty, occupying upwards of a million square miles of the most varied, fertile, and interesting portion of the globe'.[18]

The catalogue of imperial possessions, combined with a forceful representation of the magnitude of the threat, was a way of calling public attention to Britain's overseas investments, which figured consistently as a reflexive policy concern from the decades before American independence until decolonisation in the mid twentieth century. To the Radical critic William Cobbett writing in his *Political Register* (1803), such possessions were no more than 'gorgeous and ponderous appendages to swell our ostensible grandeur',[19] though Radical opposition to expansion, lacking on the colonial question the support it garnered from Whigs and Nonconformists in domestic politics, was never more than a fringe opinion in a political spectrum where there were always influential constituencies, interest groups and sub-cultures in favour of territorial and commercial expansion. While public interest in the colonies was at best fitful until the European 'scramble for Africa' fuelled the growth of popular imperial culture from the 1880s, the reception of the news of the rebellion in Britain, and the almost immediate manufacture of a language combining patriotic fervour with xenophobia, enthusiastically circulated by a burgeoning press and other popular media, anticipates middle- and working-class jingoism and warmongering of later, high imperial, decades. As *The Times* commented on 10 October 1857: 'Nothing can now undo the hold which India has, at last, taken on the minds of the people, or disabuse the people of the belief that the question is their own'; a metropolitan view echoed by an article in the Anglo-Indian *Calcutta Review* which remarked that 'the insouciance of a century on Indian questions' had ended, and that 'nothing short of the *electric shock* of this mutiny would have aroused the people of England from their culpable and mischievous apathy on the affairs of India'.[20] Beyond this, the preliminary remarks in Ball's history justify and situate the narrative project, itself a product of the 'electric shock', as part of a body of writing and public debate, which for perhaps the first time in the century bought empire home, transforming a trading venture into an arm of the British state and an extension of British nationality.

But, as the prefatory moves show, the aim to produce a 'connected statement' on the rebellion in a largely chronological narrative may not be achieved without support from an auxiliary project. As Martin's Introduction claims: 'The history of India, whether in the earliest times or during the Mohammedan epoch, is ... no less interesting as a narrative than important in its bearing on the leading events of the present epoch, which, in fact, cannot, without it, be rendered *intelligible*' (emphasis added).[21] Likewise, Ball's history begins with an excursus on 'the general history of the country – its various races and native governments', preparatory to his narrative of the rebellion.[22] In the *History of the Indian Mutiny* this prefatory move takes up less than twenty pages, but Martin's pursuit of intelligibility meanders through a 459-page detour (chapter 1) on the history of India from the Macedonian invasion of the third century BCE, through the Ghaznavid invasion of the tenth century CE, to the arrival of the British in the land, with passing mentions of Portuguese, Dutch, Danish and French forays. The cavalcade of invasions, Macedonian, Islamic west and central Asian, and finally Christian–European, establishes the vulnerability of the land, its habitual prostration, and provides historical precedents obliquely justifying the foundation and guaranteeing the future of the 'Anglo-Indian Empire'. Martin's account of the Indian *longue durée* ends with a review of the administration under Dalhousie. The dovetailing of two millennia into eight years is startling, if suggestive of the explanatory burden of Martin's narrative; for, in contemporary opinion at least, Dalhousie's annexation of several Indian states, especially Awadh (in February 1856), and the generally liberal-interventionist bias of his administration, were among the most likely causes of the rebellion. While this explanation stems from a complex of political ideas that will be examined in the following chapter, the final eight years preceding 1857 are the crucial springboard in Martin's narrative, for the events of those years nearly led to the undoing of an empire whose possibility, reality and indeed moral viability, given Indian readiness to be conquered and colonised, is authorised by a long arc of two thousand years.

There is, however, one twist to this tale. Coming from an area geographically to the west of the Indus, yet east of the European west, Muslim invasions and migrations were perceived to be at once like and unlike their European, and specifically British, successors. As John William Kaye, later the author of a history of the rebellion, remarked in his *Administration of the East India Company*, 'The rulers whom we supplanted were, like ourselves, aliens and usurpers.'[23] They conquered the land and the people to become the ruling elite, established their religion, forms of life, languages, architectures, modes of government and warfare, and in the case of the Mughals, an imperium too. If the intermediate Muslim period (in James Mill's influential triadic periodisation) of Indian history prefigured the idiom of the hegemony that the East India Company acquired from the mid-eighteenth century, as it stepped into the shoes of a disintegrating Mughal empire and defeated its Maratha rivals, it was also vital to distance the new imperium from its precursor.[24] Having dismissed elements of Hindu mythology and customary practices as indices of an inferior culture, Martin turns to praise the Hindu past when he compares it with India under Muslim rule, claiming that an 'extensive study of Indian records leads to the conclusion that the decay of Hindoostan dates from the period of Muhammedan incursion and conquest'. Muslim 'tyranny and sensuality pauperised and demoralised all whom they subjected to their sway', and under Muslim rule the condition of the Hindus and of India was 'not dissimilar to the destruction and demoralisation of the Greeks, and the desolation of the fair region of Asia Minor by the Turks'.[25]

While this little vignette represents an aspect of British historiography and European Indology that inspires the Muslim-baiting of Hindu cultural nationalism to this day, Martin's analysis of the long-term history of India turns upon the triadic Hindu–Muslim–European/British model that James Mill's *History of British India* (1817) had given great explanatory power. The Hindu predisposition to defeat explained the successive conquests of India from the west, including those over the Islamic interregnum. But since Europeans, and especially the British, replaced 'Muslim rule', that interregnum becomes integral to the history of a characteristically supine land. The mapping has its uses, for it constructs at once a genealogy of conquest and hegemony of which the British are the legatees, and a hierarchy of political value where the 'tyranny and sensuality' of the preceding empire will be erased and replaced by applications of the rule of law. Configured as the strong precursor of 'enlightened despotism', the dominant imperial imaginary from the first Indian tenure of Cornwallis (1786–93),[26] Asiatic and especially Muslim despotism turns into the Other, to be preserved as an enabling historical condition and exorcised as a threatening mirror-image.

That the historical narratives in Martin and Ball are prefaced by observations on geography, geology, climate, demography, society and language is a pointer to the proximity – in method and application – between historiography and the contiguous concerns of (geological, cartographic and revenue) survey work and ethnography. This detailing is, as Martin argues at the end of his long view of Indian history, necessary to 'make the narrative of the mutiny, and its attendant circumstances, more easily understood than it could be without such . . . information'.[27] Like Alexander von Humboldt and his botanist colleague Aimé Bonpland, who explored south-central America between 1799 and 1804, Martin was a collator (though not surveyor) of the natural, economic and ethnographic features of colonial possessions, the author of *The History, Antiquities, Topography, and Statistics of Eastern India* (1838) and the *Statistics of the Colonies* (1839), and his observations on the economic draining of India under British rule are appreciatively cited in the Preface to Dadabhai Naroji's *Poverty, or Un-British Rule in India* (1901). The source material and organisation of Martin's first work, as of the first volume of *The Indian Empire*, are largely based on the pioneering survey of the Bengal and Madras presidencies and the kingdom of Mysore by the Company surgeon, Francis Buchanan, following a Company directive of 7 January 1807. Organised around categories such as topography, antiquities, people, natural products, agriculture, manufactures and arts, the rise of surveying as a genre is coeval with demands for hard knowledge of Indian conditions, as the Company's territorial holdings swelled rapidly in the decades between the Battle of Plassey or Palashi (1757), and the final defeat of the Maratha feudal states of western and central India in 1818.[28]

With these resources Martin's introduction to the rebellion certainly yields more administrative detail than Ball or Nolan. The preliminary description is more than a matter of local colour, and as the evolving methods of positive history writing from the *philosophes* to the Scots enlightenment shows, natural history constructs, delimits and individuates a region, preparatory to the social and political history of its inhabitants. As a method, regional detailing is common to history writing, district gazettes, surveys and ethnography, whether amateur or specialist, and flags the epistemic possibility for environmental and determinist elucidations of race and culture, and their variations. Located between Buchanan's early survey and the Statistical Survey of India project of 1869 (later condensed into the fourteen volume *Imperial Gazetteer of India*), and attached to a narrative of the rebellion, *The Indian Empire* is an example of empiricist – as distinct from orientalist or missionary – historiography, underscoring the need for systematic information, and using techniques whose applicability was as much metropolitan as colonial.

While this framing device is closely allied with the aims and methods of survey work, the discussion on the population that usually follows shows a family resemblance with the concerns of colonial ethnography. Ball begins with the Hindus, the 'original inhabitants' of the land, and suggests that 'subsequent conquests' may have led to substantial 'intermingling of foreign races with the aborigines'. Disregarding the consequences of this miscegenation, Ball fixes the essence of Hinduism – ingeniously, but not unusually, identified with 'race'[29] – in the institution of caste. Thus, 'from the earliest period of which any records are extant, the Hindoo races have been divided as a people into four distinct classes or *castes*; designated Brahmins, Kshatriyas, Vaishyas and Sudras'.[30] In Martin, the ethnographic third chapter begins with tables of population figures for the districts and provinces under British rule; the organisation and interpretation of data confirms Bernard Cohn's suggestion that British census operations – part of what he calls the 'enumerative modality' of colonial knowledge – produced the 'social categories by which India was ordered for administrative purposes', for they were assumed to reflect 'the basic sociological facts of India'.[31]

Demographic tabulation constructs the empirical scaffolding for an ethnography that, unlike Ball's urge to unify, emphasises innate heterogeneity. As Martin notes: 'It is natural to speak of India as if it were inhabited by a single race: such is not the case; people are more varied in language, appearance and manners, than those of Europe.'[32] He next locates India's 'twenty' languages (compared unfavourably to Europe's fifteen) regionally, and stresses the varieties of dietary habits, religious practices and kinship patterns. Beyond the differences of caste and religion, 'there are other diversities, arising probably from the origin of race, and the peculiarities engendered during a long course of time by climate and food', so that the Maratha and the Bengali, though Hindu (and even when they belong to the same caste), are distinct in many respects. Martin then describes the two Muslim sects of the Shias and the Sunnis ('who abhor each other as cordially as members of the Latin and the Greek Church do'), the Buddhists, Jains, 'Seiks', Parsees, Eurasians and the tribal population of India. Like others before him, the survey of regional, customary and religious differences leads Martin to the conclusion that: 'there is no homogeneity of population in India, no bond of union, – no feeling of patriotism, arising from similarity of origin, language, creed, or caste, – no common sentiment, founded on historic or traditional associations . . .'[33]

Ball and Martin's use of ethnography draws on a body of empirical and speculative enquiry, relevant for administrative and political purposes, that leaned heavily on observation and on indigenous textual sources often mediated by indigenous informants such as Sanskrit and Arabic–Persian scholars. But it is noteworthy that the frames of observation and theorisation which the British in India began to hone from roughly the last quarter of the eighteenth century were derived from and contributed to the methodological core of a coeval European ethnography, with national, colonial and global layers of application, and an insistence on classifying 'types', physiognomies, races and nations in lateral schemes and into hierarchies.[34] Using criteria such as race, language, religion, region and caste, the 'enumerative modality' supports a view of many monads within the population, emphasises difference and discontinuity and sets up an analytic order where variation may be ordered geographically, historically and in terms of the interrelations between mutually exclusive categories and groups. There is moreover no ready homogeneity in nineteenth-century ethnographic thinking about India. Alongside missionary ethnography, bent chiefly on attacking Hindu forms of worship and the caste organisation of Hindu society, were orientalist attempts to trace racial and linguistic continuities within the Indo-Aryan family, and an empirical-experimental ethnography locating Indian 'types' within evolutionary and acculturative race theories. While these diverse and sometimes overlapping systematisations are the general means by which colonial knowledge ordered indigenous society and history, the value of such schemata is especially prominent at a time of crisis. As the colonial state began reconstructing the period of its absence and interpreting the rebellion, ethnography provided a crucial explanatory resource for explaining the failed rebellion.

The diptych of Hindu and Muslim culpability appears in historiography, as in the Mutiny novel, with varying emphases. Viewing the rebellion primarily as the work of Hindus, Ball argues that 'the most frequent and formidable ground of discontent has been that which presents itself at the present crisis, namely, a suspicion of meditated interference with the inviolable immunities of their faith and the privileges of *caste*'.[35] Nolan, on the other hand, dispenses blame evenly when he suggests that the British in India were hampered by caste *and* 'Mohammedanism', and warns that in the coming years the government should ensure that caste does not 'obtain official recognition', especially in the Bengal army where recruits were mainly high-caste Hindus from the Awadh region, and insists that the army should make allowance for the customary practices of Hindu and Muslim troops. As for Muslims, Nolan claims that the former ruling elite still hated their successors, and ought to be 'kept down by all possible means' in order to 'curb the licentiousness of all fanaticisms in India'.[36] The Preface to *Chambers History* is more nuanced in assigning blame. A complete 'chronicle of events', the Preface hopes, will raise questions on why the 'lower castes' were quiet while the upper castes rebelled, or why the 'Punjabis' and the armies of the Bombay and Madras presidencies stayed loyal. From these differences the narrative will 'trace the influence of nation, caste and creed' on the rebellion, issues that 'it behoved the government to solve, as clues to the character of the government, and to the changes of discipline needed'.[37]

But the list of internal variation is more than the source of the series of negations in Martin's ethnography; the lack of a 'bond of union' or 'common sentiment' ensures 'more security for the preservation of British authority'.[38] The deep contradiction between the postulated social formation and history that simultaneously caused the revolt and created conditions for its successful suppression is an important source of the legitimacy of empire after 1859. Based on religious and customary scruples, the Hindu and Muslim soldiers' refusal – albeit for different reasons – of the greased cartridges issued for use with the new Minié-Enfield rifle functions as a metonymy for the culture of a pre-modern society locked in an 'invincible immobility'.[39] In post-rebellion assessments, Indian resistance to technology, to rationalisation (in politics, jurisprudence and cadastral methods) and to European modernity (in education and social reform) led, as Metcalf notes, to 'a conception of empire grounded ever more firmly in notions of Indian "difference", and a revitalized conservatism that gave that empire a central place in Britain's vision of itself'.[40] The idea of difference emphasised India's historical decline or its perennial hypostasis, and produced conceptions of a feudal-medieval India that was seen as comparable to Britain's past; a tropological encounter between civilisations that continues powerfully to inflect western conceptions of Islam and of west Asia. But Metcalf's proposal that the theory explaining this difference was based on 'racial, rather than environmental or cultural, terms'[41] is only partially correct. While popular race thinking does not usually go beyond stereotypes, in 'scientific' enquiries race as a category is often overdetermined by 'climate and food', or decipherable from cranial anthropometry. These environmental and biological frames yield a global hierarchy of regionally individuated societies, to be used in justifying expansion and colonial conflict, to administer territories, or to differentiate between Gallic, Teutonic and Anglo-Saxon types. Alongside the *extrinsic* difference between India and Europe/Britain, the formulation of *intrinsic* differences of 'nation, caste and creed' to classify and explain Indian society underlines the need for control and guarantees its effectiveness. India's pre-modernity and the mosaic of internal differences are thus complementary: the one may have produced the revolt but the other explained its failure, and so vindicated the necessity of governing a people who had signally failed to take a united stand.

Such preliminaries are particularly significant in the representation of an event that had exposed the inability of the colonial state to predict, and therefore to control, the behaviour of its subjects. The story of 1857–9 prompts an analeptic return, beginning, usually, with the earliest known invasions, through an intermediate history of the Muslim centuries, to the beginning and progress of British investment in India and eventually to the consequence of this investment: the rebellion by the subject people. Simultaneously, and inasmuch as this excursus is guided by the imperatives of empire and its contemporary crisis, the analepsis is always already enacted under the aspect of an overarching prolepsis. In the cases of Martin and Ball, the prefatory journey from a many layered past to the post-Mutiny present yields a comedic meta-historical design, whereby the narrative present becomes the moment when, as Ball promises, 'the triumphs of civilisation and of peace were to recommence'. If the diachronic macro-history provides a context for the rebellion, that context is, in turn, grounded upon the syntagmata of caste, religion, race, language and geography; out of these emerges the map of a static society parcelled into discrete compartments, to be ordered and unified by administrative rationality and the machinery of the colonial state. These moves form the intellectual underbelly of counter-insurgency, and they draw on what had by the 1850s become common and authorised knowledge about India, and whose origins lay in orientalist and empirical researches, in travel writing, missionary pronouncements, in histories, ethnographies and surveys, and in such administrative debates as were raised by questions of education, law, social reform, revenue resettlements and political disputes, as the Company assumed the role of a state from the late eighteenth century. As narratives of the crisis grow co-extensive with the Indian *longue durée*, historiography employs the methods, tropes and judgements of these traditions of enquiry, to work towards a rhetorical closure transforming the rebellion into a formative, though critical, moment in the history of empire.

RECEPTION AND REACTION: CHARLES BALL, *HISTORY OF THE INDIAN MUTINY* (C. 1859)

While these closures locate the histories amidst an archive of representations and the rebellion in the densities of India's past and present, the administrative and military preparations of the colonial state following the news of the uprising were accompanied by a public debate in Anglo-India and Britain. The nature of that reception and the contours of that debate, and their implications for counter-insurgency, for the British view of India and its self-image as an imperial nation, will be explored through this book. But it must be noted here that the public outcry in Britain and in Anglo-India, with its xenophobia and shrill call for revenge, as well as more sober policy debates that the rebellion generated, bear similarities with the spectrum of public reactions to a series of nineteenth-century colonial conflicts including the Chinese War (1839–4; 1857–8), the Morant Bay rebellion (1865), the Maori Wars (1845–72), the Ashanti War (1873), the second Afghan War (1878–80), the Egyptian War (1882), the Mahdi uprising and the siege of Khartoum (1884–5), the invasion of and consequent rebellion in Mashonaland and Bechuanaland (1896) and, indeed, the Crimean (1853–6), and the Boer conflicts (1880–1; 1899–1902). Several recurring factors intersect in each instance. The resistance of the Sudanese, the Chinese, Jamaican slaves, Maoris or the indigenous peoples of 'Rhodesia' to British encroachment – whether commercial, military or settler, or a combination

of all three – and in defence of local economic, political and cultural interests produces sophisticated forms of metropolitan counter-mobilisation
structured around themes of race, religion, 'pacification', imperial identity
and a forthright binary of civilisation–savagery.

As recent studies on the intersections between late Victorian public
spheres and empire have shown, there were two main channels for the propagation of the imperial idea at home and in the expatriate communities,
in India and in the settler colonies.[42] Of these, the first comprises debates
on foreign and colonial policy in Parliament and outside, learned histories,
commentaries and travel-writing, besides periodicals such as *The Times*,
Blackwood's Edinburgh Magazine, the *North British Review*, the *United Services Journal* and *Bentley's Miscellany*. While the opinions and controversies
appearing in these media were largely of the elite circles, and based often on
a specialist knowledge shared by author, reviewer and reader, the dramatic
legislative and technological developments in print media and the growth
of the reading public over the second half of the nineteenth century created
conditions for mass circulation of non-elite newspapers, magazines and
forms of 'improving' and juvenile literature, including the 'penny dreadful'
and boys' magazines. Along with music halls, the stage and advertisements,
popular print culture constitutes the second channel for the propagation
of British overseas expansion, translating rarefied policy concerns into the
vulgate of race, patriotism, xenophobia, adventure and martial exploits.
The need to ensure sales in a fickle market, and against competition, found
a profitable solution in uplifting, swashbuckling accounts of national character and history, which produced ersatz versions of the past, encouraged
jingoism and, drawing empire out from elite circles, handed it over to
popular interest.

Circulation figures grow visibly with the increasingly frequent European
and colonial conflicts. *The Times* sold 100,000 daily copies in 1882, the
year the Mahdis temporarily ousted the British and their Egyptian clients
from Sudan, the *Daily News* and the *Daily Telegraph* sold between 150,000
and 200,000 copies during the Franco-Prussian war of 1871 and the *Daily
Mail* had a daily circulation of 540,000 in 1899, the year the Boer War
began.[43] War and overseas exploits made profitable copy at a time when the
state, increasingly mired in global policing, with numerous commitments
in colonial and foreign policy, and facing aggressive competition from other
European states, had more need of men and *matériel* than ever before. The
intersection, indeed reciprocity, between empire, nationality and popular
media in the second half of the nineteenth century is precisely the site
where, as Linda Colley observes about the impact of the Napoleonic Wars,

'impressive numbers of Britons [made] the step from a passive awareness of nation to an energetic participation on its behalf'.[44]

But if this suggests homogeneity in the new channels of public opinion, there were simultaneously often muted articulations of dissent, sceptical of the benefits of war and expansion, fearful of the consequences of militarism for the British economy and civil society, and for dependent societies, of the curtailment of liberty under despotic imperial rule. Dissent appears from several quarters. Considerations of method and expediency, though other-wise in favour of the globalisation of British hegemony, found fault with specific policies, especially the over-extension of resources, or were critical of the baneful influence of populist excitement in elite decision-making, or urged more vigorous reforms in the dependencies, or made grandiose designs for an Imperial Federation of English-speaking peoples.[45] Other sources of dissent were more fundamental, and though often making a distinction between settler dominions and India, these views centred on a discomfort with ruling other people, and with the revenue burden of supporting the colonial and war machinery. In the view of Radicals like William Cobbett, James Mill, Richard Cobden, John Bright and J. S. Mill, and separatist 'little Englanders' like Goldwin Smith, Charles Dilke and William Harcourt, there was little point and much expenditure in ruling (settler) 'nations when they are fit to be independent', though in India 'if we were to leave . . . we should leave it to anarchy'; a motive for stay-ing on that must be distinguished from the Whig expansionism of the Secretary for War and Colonies (1833–3; 1841–5), George Stanley (later, Lord Derby), and of Lord Russell, who, in speaking of New Zealand, declaimed on 'the obligation and responsibility to govern [the] colonies for their benefit'.[46]

Alongside persistent ideological wrangling over expansion and empire building were specific instances of protest arising from crises of colonial governance and the applicability of the rule of law. One of these was the controversy following the brutal suppression of the Morant Bay rebellion, when some 600 emancipated slaves were killed by the order of the governor of Jamaica, Edward Eyre. The debate, which soon went to court in London, ranged liberals and public intellectuals such as J. S. Mill, Charles Darwin, Herbert Spencer and T. E. Huxley (all of whom Thomas Carlyle contemp-tuously described as 'a knot of nigger philanthropists') campaigning for the trial and prosecution of Eyre, against supporters such as Thomas Carlyle, John Ruskin, Alfred, Lord Tennyson and Charles Dickens.[47] The colonial race in Africa from the 1880s caused another spiral of debate culminating in the Labour and Manchester Radical criticism of the Boer conflict in particular, and of pervasive militarism and jingoism in general. And while Salisbury, in his speech before the Lords as Prime Minister, urged quick deployment since 'there were four, if not five, Powers . . . steadily advancing towards the upper waters of the Nile',[48] the Whig little Englander and Chancellor of the Exchequer, William Harcourt, expressed a wider unease when he wrote to Prime Minister Lord Rosebery asking whether 'we [are] to attempt to create another India in Africa?'[49]

That large numbers of British expatriates died at the hands of the rebels may explain why the rebellion was not the occasion for serious dissent, as perhaps was the fact that India was a huge economic asset, the loss of which would have severely affected British industry, finances and geopolitical edge. Nonetheless, the reception of the news of the rebellion in both popular and elite channels, and the ensuing controversies, anticipate some of the main contours of public debate on colonial policy from the second half of the nineteenth century to decolonisation and after. The events of 1857–9 transformed British institutions and policies in India in the short run by replacing informal with formal imperialism, and, in the long run, generated a lasting iconography and vocabulary that metropolitan media, often complicit with the state, employed in representing the colonial small war, not to speak of the more recent forms of neo-colonial conflict and intervention.

As the news spread, first to government bases like Calcutta and Bombay, and then to Britain (where the news of the massacres of the British at Meerut and Delhi on 10–11 May arrived by telegraph on 26 June 1857), the debate primarily was over a language that would adequately represent insurgency, and over the modalities of counter-insurgency. The debate is an important component of the histories and other accounts, and with the early histories at least, suggests the ambiguities and uncertainties besetting the colonial state, home opinion and the narratives that aimed at producing a 'connected statement'. Coming on the heels of the Crimean War and the groundswell of interest in overseas involvement that followed, the rebellion was a widespread concern by the end of 1857, and, as Ball remarked: 'Everyone – from John O'Groat's house to the Land's End – had something to say about the Indian mutiny; and everyone with common sense, common feeling, and common intelligence, was listened to, even though his information was but scant, and his personal interest in the subject imperceptible; it was enough that his subject was India . . .'[50] The initial successes of rebels, the massacres, the prompt revival of the Mughal court at Delhi and the spiralling civil insurgency combined to generate a sudden lurch of fear and horror. The rebellion came at a time when the Company was the paramount power in India with direct or indirect control over nearly the entire subcontinent. The conquests and annexations of the kingdoms of Sind (1842), Punjab (1848), Burma (1852) and Awadh (1856) had vastly extended the borders of the Company, even as the introduction of railway and telegraph networks was meant to unify a growing dominion with networks of modern communication. Moreover, if the spectacular territorial advances of Dalhousie's tenure had proven the Company's irresistible might to Indians, they had equally demonstrated to the British the paradox underlying their power. Since the Battle of Palashi, the military and political progress of the Company had revealed the comparative fragility of Indian states; yet, these successes would not have been without the Company's mercenary Indian army. The reliance on Indians for conquering and policing India was in itself a vindication of the ethnography of internal differences, and the willingness of Indians to collaborate a sign that British rule was acceptable to, at least, the army that secured and sustained the rule. Though a few sceptics had cautioned against the overwhelming dependence on a mercenary army, and had even prophesied a revolt,[51] the general tenor of opinion before 1857 was, as Dalhousie proclaimed in his parting Minute of 28 February 1856, that under British rule 'the whole of India' was 'profoundly tranquil'.[52]

The irony of this observation is striking when set against the prolonged attacks on British life and property that ensued. A series of indiscriminate attacks on the British, European and Indian Christian population in many towns and civil stations of north and central India followed the massacres at Meerut and Delhi. The most dramatic were those at Delhi – where some fifty British were murdered in a day – and at Kanpur, where the British under General Hugh Massey Wheeler took hasty refuge in an unfinished barrack house on 6 June only to be besieged by troops under the Nana Sahib, Dhondu Pant. Though the siege failed to take the 'entrenchment' – as the cluster of unfinished barracks came to be known – there were considerable casualties, leading to the garrison's negotiated surrender on 26 June, following assurances of a safe passage by boat to Allahabad. The next day, however, the survivors of the siege were ambushed and killed at the Satichaura Ghat (a landing-stage on the Ganges) in Kanpur. Some two hundred women and children who escaped the massacre were imprisoned in the Bibighar, a house in the city, and killed on 15 July, two days before British reinforcements under General Havelock entered Kanpur.[53] While Kanpur was extraordinarily sensational not only because of the numbers involved but also and especially because at Kanpur British women had been subjected to systematic humiliation and violence, the news of such events questioned current notions of security, and the inviolability of British power, prestige and person in India. Since the Bengal Army was responsible for, or had at least created conditions for, this state of affairs, Martin's exclamation that the British were 'met by foulest treachery in the very class' they had relied on underlines hyperbolic governmental confidence and its strategic blindness.[54]

There were several conflicting aspects to the initial reception of the news in Britain and in Anglo-India. Though early reports 'were confused and disjointed, and sometimes . . . contradictory . . . there came enough of positive information to render it too certain that a terrible catastrophe had fallen upon British society in India'.[55] There were some telling controversies over the reliability of what often passed for positive information. For instance, the Earl of Shaftesbury claimed in a public speech that 'day by day ladies were coming into Calcutta with their ears and noses cut off and their eyes put out', a claim he was soon forced to retract in the face of more sober versions.[56] Early historiography too pauses dramatically over scenes of violence, and, as one of the first popular accounts, the *History of the Indian Mutiny* had no qualms in relying frequently on putative 'eye-witness' accounts and the often grisly newspaper reports. Thus Ball cites a letter from an officer in Delhi who wrote to say that: 'such horrible, indescribable barbarities were surely never perpetrated before. You in England will not hear the worst. For the truth is so awful that the newspapers dare not publish it.'[57] Later, in his description of the carnage at Kanpur, Ball sets out to verbalise some of these 'indescribable barbarities': 'There lay the hapless mother and the innocent babe; young wife and the aged matron; girlhood in its teens, and infancy in its helplessness – all – all had fallen beneath the dishonoured tulwars of the Mahratta destroyer, and his fierce and cowardly accomplices in crime.'[58] Again, while describing another massacre that took place on 6 June, Ball conjures: 'Infants . . . actually torn from their mother's arms, and their little limbs chopped off with tulwars yet reeking of their father's blood; while the shrieking mother was forcibly compelled to hear the cries of her tortured child, and to behold, through scalding tears of agony, the death-writhings of the slaughtered innocent.'[59] Having retailed for the most part a saleable mood and idiom, Ball later admits with somewhat more circumspection that in 'the early days of tumult and revolt, the terror inspired by the sudden and unlooked-for visitation, led to much exaggeration' in the press and public opinion, though his vivid and enthusiastic representation of rebel (rather than the retaliatory British) brutalities is quite consonant with the predominant tone of popular media from the last quarter of 1857.[60]

But the populism that Ball and others like him exploit turns upon a cluster of images and icons and their traumatic reversal, that deserve attention. In all such accounts, rebel violence is at once the sign and the effect of an event that had 'indescribably' upset habitual hierarchies, replacing the symbols and institutions of the British with indigenous alternatives, and physically attacking the person of the rulers. More than the causes of the rebellion, or the judicious means of containment that preoccupied the echelons of high policy, it was this reversal that dominated the popular media, bringing forth calls for vengeance, and construing the event as a confrontation between races and religions, between martyrdom and heroism on the one side, treachery and bloodlust on the other. As the narrator of a later Mutiny novel, *In the Heart of the Storm*, described the popular reaction in Britain and in Anglo-India: '[A] sort of madness seized upon the people, to whom the knowledge of Christian women and children of their own race . . . slaughtered and tortured by that inferior and subject heathen race they had been accustomed to hold cheaply, was a horror beyond endurance.'[61]

Recent studies on the discursive figuration of the rebellion have fruitfully argued how popular images of European 'matrons', 'young wives' and 'girlhood' exposed, helpless and at the mercy of the dark-skinned male rebels yields a scene of crime, showing up 'English women as innocent victims and Indian men as sadistic sex criminals', where the rebellion becomes 'above all else . . . a crime against women'; a figuration of torture and sexual violation in the early accounts that, turning upon the revival of chivalry in Victorian England, propels the urge for revenge and reconquest, while obscuring the political content of the rebellion and the history that it embodied. Enduring the wrongs done to them with a dignified calm, the suffering women evoked 'a classical and biblical tradition', and provided 'the British with their charged plots of martyrdom [and] heroism', profitably recycled in the popular imagination throughout the period of formal imperialism, and underscoring the braiding of gender and race in the rhetorical flourishes of empire building.[62] But beyond the insignias of white female sexuality there is a tableau of other meanings in the penumbra of the scene of crime, including the often sharp division between the popular and the official versions.

Besides the obvious victim and the equally obvious chivalry she summons is a simultaneous representation of the perpetrators: the 'fanatic races' whose 'past atrocities' are insignificant 'when compared with the prodigious and almost indescribable outrages' that occurred during the rebellion.[63] Derived from hoary stereotypes of Muslim sexual appetite and Hindu 'depravity', the tableau of native desire unleashed on the white woman's body, publicly, ritually and to the accompaniment of torture encodes an ethnographic proposition validated by a common perception of Indian history. As a reviewer in the *Calcutta Review* opined, the evidence of Indian history to the eighteenth century was 'sufficient to show that the Asiatic, when the hand of the master is withdrawn, is quite capable of doing all that has been done in 1857', that 'their instincts are towards disorder, and that they despise law'.[64]

All was well so long as the native propensities of the 'Asiatics' were contained by a reforming administration; once that guiding, paternal authority was suspended, ironically by the army that was its chief enforcer, there followed the return to a licence whose object and victim is the flesh of the European female. 'Dissimulation', 'treachery' and 'cruelty', the inalienable constants of Asiatic history were, according to Ball, the cause and the content of the rebellion. Since Hindus and Muslims share this inheritance, their unity against the British – notwithstanding the 'capricious distributions of language, creed and appetite' that Ball's ethnography had drawn attention to – becomes a natural but 'extraordinary combination of mutually-repulsive principles for [the] specific purpose' of erasing the British from the land.[65] Configured in the sign-system of popular reception, the mutiny of the Bengal army was not military insubordination alone but a libidinal mutiny against an alien repression; and the obsessive repetition of the figures of rape and mutilation are enactments of a nightmare underlying the megalomania of empire. Beyond their obviously sexual charge, the emphasis on massacres, mutilations and rapes also points to the symbolic economy of British India. By attacking, disrobing, dismembering and otherwise violating the immaculate persons of the rulers – long confident of their absolute mastery and assured of the complete subservience of Indians – and by subjecting them to public humiliation, setting fire to their houses, destroying their property and reducing them to fugitives, suppliants or corpses, the rebels are placed in a new relationship with their erstwhile rulers. If British advance in India from the late eighteenth century was predicated on the growing assumption of a language of agency and command that required the submission and expropriation of a subject population, then at such moments of rebel violence the colonial project, incarnate in a violated or dismembered femininity, surrenders to the 'humiliation by an inferior race'.[66]

In contrast to the prurient fantasies of captive white women, a staple in the popular versions, official, forensic records argue otherwise. While the former would not be appeased without rape, intelligence and judicial reports appear to suggest that, for a variety of reasons, including fear of caste defilement, the *sipahis* may not have violated captive women, or that, at the least, there was insufficient evidence of rape. In historiography, the contrast between popular and official versions can be seen in the contrast between the high drama of Ball and the quiet denials of John Kaye. The Secretary of the Secret and Political Department at India Office following the rebellion, Kaye wrote in his *History of the Sepoy War in India* that:

beyond this wholesale killing and burying, which sickened the entire Christian world, and roused English manhood in India to a pitch of national hatred that took years to allay, the atrocity was not pushed. The refinements of cruelty – the unutterable shame – with which, in some chronicles of the day, this hideous massacre was attended, were but fictions of an excited imagination, too readily believed without inquiry and circulated without thought.[67]

So too, William Muir, chief of the intelligence department of the North Western Provinces at Agra in 1857, confirmed that that the 'cold and heartless bloodthirstiness' of the rebels was 'at the farthest remove from the lust of desire', a view corroborated by district narratives from other sites of siege and massacre.[68]

But it was from the hysterical popular media that counter-insurgency gathered energy and momentum. Reverting again to his populist tone, Ball announced that the news and rumours from India produced a climate of opinion so that: 'Throughout the British empire, the shout of the people was for rescue and for vengeance: the blood of their slaughtered countrymen, of their martyred women and children, came welling up before their mental vision; and one desire for retribution seemed to pervade all hearts, and nerve all arms.' Prayers, funds, men, material, chivalry and jingoistic fervour in Britain and in India followed in response to the 'national cry for unmitigated vengeance'.[69] In Ball and other historians, early and late, the narrative moves along two overlapping but distinct trajectories. The speed at which the revolt spread, as one after the other regiments rose, murdered their officers, plundered the district revenue treasuries and massacred the local British community, was usually accompanied by varying degrees of civil rebellion, arson and unrest, and often by the installation of a rough and ready local government under a dispossessed regional ruler, landlord or military commander who in turn tendered allegiance to the Mughal emperor at Delhi. Where, as at Kanpur and Lucknow, the British dug in their heels – either because they believed rescue would be swift, or because of the impossibility of evacuation – there began a war of attrition, while the rebel militias devised a more comprehensive revolt, or made largely ineffectual attacks on besieged garrisons.

This, in brief, is the first trajectory describing the opening gambit of the rebels. The second trajectory is of counter-insurgency. Military mobilisation, legislation, the march of the various relief forces, their engagements with and eventual victory over the rebellious districts, the heroism of the officers, the fortitude of the men and the capture and punishment of the rebels, form the substance of this movement. But beneath the loud, gung-ho mood are susurrations of a debate that runs alongside counter-insurgency operations and overlaps with the controversy over causes. An indicator of this is in Ball's later observation that the 'impulsive and all but national cry for unmitigated vengeance' was offset by 'the prudent dictates of high policy and humanity'.[70] Emerging from both Houses of Parliament and other fora were sceptical voices declaring 'the terrible details of outrage and suffering' to be 'for the greater part utter fabrications, or wild and malicious exaggerations' that could only hamper the work of 'pacification', the euphemism for reconquest.[71] Nor was it only a question of the veracity of the reports from India, for as Disraeli, the leader of the Tory opposition, stated in a speech before the Commons: 'I protest against meeting atrocities by atrocities. I have heard things said, and seen written of late, which would make me suppose that the religious opinions of the people of England had undergone some sudden change; and that instead of bowing before the name of Jesus, we were preparing to revive the worship of Moloch.'[72] Such protests were privately echoed by William Russell, the *Times* correspondent in India who had earlier reported from the Crimean front, and who while covering the campaigns of 1858 under the commander-in-chief, Colin Campbell, deplored popular methods of dealing with the captured rebels: 'sewing Mohammedans in pig-skins, smearing them with pork-fat before execution, and burning their bodies, and forcing Hindus to defile themselves, are disgraceful and ultimately recoil on ourselves. They are spiritual and mental tortures to which we have no right to resort, and which we dare not perpetrate in the face of Europe.'[73] The criticism was chiefly directed at officers such as Brigadier Neill, Major Renaud and the Deputy Commissioner of the Punjab, Francis Cooper, who carried out indiscriminate and brutal reprisals whenever the British had the upper hand, against not only the rebels but also in the countryside, where they often used a scorched-earth tactic. Of Neill's march from Allahabad to Kanpur in July 1857 Russell wrote that 'his executions were so numerous and so indiscriminate, that one officer attached to his column had to remonstrate with him on the ground that if he depopulated the country he could get no supplies for the men'.[74] Cooper, meanwhile, summarily executed nearly five hundred unarmed mutineers (who had surrendered believing there would be a court martial) using Sikh and Afghan mercenaries at Ajnala on 30–31 July, upon which he announced vengefully: 'There is a well at Kanpur, but there is also one at Ujnalla.'[75] But against the 'effort to throw a cloak of palliation over the crimes of the native army', Ball, reverting to the role of hack historian, contends that Britain need not be humane with the rebels, and that, in any case, such protests 'did not represent the tone of popular opinion'.[76] Harsh reprisals were necessary, for the crimes of India 'will take oceans of tears, and ages of humiliation and practical repentance, to efface', while demonstrating to the subjects the might of the empire they had dared to challenge, and satisfying the passion for vengeance.

The criticism by Ball and others of the 'cloak of palliation' has however a specific referent. Though by the end of May 1857 the Whig-appointed Governor-General Canning had granted plenary military powers to Henry Lawrence, then Commissioner of the newly annexed Awadh, and had allowed a free hand to John Lawrence, the Lieutenant Governor of the Punjab, he also instituted measures and enacted legislation that drew widespread criticism in popular press and opinion. Of these, the first was his rejection of a proposal from the Europeans in Calcutta to raise a volunteer corps, prompting a public outcry against Canning.[77] A second confrontation between Canning and Anglo-Indian public opinion began when the legislative council in Calcutta introduced a Bill on 13 June proposing to monitor and control the press, Indian and British, in India. Quickly denounced as the 'Gagging Act', it caused a furore in making no distinction between rulers and subjects. While the Indian language press, especially Urdu papers, became an increasingly belligerent vehicle for anti-British propaganda[78] – exhorting readers to rebel against the threats to religion and customary practices, denouncing revenue policies, celebrating rebel victories and announcing imminent military help from Russia, Persia and Turkey – the Anglo-Indian press presented other problems. Critical of the administration under Canning, newspapers such as the *Bengal Hurkaru* and the *Friend of India* carried reports that were an embarrassment, circulating wildly exaggerated rumours of atrocities and proposals for dire revenge. These, Canning thought, would contribute to further unrest as 'Articles of the English newspapers [were] translated into the Native languages and . . . read by all'.[79]

The third and most serious confrontation was over a strategic decision to restrain counter-insurgency. The supreme council in Calcutta gave extraordinary powers to Special Commissions to capture and punish rebels in its Act XIV of 6 June 1857. However, the indiscriminate uses to which these powers were often put prompted the official Resolution of 31 July 1857, enjoining a set of guidelines for the interpretation of Act XIV. The aim of the Resolution was to ensure that even as rebellious areas were brought under civil authority, 'a spirit of animosity' was not 'engendered in the minds of people', as it must be 'if their feelings were embittered by the remembrance of needless bloodshed'.[80] To that end, the Resolution required restraint and circumspection from officials, and was a discreet rebuke to those who 'may have been carried too far' in 'restoring order'. While indiscriminate reprisals 'may induce [the people] to band together in large numbers for the protection of their lives, and with a view to retaliation', the burning of villages and standing crops in the region between Allahabad and Kanpur – a practice for which officers such as Major Renaud became renowned – could lead, the Resolution added, to 'distress and even famine . . . added to the other difficulties with which the Government will have to contend'.[81] Though the instructions were in the larger interest of the colonial state, it was soon ridiculed as the 'Clemency of Canning' in *The Times* of 17 October. Along with *Punch*, which carried a celebrated cartoon in which Canning appears pardoning an armed and bloody *sipahi* (24 October 1857), *The Times* began a campaign against the 'Indian Government [which] has thought fit to publish a silly proclamation' at a time 'when everything depends on prompt and speedy retribution'.[82]

Inserted into the narrative of counter-insurgency, the dispute is both surprising and familiar. It is surprising in showing up fissures within the conduct of counter-insurgency at a time when the security of the British in India was at stake. The disagreement between the actions of men on the spot and the supreme council in Calcutta, between high policy and public opinion, between the Company and a monitory Parliament, or even within the Parliament – as the Palmerston ministry defended itself against criticism until its fall in February 1858 – continued throughout the rebellion, intensified at the issue of the 'Oudh Proclamation' and was brought to an end with the transfer of power to the Crown in November that year.[83] While discrepancies of opinion and judgement are perhaps inevitable in a crisis whose resolution involved the men on the spot, the Indian administration, Parliament and the press, a crucial and defining moment in the conduct of counter-insurgency is the struggle between the permissions of Act XIV and the prohibitions of the subsequent Resolution.

Three months after the initial outbreak at Meerut, and long before Lucknow was relieved or the Mughal capital captured, the colonial state paused, as it were, to examine the modalities of counter-insurgency, and in so doing defined the locus of the state's authority to its agents and before an implied audience of insurgents. By invoking the primacy of law and procedure over an arbitrary, extra-legal 'retribution', the Resolution domesticated the rebellion as a law-and-order problem *internal* to the judicial and legislative territory of the colonial state, denying to the event the radical exteriority that later Indian nationalism claimed to find in the rebellion. Despite an appearance of clemency the guidelines constituted a more authoritative and authoritarian act than the reprisals carried out by the up-country freelancers. In recommending restraint and discrimination, and by containing, equally, the rhetoric (as in the Press Act) and the practices of insurgency and counter-insurgency, the state transcended its subjects and its instruments, foreclosed the scope of the rebellion and indicated an imperial future that lies beyond, and so contains, the current crisis. Disraeli's opposition to 'meeting atrocity by atrocity' signified somewhat more than a moral scruple; and in the prohibitions of 31 July, and in Canning's letter to the Queen, reprisal became a peril as great as the rebellion it promised to quell.[84] At the same time, the prohibition of indiscriminate and extra-legal military action was also the matter of a distinguishing style. Such actions, including plain looting, did in fact resume whenever the British and their allies (Sikh, Gurkha and Afghan freebooters) took rebel strongholds – as at Delhi, Jhansi and Lucknow following their capture – and were a spectacular complement to the system of authorised rewards and punishments; but the invocation of a rule of law to regulate counter-insurgency, at least in theory, speaks for a need to dissociate British-led banditry from the 'lawless' depredations of the Rohilla and the Pindari militias, the Afghan invaders of the eighteenth century and, not least, the rebels themselves.[85] Though in his thoughtful essay on colonial military doctrine H. L. Wesseling distinguishes between purely military intimidation, which he calls the English style, as opposed to the French and American method of subordinating military to political objectives, the rebellion shows the simultaneous presence of and contest between the two doctrines, with public opinion and the men on the spot clamouring for a 'purely military' solution, and the government actively trying to win over Indian opinion as in Canning offering terms of truce to the rebels and their patrons.[86]

The 'prudent dictates of high policy and humanity' that Ball criticises have, however, a deeper resonance, one that makes the controversy a familiar echo of other debates in the history of British empire in India. The trial of Warren Hastings, the quarrel between the Orientalists and the

Anglicists, the conflict between the missionaries and the Company and the more recent controversy surrounding the annexation of Awadh, had all raised fundamental questions about the British brief in India, about the degree and manner of intervention that was possible or necessary over the statist ambitions and methods of a merchant company; and usually, though obliquely, about India itself. In these precedents, as in the controversy over the modalities of counter-insurgency, are to be found the lineaments of a struggle at the core of the British project in India: a struggle between expediency and legitimacy, between the violent applications of military power and colonial aggrandisement, and the competing narratives of justification. Viewed thus, the prohibitions of the 'Clemency Resolution' are akin to Burke's monumental indictment of the Company's 'geographical morality' and the arbitrary 'excesses' of its pro-consular protagonist, Warren Hastings, and to Cobden's Radical uncertainty as to whether the British could 'play despot and butcher' in India without 'finding [their] character deteriorated at home'.[87]

While maintaining an uneasy balance between the troubled moderation of the government and the enthusiasm of its instruments, the *History of the Indian Mutiny* is laced with criticism of policy that underlines the dichotomy between expediency and legitimacy. Ball claims that the 'acquisition of sovereignty' in India was unintended and accidental, adding that 'the officers of the old-established English Company' had no 'inducement' to conquer or rule India.[88] It is an old argument, a disclaimer among the commonplaces of British historiography of India, and a view that in insisting on the absence of an original and controlling volition, seeks to legitimise territorial acquisition and *de facto* statehood before a fretful Parliament. India was an empire of consent, not conquest, so the argument went; for, quite apart from the fragility of Indian polities, and the fact that Indian states often sought British meddling in their affairs, was the need to secure trade by pacifying the country. The claim is important as a defence against the accusations of those like Burke who had argued that the Company, led by unscrupulous if not criminal functionaries, represented an excessive and arbitrary exercise of power that, even as it rode roughshod over Indian society and polity, threatened metropolitan politics. In his introduction to *The Administration of the East India Company* – an apologia for the Company and a celebration of its achievements in India – John William Kaye had similarly claimed the absence of volition. The territorial imperative of the Company was, Kaye argued, 'in accordance with a law of nature, universal and immutable', and it was as the result of such a law that the 'empire should have so expanded'.[89] The locution 'law of nature' conceals and reveals the cycle of 'defence' and 'aggression' in which the Company was caught in order to protect its possessions and commercial interests from European and Indian competitors, in the general clawing for dominance following the disintegration of the Mughal empire by the second half of the eighteenth century. Yet if the masquerade of natural law disguises the Company's will-to-power and its pursuit of expediency, liberates empire from the burden of an original culpability and enables Kaye's narrative of justification (appropriately subtitled 'A History of Indian Progress'), the spectre of guilt returns with the trauma of the rebellion.

Though veiled by the rhetoric of heroic and vengeful counter-insurgency, guilt is often a motif in historiography. Ball's history opens with a survey of the contentious relations between the Company and Parliament, followed by criticisms of legal discrimination against the subject population, of the contradiction between the initial trading brief of the Company and its growing militarism, its inherent corruption and the tortuousness of procedure, and of the widespread discrimination against Indians in the army and the civil administration. At the end Ball also addresses the racial prejudice of Anglo-Indians, observing that the 'want of sympathy between the two races had induced an isolation of the dominant class', and had led to a situation akin to the relation between the 'Anglo-American' and the 'Negro'.[90] Again, while describing Home opinion at the end of the first volume, Ball admits that 'the sepoy mutiny was only another name for fierce and sanguinary war of races', but suggests that the war had its reasons.[91] Notwithstanding the attempts by the Court of Directors to minimise the grievances of the soldiers, the government had deprived soldiers of deserved benefits and honours, so that they began to 'detest the rule . . . of the Feringhee subjugators of their native princes'.[92] Moreover, the administration, led by a cabal of officials who deliberately misled Parliament, had instituted laws and policies of revenue reform that impoverished the peasantry. Thus, 'in Bengal an amount of suffering and debasement existed which probably was not equalled, and certainly not exceeded, in the slave-states of America'.[93]

Ball's history is divided between a narrative of justification and the facts of 'suffering and debasement', between the 'prudent dictates of high policy and humanity' and the 'cry for unmitigated vengeance'. The ambiguity is also evident in his observations on Indian violence during the rebellion: if 'the past atrocities of these [Hindu and Muslim] fanatic races fade into insignificance when compared with . . . indescribable outrages . . . associated . . . with the sepoy mutiny of 1857'[94], that somewhat culture-specific formulation is made relative by a reminder of intolerance at large:

> The rancour and bitterness that spring from religious fanaticism, have produced in all ages, and still produce, the same fruits in all parts of the world. Spain, America, the Low Countries, France, and even England itself, can testify to this fact; for the annals of each are red with the stains of blood poured out in the wars of creeds.[95]

The ambiguity reveals the predicament of historiography, faced with the task of writing the rebellion from the vantage of the victors, and forced by the vector of narrative to confront a culpable past. Reconciling the expedient application of power with the labours of legitimation is the primary theme of the self-representations of empire, replayed no less in the pages of Mutiny historiography. Written after the fact and buttressed by the investigations of the state, the *History of the Indian Mutiny*, like other early histories of the event, is primarily a testament of power. It derives authority from the recent success – indeed, the vindication – of empire, and renders to empire a 'connected statement' of that success. In this, the discourse of counter-insurgency gives a rubric, a form and a meaning to colonial insurgency, and altogether expropriates the rebellion as effectively as the combination of Act XIV and the 'Clemency Resolution' had done. At the same time, and since the fact of the rebellion cannot and does not deter the imperial agenda, historiography, like the colonial state it serves, requires the discovery and prosecution of a symbol to exculpate empire and to reaffirm its legitimacy.

It is in a sense a fitting end: by making the East India Company the symbol of culpability, by ascribing to the Company the excesses of arbitrary power and the consequent transgression of the ideal of trusteeship in which India was to be held, the Crown and the Parliament finally ended the fearful licence of the merchant as state that Burke had brought to notice at the end of the eighteenth century. And even as the Company was blown from the mouth of a cannon with its aide and associate, a mercenary army turned rebel, Ball offers final counsel: that 'it had become necessary, for the future safety of the country, that the bearing of Europeans of every class, towards the native races of India, should be very considerably modified'.[96] Nor is this only a matter of the racial prejudice that had contributed to a 'want of sympathy' between the Indians and their Anglo-Indian masters. On the next page Ball argues against those who maintained that there would have been no rebellion if missionaries had converted sufficient numbers of Indians, that the keystone of British policy in India was a policy of non-interference, and warns of future conflicts if the suppression of the rebellion encourages renewed interference. There is, of course, some fiction in this formulation, for British advance in India, if Dalhousie's tenure is taken as an example, was nothing if not interference. Yet the formulation epitomises a new orientation, as the metropolitan state, at once the inheritor and the repudiator of the Company's aggrandisement, recoils from the project of reform, and refashions a traditional India that had betrayed the expectation 'that [it] could be transformed on an English model'.[97]

2

Reform and revision

Strike our roots into the soil, by the gradual introduction and establishment of our own principles and opinions; of our own laws, institutions,
and manners; above all, as the source of every other improvement, of
our religion, and consequently of our morals.

William Wilberforce, speech on the East India Company's Charter Bill
(House of Commons, 1 July 1813)

We have to consider what countries must be developed either by
ourselves or by some other nation, and we have to remember that it
is part of our responsibility and heritage to take care that the world,
as far as it can be moulded by us, shall receive the Anglo-Saxon and
not another character. . .

Earl of Rosebery, speech at the anniversary banquet of
the Royal Colonial Institute (1 March 1893)

LINEAGES OF AN AETIOLOGY

The idea that the Company administration had, through its failings, produced conditions for a revolt was initially put forward by the Anglo-Indian
military, anxious to underplay the mutiny and deflect attention to civilian
resistance. The idea meshed well with long-standing parliamentary discomfort with a mercantile company acting as a state, leading eventually to
the Charter Act of 1833 which ended the Company's right to trade, after
some eighty years of acrimonious public and legislative wrangling stoked
by a broad spectrum of interests. That this legislative fretting could work as
cover for merchant lobbies and partisan interests, or to keep a jealous eye on
audit and preferment in a monopolist corporation with *de facto* statehood
in a faraway land, ought to be seen alongside normative criticism of overseas
investments by a Whig oligarch such as Burke, by free-trade theorists and
by the Radicals, philosophic and otherwise.[1] But the fretting over India in
and out of Parliament is only one instance of a fretful metropolitan negotiation with an array of dominions, settler colonies, dependent territories,

client states, as well as European nations, and later the United States of America. If this history shows up strains and overlaps between foreign and colonial policy on the one side, and domestic economy and politics on the other, it reveals, too, continuities between Cobbett's scepticism of British purpose in India, Harcourt's over Africa and Goldwin Smith's reluctance to hold on to settler colonies when they were 'fit to be independent'.

But the register of moral and economic dissent against expansion and colonial possession, audible from the late eighteenth century, was never quite in favour of relinquishing India, and keen separationists in the case of settler colonies often proposed better, meaning more, governance in the east. Notwithstanding Goldwin Smith's acerbic remark that a '"mission", historically speaking, is little more than another name for a tendency to rapine', the responsibility or trust that the project entailed meant, beyond liberating those fit for independence, a watchful scrutiny of commercial, political and legislative proceedings in at first India, and, towards the end of the century, in Africa.[2] The call for vigilance over procedure and for the universality of the rule of law is something that Canning's much reviled clemency appears to share with the Jamaica Committee trying to prosecute Governor Eyre, and with historians, publicists and administrators who argued against bullying and chicanery in proceedings with states and people, whether in eastern India or in 'Rhodesia'. The principal criticism of expansion was not the fact itself, but that for such investment to advance through breaches of contract or confidence was morally unsound and could have baneful results. And it is from this coign of vantage that dissenters, early and late, are precursors of the early nationalist lament that while British government of India was in theory beneficial, it was in fact neither representative of the people nor healthful for its economy.

That the Company was to blame for one thing or another was not therefore a new idea, being shared periodically by conservatives, Whigs and Radicals, and by free-trade theorists, orientalists and missionaries, though the rebellion gave a new spin to an old indictment. What is curious, however, is that an idea, mooted by army apologists but with a longish historical record, should reappear in Indian writing on the event in vastly different ways between 1858–9 and the early twentieth century.

The first account by an Indian was the *Causes of the Indian Revolt* (1858) by Sir Syed Ahmad Khan (1817–98), then a government sub-judge who aided British fugitives in his district, and later better known as archaeologist, educationist, publicist and leader of Indian Muslims.[3] Published in a print run of 500 copies, Sir Syed sent most to London, one to the supreme council in Calcutta, and kept a handful with him, keeping the book out of public circulation until the English translation of 1873. The primary aim of the *Causes* was to show the loyalty of Muslims, who in the years following the rebellion were viewed with suspicion and disfavour. But apologetic accounts like Sir Syed's – and there were others like him – with their special pleading for Bengalis, Parsis or Muslims and their air of grateful loyalty, grew politically and intellectually vestigial with the accelerated transformation of identities, politics and forms of protest over the turn of the century.[4] Increasingly broad-based and radical demands for independence replaced elite-led nationalism over the first partition of Bengal (1905–7), honing in the process theories of nativism and nationality, and the practices of protest, from urban terrorism to village industry.[5] The reinterpretation of the rebellion that began some fifty years after the fact, and within the broad field of cultural rediscovery, political praxis and nationalist history writing, is a result of fundamental changes among the actors in Indian politics, amplifying adversarial politics in the imperial formation, and revealing the ambiguities besetting theories of nationality.

The exemplary rereading from this period is *The Indian War of Independence in 1857* (1909) by Vinayak Damodar Savarkar (1883–1966), an exponent of armed protest who associated with expatriate Russian revolutionaries in London around the time he wrote the book, and, from 1937, leader of the chauvinist Hindu Mahasabha, accused but acquitted of the assassination of Gandhi in 1948.[6] In his polemic against stuffy high imperial historians who insisted on using the term 'mutiny' – the dust having by then settled over a specific inter-service rivalry, and with a formal empire in place – Savarkar argued, much as Malleson did on the evidence of civil 'disturbance', that there was more to the rebellion than a mutiny.[7] Though unlike army apologias in that the nationalist version did not fuss too much over the military and the civil arms, or between the discontent among soldiers and of the people at large, the conclusions are nearly identical. Malleson's view that the civil service had 'completely failed in attaching even one section of the population to British rule'[8] was an acceptable, even necessary, proposition for the *Indian War*; only the former insistence on blaming the civil service becomes in Savarkar's hands, or in the hands of a nationalist imaginary that now lingers in school history books and old-fashioned novels, a broader indictment of the panoply of the institutions, policies and effects of British rule in India, whether under Company or Crown.

Quite apart from the motivations of the soldiery, the multiple instances of civil rebellion made it possible for Savarkar to jump several intermediate steps with the claim that 'war of independence' was a more apt rubric than either civil rebellion or mutiny; for, beyond all local grudges and fears, the rebellion was fundamentally the combined refusal of Hindus and Muslims to be ruled any more by the British. The title of Savarkar's book was based on an analogy between the liberation of the thirteen American colonies and the hoped-for liberation of colonised India, in that the racy, impassioned story that Savarkar writes is the inspiring, albeit distorting, mirror of contemporary armed resistance by western-educated Indian elite and middle-class intellectuals, sharing an ideological and geographical (Amsterdam, Paris, London, New York) platform with forms of militant anti-state resistance in Europe.

As a remembered figure, the rebellion gives lineage to the violent underbelly of Indian nationalism, from the gentleman-terrorist at the turn of the century to the professionally run Indian National Army of the 1940s, and, sometimes, aids the recovery of mass-based and emblematically secular anti-colonial resistance. Though these achievements rest often on a fideistic attitude to the 'motherland' where extrapolation and anachronism can supply what archive or evidence cannot, there is yet ambivalence in the political imagination at work which faith has not glossed over. The contrast between the cautious and loyal *Causes* and the programmatically disloyal *Indian War* seems clear enough. The former discounts three causes of the rebellion that could suggest a radical opposition: that it was religious war or *jehad*, that it was a Hindu and/or Muslim conspiracy and, finally, that it had nationalist or racial character. The one cause of the rebellion was the absence of Indian representation in government, a typically Whig concern prudently balancing limited representation in government with a cagey preservation of the status quo. People, Sir Syed says, 'should have a voice in its [government] Councils' to 'warn us of dangers before they burst upon and destroy us'.[9]

That Savarkar's case should rest almost wholly on the aetiology Sir Syed rejects is a sign of the political radicalisation of the educated urban Indian in the decades in between.[10] But there is more to the difference and more than difference in what they like and what they deplore. Sir Syed was decidedly not in favour of a simple return to the Mughal-Muslim, and even less to a Hindu, political order though, as grandson of a Mughal prime minister, there are traces of pathos over decline and nostalgia for the former preeminence of *sharif* culture.[11] His refusal to support the rebellion is the pragmatic decision of a Mughal nobleman seeking a timely integration with the new regime. Aware of the resources of the British nation and the administration, it is unlikely he could have shared the optimism of those who believed that a spate of rebellions and massacres would rid them of their rulers. But if this wide-eyed decision is similar to the pragmatic avowals of loyalty from the western-educated Indian intelligentsia in Bengal or in Bombay for whom, as for Sir Syed, the colonial regime held the promise of progress and modernity, his loyalty is already the tool of his representation of exclusively Muslim interests. In order to progress, Muslims must quickly adapt to western science and education, using the British to counter the growing presence of Hindus in government, and to prevent a slide back to the political instability of the eighteenth century. There is certainly criticism of the deliberate government neglect of Persian learning, as of the disruption of precolonial rent and revenue practices in the *Causes*, though these are no more or less radical than those already published in accounts and commentaries by the British, and in the English press.

When they return again after a long hiatus lasting from 1857–9 to the turn of the century, radical demands for political change share in the violence of their precursors but not their vocabulary, nor do they imagine a return to the world of rajas, sultans and the *jahanpanah*, without the accoutrements of modernity, without rule of law and without the charming reasonableness of western institutions, cultures and discourses. In the case of Savarkar or the Swadeshi activists and ideologues, as indeed in the case of Hindu chauvinists and Muslim separatists, the hope and the demand are for a republican future resting on institutions and protocols framed by the British, but governed directly by the citizens of a free nation. But where the author of the *Causes* emphasises the benefits of British rule, the western-educated and republican nationalist Savarkar, having gained political conceptions from a regime Sir Syed had defended, and with links to European revolutionary movements, eulogises in 1909 the rebellion as a war of independence while excising the political freight of that war and the religious energy of the warriors. This perhaps is again a pragmatic move. For Savarkar, recovering a story of heroism and martyrdom is to give legitimacy to contemporary armed resistance. And if *The Indian War* is the beginning of a deliberate relocation of the rebellion in the nationalist imaginary, it is also suggestive of a late nationalism swinging, sometimes erratically, between Eurocentric republicanism, and precolonial forms of political and social being.[12]

The likeness between the army apologist's criticism of the administration and the radical nationalist amplification of that criticism to attack British rule in India as such, and the unlikeness between Savarkar's republicanism and his laudatory account of a resistance that was largely feudal-monarchical in form and practice is useful for this chapter. Though obliquely, these interpretive overlaps and anomalies give an added significance to the early debates on reform and colonial modernisation, even as they show how such projects yielded in time the loyalty of Sir Syed, a sub-judge in the 1850s, as much as the revolutionary terrorism of Savarkar, sent to the island prison of the Andamans for an assassination attempt on a British judge in 1911.

The project of reform and its rhetoric was as old as the formal arrival of the Company as a territorial power.[13] Four years after the Mughal Emperor Shah Alam II made the trading corporation his governor and revenue collector in the provinces of Bengal, Bihar and Orissa, the Company historiographer Alexander Dow published 'An Enquiry into the State of Bengal; with a Plan for restoring that kingdom to its former Prosperity and Splendour', as the second volume of his *History of Hindostan* (1768). Designed to introduce the country to Home opinion and justify territorial acquisition with plans for reform, Dow's work marks the beginning of a series of representations of metropolitan interests that often double as histories of India. To what degree the plan turned out successfully for either party can be gauged from the famine of 1769–70, and from the parliamentary debate on Fox's India Bill in 1784, in which Burke accused the Company of systematically betraying and ruining Indian states. Beyond fiscal and contractual impropriety the speech highlighted the contrast between the British state at home, and a mercantile corporation deriving corporate being from the former, and acting as state elsewhere. While 'the *Magna Carta*', the *ur*-text of Whig political history for Burke as much for T. B. Macaulay later, 'is a charter to restrain power, and to destroy monopoly [the] East India Charter is a charter to establish monopoly and to create power'.[14] The burden of the comparison certainly overlaps with Adam Smith's anti-mercantilist advocacy of free trade, but has a more purely political ring in pitting power against an implied theory of rights and freedom. Monopolist power being the case in Bengal, there remained for Parliament to check its exercise, to ensure that a normative responsibility was not obscured or set aside in favour of expediency. Premised on theory rather than geography, and the only admissible justification for holding on to India, the watchfulness Burke demanded is crucial where people are not free and government non-representative, for 'all political power being set over men, and . . . all privilege claimed or exercised in exclusion of them, being wholly official, and for so much, a derogation from the natural equality of mankind at large, ought to be someway or other exercised ultimately for their benefit'.[15]

The promise of benefit to justify expansion and intervention has three main sources in the nineteenth century: the Evangelical Revival, already encouraged by its intervention in the anti-slavery movement; liberal-utilitarian theories of home and colonial improvement; and the bi-partisan high imperial sense of racial-national mission. But there is one caveat to

Burke's view of benefit that distinguishes him sharply from these later positions, of which some were Whig like Burke's, but less chary of theory-driven
models of social transformation.[16] In his speech on Fox's India Bill, and
later during the trial of Warren Hastings, Burke repeatedly makes the point
that beyond the benefit that even a despotic government owes to its subjects is the foundational matter of cultural singularity. As he observed at the
trial: 'Faults this nation [India] may have, but God forbid we should pass
judgement upon people who framed their laws and institutions prior to
our insect origins of yesterday.'[17] The argument of antiquity, so forceful in
Burke's other writings on politics, is perhaps less important here than the
fact of judgement, especially of one society by another, using categories and
norms extrinsic to the former. Love of power and monopoly leads to despotism, to justify which the Company and its apologists began representing
the backwardness of India.

The possibility of judging other societies, or past eras in history, is not,
however, peculiar to the Indian case, nor is it self-contained. The possibility
stems from a serial arrangement of the past, that typically Whig view, elaborated in the 'stage-theory' of the Scots historians, Adam Ferguson, John
Millar and William Robertson, and carried forward through the nineteenth
century by historians from Henry Hallam to John Seeley, which configured
all history as a story of progress and improvement, and in which different
societies could be graded according to the stage of political, economic and
institutional development they had reached.[18] It is a view that disallowed
organic historicism as a method for studying the past, while ruling out
the possibility of conceiving of cultural difference as incommensurable,
or cultural and social worlds as self-referential wholes; and, notwithstanding Burke's poignant, rearguard resistance, the view gave to expansion and
colonisation an irrefutable historical necessity throughout the nineteenth
century.

While Burke in his speech referred to the British in India as 'schoolboys
without tutors', or 'minors without guardians', evangelicals, liberals, and
high imperial spokesmen routinely invert the referents of the metaphor,
giving the metropolitan state the responsibility for educating a colonised,
backward people.[19] But there is more than a metaphor at work in the liberal
theory of colonial government. As the Examiner of Correspondence at
India House, James Mill, explained his narrative venture into his employer's
territory: 'To ascertain the true state of Hindus in the scale of civilisation, is
not only an object of curiosity . . . but to the people of Great Britain, charged
as they are with the government of that great portion of the human species,
it is an object of the highest practical importance.'[20] It is the philosophical

Radical-turned-historiographer who will determine the scale; for whom cultures and societies are advanced in so far as they have come to the consciousness of utility, where civil society is organised around contractual ethics, codified law, representative government and economic rationality. Where these are absent, an absence compounded by non-representative, despotic government, there is need for intervention, for in the liberal-Radical eschatology all societies must be hitched to a rationalist spiral of progress whose vanguard is liberal and, sometimes, Radical Britain. That all societies *can* be hitched to this project is a non-parochial heuristic, like the gospel in evangelicalism, outside the historical time in which all societies are enmeshed, that hopes to reform when it cannot erase the local, singular and specific. It is not a clash of civilisations, but rather encounters between many local histories and a global theory, where the parochial is the site of deficiency or perversion to be rectified by a reforming intervention. And it is a zero-sum encounter, for either the theory of history with its anthropological premises was universal, in which case all societies already partook of it, or they had to be changed to fit the theory.

This needed government, necessarily non-representative. But as John Stuart Mill explained in 1861, authoritarian government was 'as legitimate as any other, if it is the one which in the existing state of civilisation of the subject people, most facilitates their transition to a higher stage of improvement'.[21] The formulation reconciles the nagging contradiction between empire and liberty by tying present subjection to future emancipation, even as it shows the basic continuity in more than half a century of liberal-Radical theorisation on the state. And it has further use in employing a language agreeable to several political positions, often in disagreement over domestic affairs, but united on the need to introduce a new 'moral and political basis in the vast expanse of the Asiatic regions'.[22] The Whig M. P. Macaulay argued energetically against Radical social theory and epistemology in his review of Mill's *Essay on Government* (1819), pointing out a perversely reductive model of the human subject that Mill shared with Jeremy Bentham, and warning against the dangers of universal suffrage which the latter proposed in the *Plan of Parliamentary Reform* (1817).[23] The argument Macaulay had made in an earlier review was that 'in all movements of the human mind which tend to great revolutions there is a crisis at which moderate concession may amend, conciliate and preserve', making it possible 'to protect vested rights, to secure every useful institution, every institution endeared by antiquity and noble association, and, at the same time, to introduce into the system improvements harmonizing with the original plan'.[24] It is a patrician method of riot control, defending property from the clawing of the propertyless with timely let-offs, and the ruling imaginary of gentlemanly capitalism with country seats, landscaping the globe.

Yet, as law member of the supreme council in Calcutta between 1834–8, Macaulay's assessment of the value of vested rights and traditional institutions is no different from the Radical view. Macaulay's Minute on Education (1833) was a plan to prise open local cultures, to alter or else erase their specificity and assimilate them into the liberal-Radical teleology. Similarly, the draft code of Indian criminal law, which eventually took effect in 1860, drew heavily on Bentham's schemes of deductive jurisprudence wholly independent of existing or customary law. For the law commission Macaulay headed, the criminal code of 1837 was a first step in reforming substantive civil law and laws of procedure, which varied wildly even within British-ruled territory, and was factored by religious, caste and regional differences.[25] Sent out to India following the Charter of 1833, which sanctioned a full reform package that evangelicals had demanded for nearly three decades, Macaulay's educational and legal theses are not new or original, being derived from the 'Clapham Saints' with whom he shared family connections, and from the Radical Westminster, which he otherwise found too extreme and wrong-headed in metropolitan affairs. But combined with concurrent changes in revenue administration and in administrative and judicial procedure, with expansion and militarism, they amount to a panoptic exercise where, unlike in England, 'improvement' must work against the layout of the parochial 'original plan'. Beyond profit or revenue was an incontrovertible good. The metropolitan state needed to intervene in 'the work of Colonization', for in it 'lay the future and permanent interests of civilisation itself', a project that 'should be considered in relation not to a single country, but to the collective economical interests of the human race'.[26]

Malleson's attack on the civil service, which became the minister of liberal-Radical theory, Sir Syed's, belief in the promise of progress and modernity, and Savarkar's rejection of everything empire meant, form a series of responses to the British project in India, dissimilar yet all equally mediated by an event that had overturned a theory. The generic liberal belief that the 'great cause of revolutions is . . . that, while nations move forward, constitutions stand still' led to reforming intervention in India.[27] But intervention paradoxically spawned a resistance that in the vernacular signified native 'ingratitude', though in more thoughtful accounts signifying a return to the irrepressible singularity of cultures that Burke the Whig oligarch had noted.

THE AETIOLOGY OF RESISTANCE

The *History of the Sepoy War in India* by J. W. Kaye is incomplete, for he died after writing the first three volumes, which took the narrative to the end of the first year of the rebellion. Kaye's career in India and at the India Office, besides his large output as Anglo-Indian historian, editor, reviewer, biographer and novelist, make him a significant historian. He was an officer in the Bengal Army (1832–41), founded the *Calcutta Review* in 1844 and in 1858 was appointed Secretary to the Political and Secret Department at the India Office. Before *The Sepoy War* Kaye had already written a history of the Company's Afghan wars, a history of the progress of Christian missions in India and *The Administration of the East India Company*.[28] The combination of administrative concern and scholarly interest in *The Sepoy War* is also evident in the six-volume *Peoples of India* (1868), which Kaye edited with J. F. Watson. Originally a collection of photographs of Indians taken in the course of government surveys and by amateurs, and formally commissioned in 1856 by Canning as a souvenir he wanted to take back to England, the photographic assembly of colonial subjects became the brief of the Political and Secret Department following the rebellion. With short notes on 'type', tribe, race, caste, class, profession, deportment, the compilation is an act of surveillance and record that drew on and reinforced ethnographic categories, while answering specific security objectives of the colonial state, keen to learn more about a recently rebellious population.

While Malleson, who completed the work as *Kaye and Malleson's History of the Indian Mutiny* (1878) changed the title, the original is a compromise between the two chief schools of thought. The 'sepoy' is a nod to the mutiny, and 'war' suggests an event more critical than a law and order problem. Though as title 'sepoy war' is both awkward and a little vague ('sepoys' being meant to fight wars, the phrase is very nearly tautological), it underscores the trouble in naming a series of events that represented the intersection of a number of histories, political disputes, ethnic specificities and administrative-legislative institutions. The phrase 'sepoy war' hardly addresses this density, but is an admission of the failure of a mono-causal explanation, striving towards a more comprehensive semantic containment than that available in the narrowly partisan views.

Whereas earlier historians began with a general introduction to the country, Kaye's starting point is an extended reflection on the causes of the rebellion, which is really a criticism of British policies in the decades before 1857. Earlier the partisan of an improvement he now questions, the argument on causes is at the cusp of two representations of India and the British self-image in India, even as it shows how the rebellion was instrumental in the transition from the one to the other. Though Kaye admits other causes such as the service grievances of soldiers, or the controversy over greased cartridges, which was the immediate provocation, these are subsumed by an overarching design in which Radicalism, or Radical influence on the civil service, appears as the real villain.

The arrangement of the main causes of the rebellion in the first volume suggests Kaye's political location as a historian of India. Book 1 begins with the conquests of the kingdoms of Punjab and Burma (chapter 1), followed by an account of the annexation of several Indian states, and the dispossession of several royal families, including the Nana Sahib of Bithoor, under the Doctrine of Lapse (chapter 2). The third chapter is a criticism of the policies that led up to the annexation of the kingdom of Awadh, and the fourth is titled, the 'Progress of Englishism'. The four chapters are a reading of the 'extension of British rule' from the 1820s; an extension that was 'followed always by a reconstruction of the administration . . . fashioned upon our own models and composed of our own people'.[29] Expansion was often prompted by the fluidity of Indian states and frontiers, and by the need to protect the Company's revenues and trade flows, but acquired ideological legitimacy in theories of colonial transformation, evangelical or liberal-Radical. Unlike *The Administration of the East India Company* where Kaye had charted the success of intervention, *The Sepoy War* is more chastened and circumspect, indeed revisionist, with the 'progress of Englishism' emplotted as an ironic failure. And against liberal-Radical authoritarianism, Kaye resurrects an earlier approach to India where political and military caution had combined to dissuade the Company from interference in Indian life and polity, and from large territorial investment.

'To be invaded', Kaye writes, 'and to be conquered is a state of things appreciable to the inhabitant of India', for he finds in defeat 'his "kismet"; his fate; God's will'. But the Doctrine of Lapse which was used to annex kingdoms by administrative fiat was a more disturbing violence for it 'pursue[d] the victim beyond the grave'.[30] The Doctrine was first framed and applied on the Maratha kingdom of Satara in 1849 when, after the death of the king, Appa Sahib – who had no direct male heirs – it was decided by the government to disallow the successor, adopted by the late king without British consent, and to annex the kingdom. A handy tool of an expansionist colonial state, the Doctrine could do with subsidiary states what it took war to accomplish against states outside the British sphere of influence. While war was needed at the frontiers, against Nepal, Burma, Sindh, Punjab and Afghanistan, the Doctrine could absorb what

Dalhousie described as 'petty intervening states', otherwise peaceable and loyal to the British, whose independence served no purpose and whose military resources were either in British hands or negligible. Hence, 'on all occasions, where heirs natural shall fail, the territory should be made to lapse, and adoption should not be permitted, excepting in those cases in which some strong political reason may render it expedient to depart from this general rule'.[31]

Following Satara, the Doctrine was applied against the dynastic houses of Sambalpur (1849), Bithoor (1853), Jhansi (1854), Nagpur (1854), Carnatic (1854) and Tanjore (1855); and of these, the annexation of Jhansi, and the government's refusal to allow the Nana Sahib Dhondu Pant of Bithoor – the adoptive successor of Baji Rao – to inherit the title of Peshwa and his father's pension are crucial from the perspective of the rebellion.[32] As elements in the pre-history of the rebellion these events explain the sources of Indian resentment and fear at the methods and intentions of the government. Simultaneously, Kaye's reflections on the Doctrine question the practical effects of the policy of expansion supported by 'leaders of the New School' such as Mr Thomason (later, Lieutenant-Governor of the North-Western Provinces, and the first to dismiss the Nana Sahib's claim to inheritance), who was 'no friend to the princes and nobles of the land'.[33] But instead of an argument, Kaye constructs the genealogy of an alternative British politics in India. It begins with John Low's Minute of 10 February 1854, in which Low, a member of the supreme council in Calcutta, expressed dissent to the motion to annex Nagpur. As a Resident with long experience of Indian courts and kingdoms, including Lucknow, Low 'knew what were the vices of Indian Princes and the evils of native misrule':

But he had not so learnt the lesson . . . as to believe that it would be either the duty or the policy of the Paramount Government to seek 'just occasions' for converting every misgoverned principality into a British province . . . Nor had he . . . ever cherished the conviction that the inhabitants of every Native State were yearning for the blessings of this conversion.[34]

The Minute in turn referred to a general principle that guided an earlier school of administrators. Thus, Low recalled how 'many eminent statesmen have been of the opinion that we ought most carefully to avoid' making the 'whole of India . . . a British province'; and citing authority for this view, Low went on to write that: 'it is within my own knowledge that the following five great men were of that number – namely, Lord Hastings, Sir Thomas Munro, Sir John Malcolm, the Hon. Montstuart Elphinstone, and Lord Metcalfe'. Low's argument against annexation is prudent. Since in

British-administered territories 'the upper classes were invariably trodden down, it was sound policy to maintain the native States', to leave 'an outlet for the energies of men of good birth and aspiring natures, who could never rise under British rule'.[35]

But the genealogy is more than British, and what added justice to prudence was the fact that adoption was legitimate in the traditional law of the land. A 'great Hindu lawgiver' (Manu?) was the authority for the equal legitimacy of 'the son begotten', the 'son given', and the 'son by adoption'. Since 'it is the duty of the son to perform the funeral obsequies of the father', and since their non-performance means that 'there is no resurrection to eternal bliss', the 'right of adoption is . . . one of the most cherished doctrines of Hindooism'.[36] In such a cultural context therefore, 'the alternative of adoption . . . is a source of unspeakable comfort in life and in death; and politically it is as dear to the heart of a nation, as it is personally to the individual it affects'. The right to adopt and to inherit the adoptive patrimony, 'ever dearly prized by the Hindoos', was not moreover 'alienated from them by the Lords-Paramount who had preceded us'. While 'in this the Mogul rulers were tolerant', it was 'reserved for the British to substitute for the right of adoption what was called the "right of lapse", and in default of male heirs of the body lawfully begotten to absorb native principalities into the great amalgam of our British possessions'.[37] Against the territorial imperative of Dalhousie and the men of the 'New School', Kaye gathers support from three directions: Hindu law and customary practice, Mughal sanction of adopted successors to subsidiary Hindu states and finally, the policy of an earlier school of British administrators, ratified ironically by Parliament in the Act of 1781, where native law was held sovereign in matters of inheritance and contract.[38] Kaye thus locates himself and his authorities in a genealogy that begins with the 'great Hindu lawgiver', that includes the Mughals and whose lineal descendant is a view of the British rule that insisted on continuity with/in India's past.

In *The Sepoy War*, Low's five 'eminent statesmen', the Marquis of Hastings, Munro, Elphinstone, Metcalfe and Malcolm, represent that earlier policy and Kaye's recognition of their work is in his biographies of the latter two. These officers, administrators and pro-consuls fought in the Mysore wars, had seen the defeat of the Marathas in 1818, served as the Company's envoys to key Indian and Asian kingdoms and had participated in the political and revenue settlement of conquered territories in south and western India. Yet even as these settlements, made possible by growing British supremacy, were aiming to bring India under a homogeneous new administration, these men posed, as Eric Stokes observes, 'a conscious alternative to an anglicized form of administration'.[39] The 'common aim of the paternal-ist school was to conserve the institutions of Indian society', and to respect what John Malcolm described as the 'fallen greatness' of Indian states.[40] Their opposition to the liberal-Radical disregard for continuity and tradi-tional association is much like the gradualism of Macaulay, the latter-day Whig oligarch, defending the rights of property and shoring up the landed aristocracy; only, while Macaulay would conserve at home what he would do away with in India, these administrators and pro-consuls were perhaps more even-handed. As Stokes summarises: the '"Romantic" generation of British-Indian history' questioned an 'unhistorical attitude, which would impose English ideas and institutions on Indian society', and they brought 'to the Indian problem Burke's notion of history, that conception which regards human society as a continuous community of the past, present, and future'.[41]

Mediated by Low, the five statesmen, Mughal practice and Hindu law, Kaye's discussion of the competing claims of the 'right of adoption' and the 'right of lapse' is tied to a context of debates over the exigencies of administration, though also bearing on the encounter between compet-ing metropolitan political ideologies, and an indigenous landscape already burdened by a long and complex history of institutions, practices and tra-ditions. As the new policy orientation that began under Governor-General William Bentinck (1828–35) took shape, a rearguard conservative resistance, unsure of the desirability of assimilation, sceptical of its possibility and inclined to preserve aspects of India's traditions, stressed the inherent dan-ger of such policies as enforced sudden ruptures with the past.[42]

In the next stage (chapter 3 of *The Sepoy War*) of the pre-history is the case of Awadh, which 'had long tempted' the British 'alike by its local situation and the reputed wealth of its natural resources'. Kaye admits at the outset that the annexation of the kingdom in 1856:

was not by conquest . . . for its rulers had ever been our friends, and its people had recruited our armies; not by lapse, for there had always been a son or a brother, or some member of the royal house, to fulfil, according to Mahomedan law of succession, the conditions of heirship, and there was still a king, the son of a king, upon the throne; but by a simple assertion of the dominant will of the British Government.[43]

Explaining this exercise of will is an extended detour into the history of the Company's relations with Awadh. Originally a Mughal province, Awadh was drawn into the Company's sphere of influence when, following the battle of Buxur or Baksar (1764), the Mughal governor of the province,

Shuja-ud-Daula, entered into a treaty (Allahabad, 1765) with Robert Clive. Though restoring Awadh to the governor, the treaty was the beginning of 'subsidiary alliance', an arrangement which Kaye describes as 'a vicious system', under which the 'Political and Military government was in the hands of the Company' while 'the internal administration of the Oude territories still rested with the Newab-Wazir'.[44] A combination of geo-political, cultural, military and economic factors enabled the transformation of Awadh from a Mughal province to a client state, whose usefulness for British interests alone ensured its survival from 1764 to 1856. And as a contemporary observer noted soon after the annexation, while 'the indignant denunciations of Burke and Sheridan . . . have become a species of lost tradition . . . the evil days of corporate rapacity and proconsular violence' were still far from over in Awadh.[45] Besides the loans and subsidies that Awadh made regularly to the Company to finance its other Indian ventures, the presence of the Company's mercenaries in Awadh – at the expense of the kingdom, and ostensibly for the defence of the realm – extended the British sphere of influence considerably beyond its political frontiers. Moreover, 'trade controlled by the Company or by European traders had channelled economic resources away from Awadh', leading to the decline of thriving centres of trade, and these, combined with the fiscal burden of subsidy payments, contributed to a cumulative economic drain.[46]

While the dual government of Awadh was a system of coercion and extortion that led gradually to insolvency and administrative atrophy, that atrophy reappears in interesting ways in official and other representations of the kingdom. For one, charges of corruption and bad governance in Awadh were additional instruments for obtaining sanction from London for the demand for further fiscal or territorial concessions from the rulers of Awadh, and for threatening them with punitive annexation.[47] Complementing this nexus of interference, extortion, corruption and bankruptcy are sensational accounts in official reports, histories, travel accounts and later, in the Mutiny novels, of (1.) the impoverishment of the Awadh peasantry, (2.) the lawlessness of Awadh in general and (3.) the decadence and profligacy of the court at Lucknow. Yet, even as these accounts constructed and popularised the iconography of an 'oriental' kingdom, at once despotic and anarchic, impoverished and profligate, horrific and picturesque, they are also rhetorical concealments of the political economy of 'subsidiary alliance' by means of which the British had cumulatively authored the referent of these representations.

These images recur with some amplitude in *The Sepoy War*. Thus, 'hedged in and protected by British battalions, a bad race of Eastern Princes

were allowed to do, or not to do, what they liked': 'The Court was sump-
tuous and profligate; the people poor and wretched. The expenses of the
royal household were enormous . . . A multitudinous throng of unservice-
able attendants; bands of dancing-girls; flocks of parasites; costly feasts and
ceremonies; folly and pomp and profligacy of every conceivable description, drained the coffers of the State.'[48] And on the last Nawab of Awadh,
Wajid Ali Shah (1847–56), Kaye writes that 'Stimulated to the utmost by
unnatural excitements, his appetites were satiated by the debaucheries of the
Zenana, and, with an understanding emasculated to the point of childish-
ness, he turned to the more harmless delights of dancing, and drumming,
and drawing, and manufacturing small rhymes.'[49] Obscuring the causes
of Awadh's decline, these strictures facilitate the enunciation of British
agency and moral responsibility to intervene and redress the condition
of a failed Indian state. Thus, by the 1850s 'it would have been', Kaye
declares, 'a grievous wrong to humanity to have any longer abstained from
interference'. The question was one of method: 'in what manner was the
improvement of the country to be brought about by the intervention of the
British Government?'[50] The elder statesmen, Malcolm, Metcalfe, Sleeman
and Low, had recommended 'that it would be as politic as it would be
righteous, to demonstrate to all States and Nations of India, that we had
not deposed the King of Oude for our own benefit – that we had done
a righteous act on broad principles of humanity, by which we had gained
nothing.'[51] But Dalhousie, driven by a 'grievous lust for annexation', not
only deposed the monarch and annexed the territory but also acquired the
revenue of the land, so that:

the humanity of the act was soiled by the profit we derived from it; and to the
comprehension of the multitude it appeared that the good of the people, which
we had vaunted while serving ourselves, was nothing more than a pretext and a
sham; and that we had simply extinguished one of the few remaining Mahomedan
states of India that we might add so many thousands of square miles to our British
territories, and so many millions of rupees to the revenues of the British Empire
in the East.[52]

In this, as in the generally ironic account of the opportunism of successive
governors-general, *The Sepoy War* gestures towards a broader indictment of
British policy. Writing after the rebellion, witness to its particular severity
in Awadh and averse to the impolitic unrighteousness of the 'new school',
Kaye questions the pursuit of expediency even as his history is complicit
with the narratives of justification that legitimise expediency. Though the
history sets up a moral drama between an act of 'humanity' and the 'lust for
annexation' among Company functionaries, the struggle is not, however,

as dramatic as Kaye's agonised rendering appears to suggest. In the end both policies serve the same end, for as Rudrangshu Mukherjee argues, the Company had conquered or annexed most parts of north and central India by 1856, and 'Awadh, though formally independent, would – with its sprawling boundaries and its own system of administration right in the heartland of north India – have presented administrative and political problems, especially in an age of expanding public works. It was expedient in such a context to bring Awadh into the British fold.'[53]

The final stage in the aetiology of the rebellion is the 'progress of Englishism', which resulted in a 'war of extermination . . . against the nobility and landed gentry of the country'.[54] While British resettlement of the Conquered and Ceded Territories in the first quarter of the nineteenth century was acceptable to the people as 'the intelligible tyranny of the conqueror', from 1833 a more systematic method of revenue assessment 'known in History as the Settlement of the North-Western Provinces' was instituted under William Bentinck.[55] Though 'benevolently designed and conscientiously executed', the project of revenue settlement was, in Kaye's view, 'marred by a Theory' – a theory which, in fact, is none other than David Ricardo's rent-theory. Originally formulated by Thomas Malthus while he was a lecturer of political economy at the Company's college at Haileybury, the law of rent was refined by Ricardo into one of the cardinal elements of utilitarian economics.[56]

Contrary to Malthus's view that the interests of the state and the landlord were identical, Ricardo argued that the 'interest of the landlord is always opposed to every other class in the community', and since economic progress benefited the landlord alone the utilitarian principle of taxation was especially directed at this class.[57] However, 'the Radical bearings of such a doctrine of taxation were rendered harmless when the Utilitarians came to apply it to English conditions', and it was in India, where 'private rent property had never been permitted to emerge' that the theory of rent found a fertile ground.[58] The proposals of James Mill and Holt Mackenzie, as Stokes summarises them, were that the Company ought to be the sole landlord with the primary cultivators as its tenants, thus culling intermediate landlords, and that it should depart from the traditional Indian practice whereby the government took a fixed proportion of the gross produce.[59] In this, the positivist bias of rent-theory served as the fiscal basis of a *sui generis* liberal-Radical state whose revenue practices derived from economic law, and not custom, tradition or the cadastral calculations of the Mughal state.

The system, Kaye insists, was initiated in 'pure good faith' and was 'intent only on promoting the greatest good of the greatest number' by guarding 'the many from the . . . interests and passions of the few'. The 'utter worthlessness of the upper classes was assumed to be a fact; and it was honestly believed that the obliteration of the aristocracy of the land was the greatest benefit that could be conferred on the people'. Yet this 'humane system of protection' based on 'a theory sound in the abstract' was defeated by its own instruments, and 'in pursuit of right, the framers of the settlement fell into wrong. Striving after justice, they perpetrated injustice.'[60] It was not only that hereditary landowners and revenue-collectors – however they might originally have acquired their rights – possessed a 'proprietary interest, perhaps centuries old', but rather the fact that:

explain their position as we may, these Talookhdars constituted the landed aristocracy of the country; they had recognised manorial rights; they had, in many instances, all the dignity and power of great feudal barons, and, doubtless, often turned that power to bad account. But whether for good or evil, in past years, we found them existing as a recognised institution; and it was at the same time a cruel wrong and a grievous error to sweep it away as though it were an incumbrance and an usurpation.[61]

Like earlier objections to the Doctrine of Lapse and the annexation of Awadh, the criticism of expropriation reveals the contiguity between the expedient and the putative ground of its legitimacy. The settlements and resumptions were a 'cruel wrong' and an 'error', for to dispossess 'chief people of their official rank and cast them adrift upon the world' was to create 'a disaffected and dangerous class sullenly biding their time', and 'to convert into bitter enemies those whom sound policy would have made friends and supporters of the state'.[62] Notwithstanding such imminent dangers and the warnings of the 'old school', 'a grand levelling system' sought to reduce 'everything to first principles' though 'the theory of the Dead-Level is against nature, and cannot be enforced without a convulsion'.[63] Thus 'a social revolution had been accomplished, to the manifest advantage of the State, and at no cost, it was said, of popular discontent'.[64]

In trying to establish the link between Radical theory and the rebellion, the plot of Book One discloses a hidden similarity between the Company's recent years in India and republican politics, whether in Britain or in France. The ironic revision of a project that denied value to prescriptive rights and received traditions, and the sympathy for property, 'baronial privileges' and monarchy, make *The Sepoy War* a Whig analysis of resistance or insurrection in civil society, which occurred whenever governments grew tyrannical or when they were too weak. There were two cardinal political errors that Macaulay had described: deductive reasoning in political system building, which was the Radical method, and the Tory error of using the past as model for the future.[65] The rebellion was an illustration of the danger of letting deductive theory run a despotic government. For Kaye, as for Burke in the *Letters on Regicide Peace* (1796), the narrative of expropriation and reform spirals into a remarkable association of liberal-Radical politics and economics with Jacobinism,[66] for:

well-read, clever secretaries, with a turn for historical illustration, discovered a parallel between this grievous state of things in Bengal and that which preceded the great revolution in France, when the privileges of the old nobility pressed out the very life of the nation, until the day of reckoning and retribution came, with a dire tyranny of its own.

In seeking to forestall a future popular outburst against a seigneurial tradition, exactly what did not happen in France, by means of timely reforms, the administration produced 'a reign of terror' in the north Indian countryside.[67] And in trying to reform the civil service – now transfigured into the *sans-culottes* of the Commission Temporaire – the government inaugurated the terror of expropriation and the 'dead level'. A '*revolution* in landed property brought about by means of English application' threw up 'disaffected and dangerous classes, who . . . bided their time for the recovery of what they had lost, in some new revolutionary epoch'.[68] Foreshadowed by its pre-history and waiting in the narrative future of the history, that moment is configured by Kaye as the counter-revolutionary 'Sepoy War' when the Indian *ancien régime* returns to reclaim its lost rights and privileges, and to bring its vengeance on the agents of the original terror.

But the problem was not only with political changes and revenue settlements. Accompanying these was the 'progress of enlightenment' in India from the 1830s as reformers turned to Indian society, religions, education and law. As Metcalf has pointed out, although constrained in Britain, the liberals and Radicals had in colonial India 'something of a laboratory for the creation of a liberal administrative state'.[69] Encompassing the political and moral economy of the subject people, the confidence behind such projects of systemic transformation was largely a function of the stabilisation of British power in India, of the industrial revolution and of Britain's international predominance following the Napoleonic wars; and it was from these that the colonial application of liberal-Radical theory drew its energy and resources. Especially in India, where the self-assigned work of the reforming civilian and the missionary was the acculturation of natives into a state of Christian grace and European modernity, 'the prospect of future equality' between the ruler and the subject made it necessary 'to devalue and depreciate' India's 'contemporary cultures', its religions, systems of knowledge and society.[70] The teleology of the liberal project is explicit in *The Admin-istration of the East India Company* where Kaye claims that '[P]hysically and morally – materially and intellectually, we are impressing ourselves abidingly on the country and on the people'.[71] A decade later *The Sepoy War* abandons the theory of progress, but not without more insights into a born-again Whiggery. An aspect of the terror like annexations and land reforms, the 'progress of enlightenment' is yet a desirable and possible end. Desirable as an ideal yet interrupted by Indians, the project of enlighten-ment is double-edged in the *Sepoy War*, simultaneously representing the colonial mission as the unwitting victim of a traditional and unregenerate orient, and through this representation seeking legitimacy at home.[72]

Kaye's model of the encounter between Indian society and Christianity and western education is simple and asymmetrical. The spread of English education and the propagation of Christianity – the latter from 1813, when against its wishes the Company was ordered by parliamentary charter to allow and support missionary work – were challenges to traditional faith and knowledge. These, according to Kaye, created a 'new generation [of Indians] . . . not to be satisfied with absurd doctrines or captivated by grotesque fables', while 'the whole [religious] hierarchy of India saw their power, their privileges, and their perquisites rapidly crumbling away from them'. To explain 'the stake for which the Brahmin was playing', Kaye declares that Hinduism 'is the most monstrous system of interference and oppression that the world has ever known . . . maintained only by ignorance and superstition of the grossest kind'. Yet ignorance and superstition was under threat from the 'pale-faced Christian knight, [who] with the great Excalibur of Truth . . . was cleaving right through all the most cherished fictions and superstitions of Brahminism'.[73]

The image of a nineteenth-century missionary-utilitarian knight is laden with a complex historical burden that points to Europe's relation with Islam as well as the latter's relation with Hinduism, and combines these two with the Victorian revival of chivalry. For if the figures of the 'knight' and the sword conjure the Crusades and medieval romance, the sword and its target also suggest a *jehad* against the idolatrous Hindu. But it is an appropriate image of its subject: the war of liberal-Radical theory and evangelicalism against all things blasphemous or contrary to utility: 'every monstrous lie exposed, every abominable practice suppressed, was a blow struck at the Priesthood', and 'every year were there manifestations of a continually increasing desire to emancipate the natives of India from the gross superstitions that enchained them'.[74] The criminalisation of *sati*, the discovery and policing of *thagi*, the prohibition of female infanticide, the encouragement of widow remarriage, the education of women, the law allowing Christian converts to inherit and the fact that 'no effort was to be spared that could conduce to the spread of European knowledge', made the 'Priesthood . . . aghast at the sight of the new things, moral and material, by which they were threatened'. In desperation Hindu priests turned to caste to mobilise their constituency; for 'if . . . the people could be taught that the English by some insidious means proposed to defile the Hindoos, and to bring them to a dead-level of one caste or of no-caste, a great rising of the Natives might sweep the Foreigners into the sea'.[75]

In ventriloquising the priestly plot *The Sepoy War* achieves two interesting results. One, the rebellion now appears as primarily of Hindu origin and design. Though he admits that the Muslim clergy were worried too, the elision of Muslim alarm over pig-fat to grease the new cartridges indicates that Kaye, unlike some other commentators, is more favourably disposed towards Muslims.[76] Second, the clear chain of cause and effect – from British attempts at 'enlightenment' leading to Hindu reaction to, finally, a militant mobilisation around caste – underscores the power of the colonial state, and its instrument, colonial historiography, to speak for the now-silenced rebel subjects. Criticism, however, is confined only to the reform of property and polity, while Christianity, English education and social reforms are an unambiguous good. Thus, the interest in reform that Dalhousie showed was 'simply the manifestation of such love as any clear-sighted, strong-headed man may be supposed to have for truth above error, for intelligent progress over ignorant stagnation'.[77] The earlier solicitude for landed rights and for Hindu law of inheritance does not mean sympathy for (an orientalised religious) Hinduism. This discrepancy highlights the unevenness within the critique, no longer content to let cultural singularity be, but combining, as Macaulay did earlier in English politics, a quiet defence of landed interest with the language of social reform, granting improvement but without the austere, authoritarian edge of the theorists.

The discrepancy constitutes the moral. The aetiology enables Kaye to distinguish between and valorise aspects of liberal imperialism and so to determine rebel agency. In the matter of annexations and revenue resettlements the liberal-Radical project had failed to understand cultural singularity or to realise the danger of annoying the traditional landed elite. But the narrative of 'enlightenment' is closer to the aims of the 'new school'. To change India's moral economy and to bring its people under the rule of European enlightenment was a self-evident good, and the historic obligation of empire. Hence, the 'progress of enlightenment' or 'Englishism' is distinguished from cognate reforms of revenue, property and polity, and while the latter was just cause for resistance, the rejection of enlightenment was not due to any fault in the grand theory, but – and this is the burden of *The Sepoy War* – the rebellion proved the inability of the colonised people to respond to the modernity of their masters and to save themselves from a benighted past and present.

Kaye's account of the motivation of the soldiers is a dual journey: into the history of troubles in the Company's army, and the location of the soldiers in an indigenous social context. The long history of insubordination was, Kaye suggests, partly the result of the Company's mismanagement and partly due to the fact that 'Asiatic armies had always been prone to revolt'.[78] Beyond this lay the fact that by recruiting in the Company's army, the 'native of India did not cease to be a civilian. He severed no family ties; he abandoned no civil rights.'[79] The dual allegiance of the Indian soldier – to the Company that employed him and to the social and ethnic world to which he belonged – worked well so long as the interests of the Company did not encroach upon that world. But a 'series of adverse circumstances, culminating in the annexation of Oude [Awadh] . . . had weakened the attachment of the Sepoy to his colours'. At the end of the survey of a century of mutinies, Kaye reiterates this dual allegiance when he writes that the soldier

> was a representative man, the embodiment of feelings and opinions shared by large classes of his countrymen, and circumstances might one day render him their exponent. He had many opportunities of becoming acquainted with passing events and public opinion . . . He knew what were the measures of the British Government . . . and he interpreted their meanings, as men are wont to do, who, credulous and suspicious, see insidious designs and covert dangers in the most beneficent acts. He had not the faculty to conceive that the English were continually originating great changes for the good of the people. . .[80]

By demonstrating the overlap between the Company's Indian army and the civil society to which the individual soldier belonged, *The Sepoy War* harmonises the two major but competing explanations of the rebellion. That the Indian army was located in a wider ethnic, social and political milieu gave the mutiny a subordinate place in an aetiology that primarily blamed liberal-Radical political economy and its opposite number, Indian resistance to modernity and the inability to see that the British meant well. Thus, it 'was in the over-eager pursuit of Humanity and Civilisation that Indian statesmen of the new school were betrayed into the excesses which have been so grievously visited upon the nation'.[81]

Announced in the Preface to *The Sepoy War*, this conclusion forecloses the rebellion as a counter-revolutionary war, and its real, because original, author is the proactive 'benevolence' of the colonial state. That 'causal explanation . . . served in colonialist historiography merely as an apology for law and order', and that '[C]ausality was harnessed . . . to counter-insurgency and the sense of history converted into an element of administrative concern' is true enough.[82] However, as Kaye, anticipating many histories, first-person accounts and novels of the rebellion, writes at the end of the Preface: 'If I have any predominant theory it is this: because we were too English the great crisis arose; but it was only because we were too English that, when it arose, it did not utterly overwhelm us'. There is here an expropriation of rebel agency more fundamental than the exigencies of 'administrative concern' might require, and from this breathtaking rhetoric emerges a meta-theory of cause(s) embracing all theories, civil or military. And this is the *permissive* theory of insurgency, for it is the authoritarian and beneficent colonial state that, in a fit of forgetfulness, or confidence or 'humanity', permits its subjects to rebel.

3

Romances of empire, Romantic orientalism and Anglo-India: contexts, historical and literary

Of all the unparalleled features which the English Empire in India presents, not one is so unique as the slightness of the machinery by which it is united to England, and the slightness of its reaction upon England. She (England) tries to raise India out of the medieval into the modern phase, and in the task she meets with difficulties and incurs dangers, but she incurs no risk whatever from being drawn down by India towards the lower level, or even being checked for a moment in her natural development.

J. R. Seeley, *The Expansion of England* (1883)

ROMANCES OF EMPIRE

Among the early theorists of the literary yield of British expansion was Alfred Comyn Lyall, the Anglo-Indian poet, historian and administrator, posted in the district town of Bulandshahar where the rebel leader, Nawab Walidad Khan, ousted the British in the summer of 1857. In 'Novels of Adventure and Manners', an essay he wrote for the *Quarterly Review* in 1894, Lyall traced a literary-historical lineage: from Romantic orientalism, through the oriental novels of Walter Scott, *The Surgeon's Daughter* and *The Talisman*, to contemporaries such as R. L. Stevenson and Rudyard Kipling; noting the waning of romance as 'a new class of writers . . . adopted the Novel of adventure to the requirements of latter-day taste, to the widening of knowledge, and the diversified expansion of our national life'.[1] In following this expansion, these authors drew their material 'from the colonies, from Africa, from the South Sea Islands, or from India', with the result that the 'roving life of the colonies, the backwoods, the Western States, and the Indian frontiers has created an unique school of realist fiction in which Mr Kipling is the chief professor'.[2] One difficulty with this school was, however, the habit of 'verifying by documentary evidence the details of a story', a habit incipient in Scott but full-blown in these novelists, and essentially anti-literary in cutting adventure narratives off from their roots in romance.[3]

The essay located this tendency amidst the contemporary proliferation of popular media, the enlargement of the reading public and an energetic public interest in colonial affairs, all of which had opened a 'flood of lucid narrative and inflexible facts . . . upon recent events' through 'complete histories, personal memoirs, public documents, war correspondence, and all-pervasive journalism'. But these developments had consequences for quality, with the 'rule of Realism . . . becoming so despotic that the story of adventure is reverting more and more to that shape which lends itself most completely to life-like narrative, the shape of a Memoir'. This for Lyall explained why 'the Crimean War and the Indian Mutiny . . . have furnished no fresh material contributions of importance to the romance of war, either in prose or poetry, to stamp the memory of a long weary siege, or of a short bloody struggle, upon the popular imagination'.[4] The essay takes issue with this insistence on verifiable facts amongst authors and readers of the colonial adventure novel; an insistence that otherwise bears a family resemblance with the 'windless closure of high naturalism',[5] and indeed, with Leopold von Ranke's call, in the *Histories of the Latin and the Teutonic Nations* (1824), that reconstructing the past as it must have been from documents and evidence was the only legitimate pursuit for historiography.

Though Lyall identified 'taste', 'knowledge' and the extension overseas of 'national life' as the three areas of change, it is the last that really drives his argument, distinguishing the novel of adventure from the mainstream 'Little England' novel of manners, and explaining the achievements and aberrations of the former. Where a Radical such as James Mill had underscored the corrosive correlation between expansion and war in his article on the 'Colonies' in the 1824 edition of the *Encyclopaedia Britannica*, Lyall's reading of the colonial adventure novel seventy years later turns on the persistence of the type of conflict Mill had in mind, while suggesting openly a new, laudatory correlation between such conflicts and metropolitan literary culture. Lyall had personal experience of colonial adventure. He joined a corps of Volunteer Horse at Meerut in 1857 that served in defensive and counter-insurgency actions, and, after the rebellion Lyall was thrown on his own resources to restore British authority in Bulandshahar, a task for which he acquired a reputation for hanging far too many natives. Moreover, writing in a decade that produced a large count of Mutiny novels, Lyall was certainly aware of the opening of Africa for a new generation of colonial adventurers and administrators, and the near-constant skirmishing with local peoples and European competitors in Africa. Gunboat diplomacy, warmongering and obsessive campaigning prompted much critical analyses from Manchester Radicals and socialists, of which the most influential were *The Psychology of Jingoism* (1900) and *Imperialism* (1902) by John Hobson. There is very little in contemporary literary writing, Decadent or otherwise, to match the analytical rigour of Hobson, and generally, of Manchester dissent, though Joseph Conrad, the expatriate Pole makes up for the lack with *Lord Jim* (1900), *Heart of Darkness* (1902) and *Nostromo* (1904), the last an arresting long historical perspective on the integration of Central and South America into the economic 'world system'.[6]

Like Kaye's reviews in the *Calcutta Review* and the *North British Review* in the late 1840s, Lyall's aesthetics of colonial adventure and warfare supplements high imperial theorisations of colonial conflict. Five years after the review appeared, Colonel Charles E. Calwell wrote *Small Wars: Their Principles and Practice* (1899), a specialist tactical handbook in a fairly long line of military studies and campaign accounts that routinely appeared in the *United Services Journal* and in histories of war and colonial diplomacy that in the Indian case began with Robert Orme's *History of the Military Transactions of the British Nation in Indostan* (1780). Calwell, who also wrote an account of the Tirah expedition of 1897–8, examined in *Small Wars* the tactical and doctrinal features of 'irregular' conflict in the unfamiliar terrain of Africa and Asia, with states or people lacking in European forms of organisation, and against armies, militias or guerrillas who used tactics and techniques other than those of European warfare. As a matter of fact, conquest, annexation and 'pacification' in India had long pre-dated the Calwell thesis, with serviceable Irregular corps, usually made up of Eurasian, British and European mercenaries, and the Irregular 'troops' of crumbling Indian kingdoms, functioning as the thin end of an expanding territorial wedge. There is in *Small Wars* a basic distinction between conventional European and sub-conventional colonial warfare, and the methods of Waterloo or Balaclava – which are doctrinally the precursors of the Somme – were essentially unsuitable for the Hindukush or in Transvaal. Calwell's main recommendations for use against Asians and Africans were unconventional methods such as the scorched earth tactic, attacks on civilian targets, exemplary punishment, the use of light mounted brigades (instead of static defence) and psychological arm-twisting with bluff and bluster.[7]

It is possible, however, to read the historical contiguities between national expansion, documentary realism and colonial romance in a way that Lyall did not intend. In following the globalisation of British interests the colonial adventure novel drew on new resources from geography, topography, anthropology, history, political economy, warfare, technology and linguistics; a cross hatching of genres, discourses and disciplines not unique to either the nineteenth century or to British imperialism. From the letters home of Christopher Columbus, through *The Lusiads* of Luís de Camões (1572) and Richard Hakluyt's *Voyages and Discoveries* (1598–1600), to novelists such as G. A. Henty, Gordon Stables, Rider Haggard and G. M. Fenn at the end of the nineteenth century, literary representation of exploration and conquest was enabled by systems of knowledge and funds of information that resulted from and fanned European expansion to other parts of the world and into other cultures. The overlap between genres and the criterion of verifiability was the means by which an incredible expansion was configured as at once a history that appeared to possess the character of romance, and a romance that was the speculum of a verifiable material history. That traditional romance gave way to the novel of adventure reliant on journalism, travel writing and historiography is hardly surprising. For these forms of writing first followed and recorded the march of empire and its vicissitudes, and in them the lineaments of a new romance first emerged; a romance more fantastic than allegorical quests and chivalric romances, and with more promises of land, slaves, gold and profit than romance or allegory had ever offered. However one settles the question of realism in the metropolitan novel and aesthetics, the question has another valency in the colonial imagination, where, to misquote Hegel, the real is the fantastic, and the fantastic, the real, and where the memoir or history serves as a prototype for the adventure novel.

This contiguity was recognised and exploited by historians and novelists alike. In the *History of the Conquest of Mexico and Peru* (1843–4), William H. Prescott wrote of the 'inexhaustible stores of [Mexico's] material wealth; its scenery, grand and picturesque beyond example', which drew the explorer-conqueror to a project that:

was sure to win the meed of glory . . . and if he survived to return to his home, he had wonderful stories to recount, of perilous chances among the strange people he had visited . . . These reports added fresh fuel to imaginations already warmed by the study of those tales of chivalry which formed the favourite reading of the Spaniards, at that period. Thus *romance and reality acted upon each other*, and the soul of the Spaniard was exalted to that pitch of enthusiasm, which enabled him to encounter the terrible trials that lay in the path of the discoverer. Indeed, the life of the cavalier of that day was romance put into action.[8] (emphasis added)

Such apostrophes quietly recast a history of plunder and genocide by drawing a likeness between the 'peculiar circumstances of [the] Conquest' and 'any legend devised by Norman or Italian bard of chivalry'.[9] The likeness is in a suspension of disbelief that the Conquest and the protocols of romance require equally, and it sets up a circulation of signs whereby the experience of colonisation in the periphery is recorded in a metropolitan literary-cultural idiom, even as the pre-modern roots of that idiom were transformed by mercantilist or 'capitalist adventure'.[10] The homology that the *Conquest of Mexico and Peru* draws is perhaps a historicist gesture, yet Prescott's insistence on figuring Iberian expansion as romance in an otherwise positivist mid nineteenth-century historical narrative resting on archival evidence reveals the schizophrenia within a project where 'romance and reality acted upon each other' to yield the phenomenon of empire.[11]

Prescott is not, however, an isolated instance. On the other side of the globe, and in the same year that the *Conquest of Mexico and Peru* appeared, another conquest was hatching into historical narrative. Reflecting on a spate of recent wars against Afghanistan (1832–42) and the Sikhs (1845–6), an article in the first issue of *Calcutta Review* noted that: '[T]he history of the English in India, during the last six years, is one of extraordinary interest . . . Contemplating the whole, it is difficult to believe that we are not poring over some highly wrought narrative of fictitious adventure.'[12] Nine years later, contemplating a hundred-year vista enlarged recently by the annexation of the Punjab, 1848–9, Kaye observed that:

If one of the little handful of European officers, who, a century ago, in gaiters and perukes, followed the fortunes of Lawrence in the Carnatic, were now to stand again on Indian soil, and in one of our North-Western cantonments, to spread out before him a map of our Eastern Empire as now established, he would be overwhelmed with astonishment and incredulity. He would declare, that not one of his contemporaries, in the wildest flight of imagination, ever contemplated the possibility of the erection of such an empire as we have now built up in the East.[13]

In Kaye as in other apologists of expansion, the delighted incredulity is accompanied by a close focus on the nodal moments of expansion. A colleague of Stringer Lawrence in Madras was Robert Clive, who began as a Company clerk in Bengal and later acquired fame as an extraordinary military commander who protected and advanced the Company's interests from competing Indian states, besides clipping French ambitions in India.

Clive was a founder hero for the British in India as Hernando Cortes and Francisco Pizarro were for the Iberian empire, and the celebrated nineteenth-century hagiographer of Clive was T. B. Macaulay. A review of *The Life of Robert, Lord Clive* by the former Bombay governor, John Malcolm, Macaulay's 'Lord Clive' appeared in the *Edinburgh Review* in

1840, announcing at the outset that 'every Englishman who takes any interest in any part of history would be curious to know how a handful of [our] countrymen . . . subjugated, in the course of a few years, one of the greatest empires in the world'.[14] This piece of national history played out in the tropical periphery centred on Clive's campaigns in Madras and the Carnatic, and climaxed in Bengal, then under the rule of the Nawab of Bengal, Siraj-ud-Daula, when with 'nine hundred English infantry, fine troops and full of spirit, and fifteen hundred sepoys' Clive 'sailed to punish a Prince who had more subjects than Lewis the Fifteenth or the Empress Maria Theresa'.[15] The relentless traversal of a supine land, the successful contests against Indian states, the sudden ascent to fame and fortune and the moral dubiety of Clive's end established his resemblance as a founding hero with the *conquistadors*. For Macaulay, British exploits in Bengal in the mid eighteenth century were hardly atypical in a history of progress elaborated later in his *History of England* (1849–61); and the simple, telling model of colonial contact and conquest it turns upon became the engine of the colonial adventure novel later in the century. As the prolific boy's novelist G. A. Henty admitted in the Preface to one of his Indian novels, *With Clive in India*, he had 'devoted a somewhat smaller space to the personal adventures of my hero', for 'the events were of such a thrilling and exciting nature that no deeds of fiction could surpass them'.[16]

There is a similar valorisation of history as the region of extraordinary adventure and national achievement in the Mutiny novel, with 'events' taking priority over 'deeds of fiction'. Notwithstanding Lyall's later judgement that this made for bad novels, the literary potential of the rebellion was recognised and exploited almost immediately; and, it was the historian Ball who remarked that: 'if a writer of fiction were to imagine the circumstances under which the national fortitude of a body of men could be most severely tried, he could hardly invent conditions better calculated for the test than those, under which, in May and June 1857, our countrymen were surprised in Hindostan'.[17] While the diptych of insurgency and counter-insurgency was the primary scaffolding of the plot of Mutiny novels, it was the latter that became salient in the high imperial imaginary. Counter-insurgency in the Delhi region, in Bundelkhand, Rohilkhand, Awadh and in the country between Allahabad and Kanpur provided material as much for theorisations of the 'small war' as for the Mutiny novels of the 1890s and after. In representing these campaigns – often reinforced by Volunteer and Irregular corps, and accompanied by sub-conventional methods such as the burning of villages and farmlands, and summary executions – which continued until the spring of 1859, the novels employ the heroic *fabula* of European expansion from the fifteenth century. The story of counter-insurgency is garnished richly with demonstrations of racial, religious, national and technological superiority; it closed with re-conquest, and bore a close similarity to the representation of numerous European intrusions around the world in the late nineteenth century.[18] While rebel actions threw into relief a beleaguered 'national fortitude', counter-insurgency allowed the recovery of the idiom of proactive heroism and armed 'pacification'. The interplay of the two constituted the narratology of histories and novels alike; and, as historiography proclaimed the surpassing 'literariness' of its subject, fiction unhesitatingly pointed to the historical verifiability of its invention. Complementing Ball's view, the novelist J. E. P. Muddock, pre-empts criticism of her Mutiny novel, *The Great White Hand* (1896), by drawing attention to its historical basis, and in her Preface she argues that if the

dramatic situations in which my characters become involved are overstrained and improbable, I shall claim *the authority of history* that the thrilling times of the Revolt were rich in situations so sensational, so dramatic, so tragic and pathetic, that they put fiction in the shade. The bare ungarnished story of the Rising is in itself one of the most sensational records the world has ever known. Not even the Crusades, not even the wonderful defence of Malta by the knights of St John of Jerusalem, against the infidel Turk, present us with a more thrilling, romantic, and stirring panorama of battle scenes and incidents than the Indian Mutiny.[19] (emphasis added)

The transvaluation of colonial historiography and the literature of colonial adventure is among the ways in which the progress of empire was imagined, made popular and legitimised, and it created in the process new, more aggressive forms of metropolitan nationhood. The contiguity and overlap of genres has significant implications for the present argument. For, as historiography construed its referent as romance, English-language fiction of colonial adventure (in the Americas, in Africa, Asia and Australia, and the south seas) discovered, especially from the mid nineteenth century, the matrices of its invention and action in the history of expansion and colonial globalisation. History-as-romance and romance-as-history thus came to share an identical protagonist, namely European, and specifically British, imperialism, and an identical plot: the elaboration of this history through tropes of exploration, conquest and occupation, followed in time by a projected or an achieved colonial transformation. In tandem with the hardening of nationalities in Europe, with social Darwinism and racial anthropology, and with the globalisation of metropolitan arms and interests, the contiguity of history and fiction appeared most prominently in the sub-culture of popular and juvenile literature from the 1830s to the First

World War. As Patrick Brantlinger notes, reworking a genealogy that Lyall had first traced, 'Marryat's novels set the pattern for the imperialist adventure fiction that flourished from the seafaring writers who emulated him in the 1830s . . . through the Mexican westerns of Captain Mayne Reid, the "Robinsonades" of R. M. Ballantyne, and the historical romances of Charles Kingsley, down to Haggard, Stevenson, Kipling, and Conrad.'[20] This popular literary practice provided the formal templates for ex-colonial and settler novels like those by Gilbert Parker in Canada, or Rolf Boldrewood in Australia, and for the Anglo-Indian novel, where military-colonial adventure found most fulsome treatment in the novels of the rebellion. Yet, even as the Mutiny novel exploits and insinuates itself in a longer history of colonial adventure, it has too a local context in the history of the British in India: their politics, idioms of representation and the often complex negotiations with indigenous states, societies and forms of life.

ROMANTIC ORIENTALISM AND *THE MISSIONARY* (1811)

A major difference between the colonial adventure novel and Romantic writing on India and the Arab-Islamic world is in their representation of overseas expansion. Emerging out of a fairly long and hybrid tradition of the oriental tale, and influenced by the Gothic fiction of Walpole, Anne Radcliffe, Charles Maturin, 'Monk' Lewis and others, Romantic use of the orient is frequently oblique and a sublimation of the facts of expansion, trade and conquest.[21] The journey into non-European spaces and times that occurs in William Beckford's *Vathek* (1786), Robert Southey's *Thalaba the Destroyer* (1801) and *Curse of Kehama* (1810), Sydney Owenson's *The Missionary* (1811), Thomas Moore's *Lalla Rookh* (1817), Shelley's *Revolt of Islam* (1818) and *Prometheus Unbound* (1820) is of course an expansion of the resources of metropolitan literature, increasingly informed by knowledge fashioned, formulated and translated at peripheral locations such as Calcutta, Srirampur, Madras, Bombay and Banaras, where institutions and practices of colonial enquiry interpreted the lands and peoples that the Company had begun to rule from 1765.

The Asiatic Society of Bengal (1784) and its first president William Jones formed an important, enabling link between territorial and commercial expansion in India and the trafficking in knowledge and artefacts which produced Romantic orientalism, with Jones as a founding figure for British knowledge of India, as Clive and Lawrence were for the British military machine in the land. A comparative philologist and translator of religious and literary texts from classical Sanskrit and Persian, Jones was the Chief

Justice of the Company's court at Calcutta, and among the first English translators/compilers of Hindu and Islamic law.[22] His array of interests and practices shows a conjunction of administrative, cadastral, judicial, linguistic, antiquarian and ethnographic enquiries that coexisted within the baggy folds of a multi-disciplinary orientalism. It was moreover Jones who proposed in 'An Essay on the Poetry of the Eastern Nations' (1772) that 'a new set of images and similitudes' might be derived by English poets from the 'principal works of the Asiaticks' and from the 'language of the Eastern Nations'.[23] The literary potential of the 'Eastern Nations' (analogous to the mercantile potential of the assorted exotic raw materials and goods the Company trafficked in from the seventeenth century) had figured somewhat light-heartedly as decor and heraldry in eighteenth-century oriental tales, but its recognition in turn-of-the-century orientalist scholarship and historiography, and its realisation in Romanticism occurs via a new look at the old archive of the orient. The transformation of the East India Company into a territorial power by the end of the eighteenth century had several long-term consequences: structural changes in Indian society thorough property and revenue reassessments at first, and later through education, census surveys, acculturation and conversion, all important economic and social prerequisites for tapping the Indian market and revenue. As Martha Conant notes in *The Oriental Tale*, it 'was not until the victories of Clive in India and the era of expansion under the elder Pitt that England took any vital [literary] interest in the Orient'.[24]

Unlike the popular boys' novel from the 1890s to the First World War, with its virile and technophile celebration of imperial conquest, Romantic interest in the orient tended to disguise the manifest content of empire. But as Nigel Leask has cautioned, though anti-commercial and anti-expansionist, the political core of the Romantic orientalism of say, Shelley, is not necessarily anti-interventionist, approving the civilising mission and foregrounding republican ideologues such as the 'Veiled Maid' in *Alastor* (1816) to justify transformative agenda with an eclectic mix of Hellenism and Godwinian radicalism.[25] Romantic journeys into non-European space and time applied the nuts and bolts of orientalist fieldwork from a metropolitan location. But while orientalist scholarship combined studies of the Brahmi script or classical Sanskrit drama with empirical observation of routes, topographies, minerals and indigenous revenue systems, and thus represented a remarkable conjuncture of antiquarianism with such researches as were of direct use in advancing the Company's statist ambitions, the procedures of Romantic orientalism were more selective and its interests less diverse. For, in nearly all the works listed above, the aesthetic-antiquarian aspects of the 'eastern nations' are thrown into relief even as the pragmatics of empire building – the enabling context of production and reception of these works – are substantially elided or disclosed by the indirections of allegory.

Some of these issues and methods appear in Sydney Owenson's *The Missionary*, an influential Romantic orientalist novel in which seventeenth-century Iberian presence in India works as a prism for reviewing recent forms of European intervention.[26] Owenson was the daughter of a Shrewsbury tradesman born and educated in Dublin, and her other novels include *St. Clair, or the Heiress of Desmond* (1804), a tepid imitation of *Werther*, *The Wild Irish Girl* (1806) which went into seven editions in two years and became a subject of debate in Dublin, where it was championed with equal fervour by Catholics and Protestants alike, and *Woman, or Ida of Athens* (1809), which anticipates Grecianised romances like Byron's *Childe Harolde* (1811) and Thomas Hope's *Anastasius* (1819).

Her only Indian novel, *The Missionary* exerted an impressive influence on Romantic engagement with Asia. The publishing history of the novel indicates its runaway success. Five editions came out in 1811, of which four were published from London and one from New York. Then, in 1812 a French translation appeared in Paris, followed by another English edition, published from Paris in 1834. The editor of *Lady Morgan's Memoirs*, W. H. Dixon, claims that 'a more romantic or foolish story' than *The Missionary* 'could scarcely be imagined', but the novel's reception by, among others, Shelley and Moore and reviewers such as Charles Kirkpatrick Sharpe tells another story.[27]

In a letter to Lady Charlotte Campbell, Sharpe, then a reviewer for *Quarterly Review*, wrote: 'I have read Miss Owenson's things, till I dream of the moon beaming through a gauze curtain upon the immaculacy of a Circassian's back', and compared the novel with the novels by Matthew Gregory Lewis and Mme Cottin.[28] Moore began his *Lalla Rookh*, partly based in Kashmir, with 'a long and laborious reading of it [*The Missionary*]. To form a storehouse, as it were, of illustration purely Oriental – was, for a long time, the sole object of my studies'.[29] Shelley first read the novel in 1811, when he was nineteen, and soon wrote to T. J. Hogg: 'Will you read it, it is really a divine thing. Luxima the Indian is an Angel. What pity that we cannot incorporate these creations of Fancy; the very thought of them thrills the soul. Since I have read this book I have read no other – but I have thought strangely.'[30] It is likely such reflections contributed to *Alastor*, *The Revolt of Islam* and *Prometheus Unbound*, which show the influence of *The Missionary*, in particular the character of Luxima and topography of Kashmir. Possibly at Shelley's urging, Byron read *The Missionary* in Italy in 1817, the year he wrote *Manfred*, his Faustian drama of guilt and remorse compounded by a problematic Romantic subjectivity, while Charles Maturin, who had already followed Owenson in *The Wild Irish Boy* (1808), used *The Missionary* for his *Melmoth the Wanderer* (1820), the adventures of an Irish Faust, to which Balzac wrote his ironic sequel, *Melmoth Reconciled* (1835).

The Missionary is, however, relevant to the present discussion for other reasons.[31] Unlike the majority of Romantic orientalist writing, *The Missionary* is a novel, the favourite genre of high imperial adventure. Again, unlike the oriental forays of British Romanticism, which sought to construct the 'orient-in-itself', Goa and Kashmir function in this novel as the sites of colonial contact, where cultures are tested against one another. The confrontation of cultures does not, however, work along a unilateral axis in *The Missionary*; and the ambiguities that contact brings to view make it possible to read *The Missionary* as a failed colonial adventure. Finally, the novel is about Indian resistance to European presence, and, if its reappearance in 1859 as *Luxima, the Prophetess* is taken into account, it is among the earliest literary representations of the rebellion.

Like contemporary writers of oriental romances, Owenson did her homework before writing the *Missionary*. A clue to that can be found in the use the novel makes of footnotes to invoke the authority of historical and other writings on India. As mentioned earlier, the action of the novel takes place in mid seventeenth-century India when the future Mughal Emperor, Aurangzeb (1618–1707), was fighting a battle of succession (1658–9) against his brother, Dara Shukhoh. To buttress this historical location, the novel appends a footnote that mentions the *History of Hindostan from the Death of Akbar to the Complete Settlement of the Empire under Aurangzebe* by Alexander Dow, and the travelogue-chronicle by François Bernier, the seventeenth-century French traveller in India.[32] Later in the first volume, and in the course of a digression on Hindu womanhood to explain Luxima's status as a widow and a saint, another footnote refers to 'The Duties of a Faithful Hindu Widow', a Sanskrit text translated by the orientalist scholar, Henry Colebrooke, and published in the *Asiatic Researches* in 1794. Similarly, on the difficulty of converting sixty million Indians – a problem that dogs the missionary and the narrator alike – yet another footnote in the third volume mentions an obscure and possibly contemporary work, *Sketches of the Religion, Learning and Manners of the Hindus*. The scholarly annotation gives an aura of verifiability, making the novel appear truer than eighteenth-century oriental tales to a readership better attuned to

Indian affairs after the long-drawn-out trial of Warren Hastings (1788–95) and the Battle of Seringapatam (1798). They testify, moreover, to a historical imagination, at once nostalgic and positivist, already evident in the notes and dissertations attached to Scott's collection of ballads, *The Minstrelsy of the Scottish Border* (1802–3), which anticipated the historicist proclivity of the 'Waverley' series, and, despite Lyall's disapproval, the reliance on facts and events in the colonial adventure novel.[33]

The plot is simple. Hilarion, a Portuguese Franciscan, arrives in the Portuguese colony of Goa sometime in the 1650s, travels overland to Lahore and sails up the Indus to Kashmir 'to attack, in the birthplace of Brahma, the vital soul of a religion'.[34] Hilarion's missionary enthusiasm, however, suffers a setback once he meets Luxima, a widowed (and, young and beautiful) Hindu priestess with a large following. Luxima appears to be partially derived from the character of Shakuntala in the eponymous classical Sanskrit play by Kalidas, first translated into English by William Jones in 1789. Moreover, by making her a priestess (improbably, of 'Camdeo' – a literary rather than religious icon – and a Vedantin, that is, an exponent of Hindu philosophical monism) as well as a widow, the novel borrows a clutch of exotic names and terms from orientalist research on Hinduism, brought home to Britain by not only the *Asiatic Researches*, but also by historians such as William Robertson, Thomas Maurice and Mark Wilks. Luxima's religious filiation introduces Hindu and, specifically, Brahmin high culture, while her widowhood invokes, though indirectly, British iconography of *sati*, a commonplace in British travel writing and ethnography, and a practice whose regulation kept reformers in the administration busy from the second decade of the nineteenth century.[35] Hilarion is erotically drawn to Luxima but finds her a 'false Prophetess', and so considers 'her conversion as the most effective means to accomplish the success of his enterprise': the conversion of all Hindus. For her part, Luxima, despite some initial hesitation, falls in love with him, yet 'absorbed in the splendid illusion of her religious dreams' resists his religious overtures.[36] For several months he struggles with his desire while she struggles with her patrimonial faith, the prohibitions of her (Hindu) widowhood and, interestingly, against the more forthright wooing of 'Solyman Skeko', son of Dara Shukoh the exiled brother of Aurangzeb.

Finally, when they are discovered in their secret assignations by her co-religionists, and Hilarion is threatened with death and Luxima excommunicated by her people, they decide to flee Kashmir and travel to Goa. Two things happen on the way. Hilarion baptises her (though she agrees to convert because she loves him and not from conviction, and also because she is now an outcast in her society), and soon after Hilarion is arrested by officers of the Inquisition for heresy and for the 'seduction of a Neophyte'.[37] Brought back to Goa under guard, Luxima is put to a Franciscan nunnery while the Inquisition finds Hilarion guilty and sentences him to be burned at the stake. However, events take a dramatic turn on the day of the execution. There is, first, the news that Portugal has regained independence from Spain, which turns popular sentiment against the Spanish overlords of Goa and against the officers of the Inquisition. Second, 'Indians were ripe for insurrection', for 'the coercive tyranny of the Spanish government had excited in the breasts of the mild, patient, and long-enduring Hindus, a principle of resistance'.[38] Just as the stake is about to be set afire, Luxima (suffering from the 'melancholy insanity of sorrow') leaps on it – imagining herself a *sati* dying on her husband's pyre – but is fatally wounded by a guard. She falls shrieking 'Brahma, Brahma', and at this 'the timid spirits of the Hindoos rallied . . . roused . . . from their lethargy of despair'.[39] While the Hindu population and the Indian troops battle with the Spanish soldiers, Hilarion and Luxima escape. She dies soon afterwards, loving Hilarion to the end but a lapsed Christian, and following her death Hilarion retires to Kashmir, a disconsolate recluse who has renounced his mission and his nation.

In this fantasy of a failed intercultural love, which anticipated Meadows Taylor's Mutiny novel *Seeta* (1872) and Kipling's short story 'Beyond the Pale' (1888), *The Missionary* is, as Leask notes, 'a source-book of orientalist stereotypes articulated as metaphors of gender'.[40] While these powerful and persistent stereotypes of a Hindu and feminine India (and Luxima is consistently identified with the land and its people), alluring, unreasonable and weak-kneed before Europe, and of Europe as Christian, masculine, rational, etc., constitute a familiar array of figures and motifs that appear in the later adventure novel as in the antecedent oriental tale, the novel's reconstruction of a history available from other sources is significant, as are the suggestions of presentist concern. The journey into seventeenth-century India fed a contemporary taste for literary representations of the remote in time and geography, though the unfamiliar was mediated by a Christian (though Catholic) and European (though Portuguese) hero, and by the Portuguese maritime empire in India. For, as Catholic missionary activity in India and elsewhere was the precursor of evangelicalism, Portuguese naval and mercantile dominance on the western seaboard of India was the precursor of the East India Company – well on its way to being the paramount power when the novel first appeared. These parallels punctuate an otherwise historicist reconstruction of seventeenth-century

India, inserting the signs of contemporary investments in India through the detour of a relatively distant history.

It is mainly religion that correlates the two historical frames; the crucial link between the two sets of histories, and not merely a matter of private faith. The resistance of Luxima to conversion, as of the Hindus she represents, cannot be overcome without 'a train of moral and political events which should . . . emancipate their minds from antiquated terror . . . and . . . destroy the fundamental principles of their loose and ill-digested government'.[41] Hilarion's linking of conversion with the wider transformation of state and civil society had a contemporary ring in the case of Whig-Anglican evangelicals such as Charles Grant, associate of the anti-slavery and social reform campaigners William Wilberforce and Zachary Macaulay and, like them, a member of the Clapham Sect, the influential parliamentary and India House lobby. For Hilarion as for the Clapham 'Saints', conversion would be genuine when the convert's free and willing acculturation in European forms of life and simultaneous rejection of the patrimonial attended the formality of baptism.

Grant's *Observations on the State of Society among the Asiatic Subjects of Great Britain* (1812–13), a more polemical version of a 'Proposal' he first drafted for Parliament in 1792, is among the earliest defences of Company rule in India on grounds of principle.[42] Against Whig oligarchs like Edmund Burke who accused the Company of political, contractual and fiscal impropriety in India, Grant proposed a necessarily non-representative governance that would 'sedulously watch over the civil and social happiness' of the subjects. The obligation of government was the 'introduction of light'; the 'Hindoos err because they are ignorant; and their errors have never been fairly laid before them'.[43] In India as among the metropolitan poor, education was the key to reform of manner and morals for the Evangelical Revival.[44] For, with education '[I]dolatry, with all its rabble of impure deities . . . its false principles and corrupt practices, would fall', and people 'would rise in the scale of human beings and live in peace under British rule'.[45] It was a project of colonial transformation that appeared in and out of Parliament after the Company became the governor of Bengal in 1765, though a clause forcing the Company to support mission work and education in India was added in the parliamentary Charter of 1813.

That Luxima relapses, Hilarion at the end gives up his vocation as a missionary and goes native and the Hindus rebel against their European rulers, may be read as an inversion of the fable of improvement by which evangelicalism and the liberal-Radical theory of colonial administration justified continued expansion in India. As Hilarion tells the officers of the

Inquisition who arrest him, 'we bring them [the Hindus] a creed, which commands them to forget the world, and we take from them material possessions which prove how much *we live for it*'.[46] That profit and revenue compromised the religious mission implicates more than the Iberian empire. For, as the Abbé Dubois described the contemporary missionary-colonial encounter in his *Letters on the State of Christianity in India*, written upon his return to France in 1823:

The Hindus soon found that those missionaries whom their colour, their talents, and other qualities had induced them to regard as such extraordinary beings, as men coming from another world, were in fact nothing else but disguised Feringis (Europeans), and that their country, their religion, and original education were the same as those of the evil, the contemptible Feringis who had of late invaded their country. This event proved the last blow to the interests of the Christian religion.

But Dubois's view that the identity between the missionary and the invader meant that 'the time of conversion [had] passed away'[47] was hardly the metropolitan view, with the multiple engagements in Indian politics, economy and society of the preceding three decades amplified in the frankly interventionist Charter of 1833, which brought forth a promissory eschatology of 'the imperishable empire of our arts and our morals, our literature and our laws'.[48] Evangelical influence contributed to what Marx described as the '*social* revolution' which the British had worked in India, one of a series of 'conversion' projects: of criminal law and the law of procedure, of revenue, land rights, markets and social practices.[49] The presence of religious conversion alongside these collateral modes of transformation suggests the convergence between the Clapham evangelicals and the philosophic Radicals, between, in other words, the gospel and the liberal theory of governmentality, opposed in metropolitan politics but united on the Indian question; and driven as much by profit and revenue as by a globally applicable model of progress. It is against this broad-spectrum package of reform that the unease of Dubois, the failures of Hilarion and the patient caution of *The Missionary's* narrator need to be read. The package was not only morally deficient in braiding profit and revenue with philanthropy; it was simple-minded to propose that conversion could erase 'a faith which resisted the sword of Mahmoud and the arms of Timur'. By the end of the novel the conversion of Hindus is a nearly impossible goal, requiring 'a power seldom vested in man, and which time, a new order of things in India . . . can alone . . . accomplish'.[50]

While Luxima's resistance to Christianity and Hilarion's surrender defer colonial transformation to an uncertain future, suggesting unease over a policy briefed with leaving very little of the orient unchanged, the 'popular insurrection' at the end of the novel introduces a new interaction between the historicist frame and presentist interests. That the uprising was reaction against the 'coercive tyranny' of Spanish–Portuguese rule, and 'the arts used by the Dominicans and the Jesuits for the conversion of the followers of Brahma', twines anti-clericalism with a typical if unfavourable representation of Iberian imperialism in Anglo-American histories.[51] As Robert Southey wrote in the *History of Brazil*, from Pombal onwards: 'a character of oriental despotism had been given to the Government in all its branches, for which the Portugueze had been prepared by the mal-administration of the laws, and by the yoke of the Inquisition . . . Caprice held the place of law, and justice was sacrificed to any consideration of interest.'[52] Though the Iberian empire and the Catholic Church were just cause for rebellion, a footnote places the seventeenth-century revolt in Goa alongside the 'insurrection of fatal consequences [that] took place in Vellore so late as 1806'. The association is short-lived, even tenuous, but it opens another window on the two historical frames. Victims of tyranny in the first case, Indians figure as perpetrators in 1806; for, as the footnote explains, the cause of the Vellore mutiny was 'the religious bigotry of the natives, suddenly kindled by the supposed threatened violation of their faith from the Christian settlers'.[53]

The exchange between the footnote and the text associates similar events and dissimilar aetiologies revealing a nexus of continuity and discontinuity between the two historical moments. The broad likeness of events makes the seventeenth century serve to review contemporary history, while disparate causes distinguish Vellore from Goa, and the Company from the Iberian precursor. A result of exchange between the text and the footnote is that the earlier disclosure of complicity between religious proselytising and commerce is now overlaid by a new, ethnographic explanation: 'the religious bigotry of the natives'. It is a charge that otherwise echoes contemporary British appraisals of the Vellore mutiny, and serves as useful defence for the Madras government of the Company in official correspondence, where the mutiny is perceived as the result of religious prohibitions warring against an innocuous military dress code.[54] But the specificity of the two histories is only partial, for the fact that in both instances the rebellion was prompted by perceived threats to religion identifies India as the site of changeless customary practices and belief-systems ever opposed and resistant to Christian and European influence. The religious explanation of indigenous resistance at Goa and Vellore turns on a view of Hinduism as the site of hypostasis, at the far end of the spectrum from the linear series represented by Mahmoud, Timur, the Iberian maritime empire and the British Company. In this, *The Missionary* shares a view of Hindu religion and society with orientalism, generally inclined to preserve cultural singularity, and with evangelicalism and liberal-Radical administrative theory, which aimed to hitch a deviant Hindu world to the teleology of progress through a sequence of conversions.

The intersection of the linear and the recurrent historical designs acquires an additional resonance in the 1859 reissue of *The Missionary* as *Luxima, the Prophetess*, in response to 'the recent melancholy events in India'.[55] As prophesy, *Luxima* extends the original series without modifying the basic explanatory model. While Goa prefigured the Vellore mutiny of 1806 in *The Missionary*, in *Luxima* Goa and Vellore together prefigure the rebellion of 1857–9. Religion is crucial in the interplay between event and type, explaining the series from Goa through Vellore to 1857, and tying them into a homogeneous set to construct a paradigm of cultural encounter from the seventeenth to the mid-nineteenth century. Though without any reference to the rebellion except a brief editorial aside, the subtitle of *Luxima* suggests the possibility of applying the old aetiology to the latest revolt, an explanation that shares a good deal with contemporary appraisal of the rebellion.

As histories and other accounts often insisted, the rebellion of 1857–9 was the resistance of a traditional social and political order, an insistence that often led to the reification of Hindus as 'superstitious', Muslims as 'fanatics' and Indians in general as irrational and ungrateful. In more sophisticated accounts like *The Sepoy War* the revolt was a reaction against the combined and intrusive meddling of liberal-administrative reform and Christianity; a cause that made the rebellion a type of counter-revolution, seeking to overturn the 'social revolution' produced by reformist intervention, with shades of a displaced, even misplaced, Jacobinism in the tropics. In *The Missionary* and *Luxima*, the implied theory of resistance is the obverse of the several failures of Hilarion: to convert Luxima, to acknowledge the rules and protocols of the Jesuit establishment and to preserve intact his national and racial identity in the cultural contact zone. Together with the persistent indigenous opposition to the projected and putative empire of consent, these failures underscore the inadequacy of a transformative project premised on a sequence of conversions. Hilarion's career swings from a Grant-like confidence to an eventual submission that recalls the wish to create means for 'reconciling the people of England to the nature of Hindostan' that Warren Hastings once expressed.[56] It is a revisionary journey, articulating 'anxieties embodied in British Romantic writing about the East – both the assertion of superiority and the fear of instability and absorption', and representing 'the tenuous nature of the East India Company rule in the late eighteenth and early nineteenth centuries . . . and its complicated attitude to indigenous idioms'.[57] Though Hinduism is 'ignorance and superstition of the grossest kind' for Kaye as for the early Hilarion, *The Missionary* shares some of the 'Whig opposition to the evangelization of India', an opposition stoked 'by a distrust of interference in cultures ruled' by laws, practices, and customs intrinsic to their history, and calling for a defence of the parochial and the singular from a global theory of progress.[58]

The failures of Hilarion, the obduracy of Luxima and their exile from their respective social worlds confound equally the evangelical and the liberal agenda. In *The Missionary* these constitute a rearguard resistance to the political and moral economies of overseas expansion at the turn of the nineteenth century, questioning the putative improvement that a broad-spectrum package of conversions promised to introduce, and demonstrating the impossibility of prising open cultures or overcoming their incommensurability. Political gradualism, the cornerstone of the Whig compromise, was for Macaulay the means for guarding British and European civil society from anarchy and tyranny. But while Macaulay chose to leave gradualism at Home and employed Radical methods in India, *The Missionary* brings gradualism to British-ruled India, tying religious conversion to wider changes in society and polity, and postponing colonial transformation to an indefinite and uncertain future. Identical in all but the title, *Luxima, the Prophetess* continues the gradualist insistence, though turning, with the analeptic subtitle, to a history of resistance to frame the rebellion of 1857–9.

The Missionary represents an interesting transitional moment between Romantic orientalism and the later adventure novel, though it is also an early example of British and Anglo-Indian historical novels on India. But there is one important difference between *The Missionary* and the adventure novel that demands notice. The failure of Hilarion to convert Luxima, a figure perhaps of the inadequacy or insolvency of the colonial project, is radically different from the articulation of similar projects in the later colonial adventure novel or the Mutiny novels. Though Owenson constructs Hilarion in terms that are martial and heroic, and that stress his physical, moral and intellectual superiority over the land and its peoples, there is in him simultaneously a weakness, and even a willingness to surrender to that metonym of India, Luxima. While this generates an unresolved tension between Hilarion's desire and his vocation that leads inexorably to the tragic end of the novel, the ambiguities and tensions compromising the European project here are wholly absent from the sanguine heroism of the adventure novel. In that body of writing, and especially in its subset, the Mutiny novel, for the European hero to have or, indeed, to conceive of, an attachment with an Indian woman is nearly always cast as a moral lapse compromising colonial security and racial purity.

The cultures of Anglo-India have been the subject of literary, literary-historical and historical readings from the late 1840s when, as the next section and later chapters will show, new, self-reflexive articulations of British identity in India were first made. Such readings of Anglo-Indian society and literature have continued into the twentieth century, though decolonisation and developments in archival research have given greater depth, density and critical insight into the career and life-worlds of a community that was never quite expatriate as settlers in Australia were. There is, however, a working consensus in this long body of reflection from literary historians and academic historians that between the 1820s and the 1840s occurred marked changes in Anglo-Indian identity, sexuality, culture and settlement patterns. For some historians the change was the result of British immigration patterns and slumps in Home economy, for others it was the result of paramountcy, which brought along a new language of command, and for still others, the change spelled disaster, alienating the British in India from the ambient social and cultural world and leading directly to the rebellion.

It is in the light of this rather long debate on identity and attitude that the distance between the erotic licence of *The Missionary* and the mandatory endogamy of the colonial adventure or Mutiny novel can be measured. The shift from a culture that acknowledged and tolerated officers and men who married Indian women (sometimes polygamously, as with the Company's colourful Resident at the Mughal court in Delhi, David Ochterlony) or kept *bibi*s, to a firmly drawn cordon sanitaire regulating British male sexuality coincided with the rising influence of the liberal-Radical and evangelical ethos, a 'purity campaign' that set about cleaning up Anglo-Indian habits and manners, and rationalising the Company's haphazard administration into a well-oiled bureaucratic machine, even as it worked on reforming the benighted natives. Put another way, Hilarion's vulnerability to an eroticised India and his eventual recusancy, while these may have been tolerable in 1811 when *The Missionary* was published, were taboo when *Luxima* appeared in 1859. The failure of the missionary project and the fact that Hilarion finally goes native suggest ambivalence towards British expansion, an unease largely absent from British writing on India until the second decade of the twentieth century. Driven by a desire to possess yet finally possessed by the object of desire, the career of the missionary is at once acquiescence to and a refusal of the imperial project, and constitutes, as such, a remarkable counterpoint to the proactive martial heroism of the colonial adventure novel.

THE LOCATION OF ANGLO-INDIA

Alongside metropolitan imaginative literature about India in particular or colonies in general, there was a considerable body of imaginative literature by the British who lived and worked in India. This double location reappears in the Mutiny novel. There are a large number of novels on the subject written by those with personal experience of India and sometimes of the rebellion, but there are also numerous metropolitan novels of the rebellion, too. This is no less true for historiography, with Charles Ball, the jobbing historian based in England, and John William Kaye, who spent a good part of his working life in India, closely involved with Anglo-Indian letters and with the administration under Company and Crown. While location and experience yielded certain visible differences in their analyses of the revolt, the duality of location acquired a disputatious overtone between the conservative-orientalist and the liberal-reformist understanding of Indian past and present.

In the Preface to his *History of British India* (1817), a work that summarily rubbishes Indian history and culture, James Mill had claimed that 'a residence in India, or a knowledge of the languages of India' were not necessary for writing a history of India. But the new Preface to a greatly extended and heavily annotated edition of Mill's history, published in 1858 by the Sanskrit scholar and translator H. H. Wilson, argued in favour of the advantages of 'local knowledge' and the 'benefits derived from personal observation'. Wilson's main target is the author he was editing. Without the benefit of lived experience and hence unsympathetic to Indians, Mill's history had a deleterious influence on official attitudes, since it was long part of the syllabus in the Company's college at Haileybury. The original *History of British India* was 'calculated to destroy all sympathy between the rulers and the ruled', and it had contributed to 'a harsh and illiberal spirit [which] has of late years prevailed in the conduct and councils of the rising services in India'.[59]

The dual location factors British representation of India in significant ways. In representing the interface between insurgency and counterinsurgency, between Anglo-India and indigenous India, the form of the Mutiny novel straddles this duality in ways more fundamental than the specific location of a particular author. This is not to efface the differences between the Mutiny novels of G. A. Henty and a novelist-administrator like H. C. Irwin, who was in the Indian civil service and knew a good bit more about the rebellion and about India than the metropolitan colonial adventure novelist Henty. Rather, the presence of the duality in the literary-ideological form of the Mutiny novel underscores the intermediacy of a representation located in the cusp between Britain and India; a cusp that opens wide when the rebellion threatens the Anglo-Indian plot of love, marriage and domesticity, or when the British hero penetrates rebel conclaves. Moreover, whether or not written by an author with Indian experience, the novels of the rebellion are sites where, notwithstanding writerly location, genres, idioms and representational traditions such as, for instance, the historical novel and the colonial adventure novel, romantic orientalism, historiography and the pictorial cultivation of the oriental picturesque, intersect. While not primarily British-Indian, these genres and idioms are among the ways in which the romance of expansion and empire was disseminated from the second half of the nineteenth century in Anglo-India and in metropolitan culture.

Moreover, the question of location and the ways in which location may inflect enunciations of identity are now prominent in a swathe of academic disciplines and political practices. In colonial discourse and post-colonial studies, the specificity of location has helped to prise open the monolithic and sometimes unhistorical thrust of Said's *Orientalism* (1978), reflecting a disciplinary move that emphasises contradiction, ambivalence and anxiety in the cultural discourses of empire, and which proposes the ineluctably syncretic nature of colonial experience. Finally, the rebellion itself throws up the question of the double locus of British India. As an attempt at ending British rule in India, the rebellion highlighted the uneasy location of Anglo-India, understood as a political formation, as a community and a cultural identity.

A recent illustration of the return to the specificity of expatriate experience is *Writing India, 1757–1990*, a volume of essays edited by Bart Moore-Gilbert.[60] In the final section of his Introduction to the volume, Moore-Gilbert points out that in *Orientalism* Said's 'argument rests to a large degree on the assumption that western representations of the Orient were based overwhelmingly upon a "textual attitude"'.[61] Though Said acknowledged the presence of another tradition of representation that drew on 'actual existential contact' with the orient, he suppressed this tradition 'perhaps because of the fracture it would necessarily open up between his conceptions of "truth" . . . as the product of discourse and "truth" as prior to discourse'.[62] Unlike Said's reductive focus on the textual archive, Moore-Gilbert introduces the essays in the volume as explorations of 'the degree to which literary texts generated by those with significant "lived experiences" of the Indian empire produced variations in, or even challenged, the dominant textuality of imperialism in *Orientalism*'. From this follows a larger point; for the 'question is necessarily linked to the larger issue of the specificity of the cultural identity of the British in India, and the degree to which their sense of Britishness was modified by exile and contact with the cultures which they controlled politically'.[63]

There is, of course, a philosophical undertow to the distinction between the 'textual attitude' and the 'existential' that the Introduction or the essays that follow do not engage with. More historically, Moore-Gilbert offers the evidence to suggest the specificity of British experience of India. The first of these is the gradual evolution of a hybrid Anglo-Indian argot recorded in lexical compilations such as Whitworth's *Anglo-Indian Dictionary* (1885) and the *Hobson-Jobson* (1886). Second, there is the emergence of 'a widespread conviction, at least within Anglo-Indian quarters, of radical differences between metropolitan and local representations of India', which prompted Kipling's satire of the 'sloppy and stereotypical Orientalist conventions of British-based writers'. Third, while the Anglo-Indian community's 'strong sense of its separate cultural identity' was evident from the persistence of 'thematic tropes' like the Calcutta 'Black Hole' and the rebellion, 'with their stress on the confinement and deprivation of besieged colonialists', these 'tropes in the literature of British India in fact respond to changes in the nature and circumstances of its relationship with its subjects'.[64]

Though these developments variously suggest the specificity of Anglo-India and its literature, exile and the consequent modification of the sense of Britishness may not altogether be a geographical issue; indeed, may prove more ambiguous than the distinction between the textual and the experiential – the markers of the two loci of British representation – would appear to suggest. To take one example: a review article in the Anglo-Indian journal, *Calcutta Review*, entitled 'Indian Faults and English Calumnies' that appeared in 1858, takes issue with Home opinion for blaming Anglo-India for the rebellion. As the reviewer sarcastically poses:

Let India provide facts, England will find theories. The most eager searchers for news could not complain that we Indians were chary of catastrophes and situations in 1857, and we may return the compliment, and say that the good folks at home have not been idle in fitting each event or rumour of event with an elaborate preface of cause and motive; and in situations where we could see nothing but blood and tears, finding 'lessons', 'warnings', 'natural consequences', and whatever else is magnificent and philosophical.[65]

To the extent that the reviewer comfortably used 'we Indians' to describe a beleagured expatriate community, these lines suggest a modification of British/English identity by the fact of 'exile', though not as the result of contact with indigenous cultures. Yet if this gives an impression of radical divergence between expatriate experience of the rebellion and Home opinion on the event, the rebellion was also the moment when in spite of such divergence some interesting convergences came to view. As suggested in the first chapter, there is clear disagreement between popular opinion and high policy on the state of security in India, and over the fate of captured rebels. That popular opinion in Anglo-India and in Britain was more shrill, more hysterical, more intolerant generally of the rebel cause, whereas high policy in London and in Calcutta tended towards caution and circumspection, and was indeed more thoughtful about and cognisant of the rebel cause, complicates an easy separation of spheres; unless one takes the somewhat absurd view that 'exile and contact with the cultures that they controlled politically' had modified the 'sense of Britishness' of the exponents of high policy in India *and* in Britain.

One more example of this complication: in an 1859 article on 'India in English Literature' in the *Calcutta Review*, the reviewer complained that while 'on Indian subjects we might fairly expect independence from Indian [i.e. Anglo-Indian] writers', they 'usually echo the misconceptions and misrepresentations of the Home Press'.[66] The reviewer then proceeded to question the habitual stereotypes in metropolitan writing on India. Thus, 'there has been for so long a tradition of the "Bengal Tiger", the wealthy upstart who wears nankeen, and whose skin is as yellow as his curry or his guineas'. On the other hand, Indians were represented as 'millions of pure-minded but partially clothed philosophers, soaring to the empyrean on the wings of contemplation, and trampled on by lawless European taskmasters – this is the state that the Palmtree-loving Public believed to exist in India'.[67] Against these stereotypes, the reviewer argued that the social composition and habits of the expatriates had changed, that while there was a time when the 'Indian exile often retired . . . with a great deal of money not very purely got, and not very prettily spent . . . now that Indians go home poor and live cleanly, the caricature becomes a libel'.[68] The review ends with the claim that the 'European and the Native inhabitants of India have a kind of common cause, a common ground on which to move the British nation for a review of judgement'. Yet if this suggests a syncretic possibility born of exile and cultural contact, and an identity distinctly non-metropolitan, there is the reviewer's remark on the previous page that the 'study . . . of Indian systems [of philosophy] should form a part not of theology . . . but of Satanology'.[69] The remark dispelled the possibility of cultural syncretism, expressed the watchfully exclusivist (and anti-orientalist) tendency that fashioned Anglo-Indian attitudes towards India from the early 1830s and articulated a missionary-reformist intolerance towards indigenous cultures.

The exception the reviewer took to metropolitan representation of the expatriate community had a wider historical compass when addressing those changes the stereotypes overlooked or misrepresented. While there was a time when the Anglo-Indian 'nabob', from Warren Hastings to Thackeray's Collector of Boggleywallah in *Vanity Fair* (1848), deserved satire and caricature for they had acquired wealth through questionable means, and had in various degrees gone native, the reviewer insists that the culture and the finances of a new generation of Anglo-Indians working the covenanted services are no longer aberrant. This transformation of attitude and culture works often as an explanatory model in social, cultural and literary histories of British India, explaining those policy changes that served as clues for understanding the rebellion, and the policy revisions that followed after. Despite overuse and the neat opposition between fore and aft that it turns upon, the model has use in locating a wide range of attitudinal shifts as functions of structural changes in the institutions and instruments of colonial administration, besides elaborating the roots of the contest between the cultural relativism of orientalism, and the cultural absolutism that drove reform. An early use of the model is in Percival Spear's *Nabobs*. Though mainly a study of the British in India in the eighteenth century, the penultimate chapter on 'Race Relations' focuses on the period between the 1760s and the 1820s, tracing the end of a brief period of syncretism and cultural contact, and the rise of new idioms and strategies of cultural and social exclusion. As the

position of the East India Company changed towards the middle of the [eighteenth] century, the character of racial relations changed too . . . The result was to set in motion a double current, of increasing contact and knowledge of Indian life, and of increasing contempt of everything Indian as irrational, superstitious, barbaric and typical of an inferior civilisation. [T]he first was typical of the period between 1760 and the return of Hastings in 1785 and is represented by such men as Hastings himself, Forbes, and Colonel Parker with its prophet in Sir William Jones; the second perhaps reaches its zenith in Macaulay's famous description of Sanskrit and Persian literature.[70]

Of the several reasons Spear advances for the transformation of Anglo-India, not least was a rapid numerical growth in the expatriate European community after the 1760s, accompanied by an influx of British women, which produced conditions for a culturally insular domesticity, the impact of the Evangelical Revival on Indian policy, and the steady assumption of a statist identity by the Company after 1765.[71] For Spear, the turning point is the tenure of the Marquis of Cornwallis whose policies anticipate a later era of reform culminating under Bentinck and Dalhousie. Cornwallis represented metropolitan rather than expatriate opinion, 'a reformer of abuses with plenary powers' who 'brought with him the view-point of the India House and the Whitehall, [with] no previous knowledge of the country, and a lack of that imaginative sympathy which would have made up for his ignorance'. Not only did he make the government 'more English and more olympian; he had no close contact with Indians and did not notice their increasing estrangement'.[72] And while neither Radical nor evangelical, the Anglo-Latin imperial imaginary of Cornwallis, rudely thwarted in America, translated into heavy-handed reforms that in tenor, though not in theory, shared a good deal with the theory-driven intervention of subsequent decades.

The dual locus of British representation of India is not only a matter of geography, but was sometimes enacted within the colonial periphery. If orientalism was an intellectually tolerant version of cultural relativism, the careers of pro-consuls, travellers and adventurers such as the Fraser brothers, William and James, of James Skinner, James Tod, David Ochterlony, among others, exemplified an exile-induced modification of an original ethnic-religious-national identity. Yet, as the history of Anglo-India shows, the experience of exile equally – and perhaps increasingly from the 1820s – results in a self-righteous recoil from indigenous cultures, yielding an exclusivity that, encouraged by policy and prejudice, serves to limit the horizon of Anglo-Indian experience, and so prepares the ground for that crisis of colonial knowledge of which the rebellion was at once the cause and the consequence.[73]

This transformation is replayed in Anglo-Indian literature over roughly the same period. As Nigel Leask shows in his reading of the three 'Company poets', John Leyden (1775–1810), Thomas Medwin (1778–1869) and Sir Charles D'Oyly (1781–1845), Anglo-Indian poetry represented the anxieties of exile and cultural contact while being responsive to metropolitan literary styles and movements.[74] An instance of the convergence and divergence of cultures is Medwin's successive revisions of his interest in intercultural sexual love. The sublime but tragic romance of 'Julian and Gizele' (1817) recurs in Medwin's later poems, 'Oswald and Edwin' and the 'Pindaree', where Oswald's love for the Indian Seta makes him willingly go native, which naturally estranges him from his own people.[75] While these poems were like *The Missionary* in their exploration of intercultural romance, the theme is radically reworked in Medwin's (self-) parody, 'A Bengal Yarn' (1842), where the orientalist 'Major B–' becomes the dupe of a child-bride he rescues from *sati*; and when a tiger kills him during a hunt, she decamps with his property. Though the moral of the 'yarn' 'is "not simply that native women make bad wives" but rather that orientalist reverence for native culture is delusory', the turn from the sublime to the ridiculous is already evident in Charles d'Oyly's anti-orientalist satire, *Tom Raw, the Griffin* (1828), a narrative poem that 'consistently debunks orientalist expectations by its negative portrayal of Indians and their customs'.[76]

The shift from a tragic-sublime to a comic-parodic register in Anglo-Indian poetry coincides with cognate developments in the Anglo-Indian novel between the 1820s and the rebellion. Though not entirely a matter of the dual location explored so far, there are two distinct representational emphases to this body of writing that suggest shifts in the representation of the experience of exile and contact with indigenous cultures, even as these texts provide templates for the later Anglo-Indian and the Mutiny novel. The first of these trends is visible in a clutch of novels of which the *Confessions of a Thug* (1839) by Philip Meadows Taylor is the most prominent, besides the now forgotten novels of William Browne Hockley, which mostly predate the *Confessions*. Little is known about Hockley, except that he was in the Company's Bombay civil service, that he was posted for a time at a remote station in the Bombay Presidency, that he knew Hindustani and Persian, and that his penchant for practical jokes led to his dismissal from the service in 1824. Hockley's first novel, *Pandurang Hari, or the Memoirs of a Hindoo* (1826), is the fictional autobiography of a Maratha adventurer who turns out to be the heir to the Maratha kingdom of Satara; and his other novels are *Tales from the Zenana, or a Nawab's Leisure Hours* (1827), *The English in India* (1828), *The Vizier's Son, or the Adventures of a Mogul* (1831) and *The Memoirs of a Brahmin* (1843).

With the exception of the fictionalised social documentary, *The English in India*, Hockley's novels are representations of indigenous society. While *The Memoirs* resembles *Pandurang Hari* in its historical period and its picaresque hero, *The Vizier's Son* is set around the wars of succession that followed the death of Aurangzeb in 1707. Despite this difference, the three novels employ an autobiographical mode and, with *Pandurang Hari* and *The Vizier's Son*, Hockley is the first Anglo-Indian novelist to use such a mode to represent indigenous life and culture. Notwithstanding this narrative interest in Indian society, Hockley's prefaces to these novels are remarkable for their antipathy towards India. In the Preface to *Pandurang Hari*, Hockley, claiming to be the editor of a Marathi manuscript translated into English, writes that while he 'went among them [Indians] prejudiced in their favour: a few years undeceived him. From the raja to the ryot, with the intermediate grades, they are ungrateful, insidious, cowardly, unfaithful, and revengeful.'[77] Similarly, Bapoo Brahmin's preface to his 'autobiographical' *Memoirs* is not only replete with denunciations of Hindu character and morals – to which his earlier life is, he readily admits, witness – but regrets the 'blindness of the English Governors who will not believe . . . the depravity of a Brahmin's heart'.[78]

Notwithstanding such prefatory echoes of missionary-reformist antipathies, these novels along with the *Confessions of a Thug* are among the first to engage with Indian history, society and subjectivity. The two Maratha 'autobiographies' and the confession of Ameer Ali the *thag* engage with a period when the Company defeated the confederation of Maratha states, and the lives of the protagonists such as Pandurang Hari and Bapoo Brahmin are located in this transition, and shaped by the collateral effects of Maratha disintegration such as *thagi* and the *pindari* campaigns. Moreover, the novels are a dense representation of this period and region, representing cults and rituals, kinship relations, indigenous polity, criminal behaviour, moral judication, topography and linguistics. In so doing, the novels are the fictional counterpart of a new historical and ethnographic interest in central and western India manifest in contemporary works such as John Malcolm's *Central India* (1823), Grant Duff's *The History of the Marathas* (1825) and James Tod's *The Annals and Antiquities of Rajasthan* (1829–32). Though British presence and the growing power of the East India Company – a power that in *The Confessions* is the enabling forensic condition of Ameer Ali's confession – hover at the edges of these texts, Anglo-India is conspicuously absent from the concerns of Taylor and Hockley. Complementing the representation of Indian life is an autobiographical mode that, in *Pandurang Hari*, *The Confessions of a Thug* and *The Memoirs of a Brahmin*, functions as the means of access into the 'polyglot density' of contemporary Indian society.[79] Immanent to the world they narrate, and therefore the guarantee of its authenticity, the autobiographical subjects of these novels do, however, stand in an ambiguous relation to that world.

Prompted and guarded by prefaces and parentheses, editors and auditors, the autobiographical subject yields a detailed ethnographic knowledge precisely because he is also a willing collaborator of the British, like Bapoo Brahmin, or a co-opted prisoner/approver, like the former *thag*, Ameer Ali. Especially in *The Memoirs of a Brahmin*, where Bapoo Brahmin admits that intercourse with the British in India has made him 'deplore the errors of Hinduism, and although a Brahmin myself, pronounce the religion, as absurd as it is wicked', the autobiographical ruse is at once a route into the alien density of the indigenous, and a rejection of the indigenous by auto-biographical subjects now in the process of being reconstituted as British subjects.[80] The two-way traffic into and away from Indian society in these novels is noteworthy for several reasons. That a succession of Anglo-Indian novels between 1826 and 1843 – a period that follows the heyday of orien-talist relativism, and that coincides with the emergence of a interventionist state, and with such indigenous reformist and modernizing movements as the 'Young Bengal' and the Brahmo Samaj – should take the form of native autobiography suggests at once a fascination with an India *qua* India evident from the fact that these novels are based in Indian states and not in British-governed provinces, and a containment of the fascination ven-triloquised, paradoxically, by the indigenous autobiographical subject. A native autobiographer/informant like Bapoo Brahmin is the literary con-temporary of the 'new type of munshi', which, as C. A. Bayly suggests, appears between 1820 and 1850. Usually diplomats and men of letters, and embodying traditional knowledge, new *munshi*s like Mohan Lal, Shahamat Ali and Raja Shiva Prasad are the 'mediator[s] of colonial knowledge' even as they occupy an ambiguous middle ground between collaboration and resistance.[81]

The containment or rejection of the indigenous, which orientalism was inclined to view somewhat more positively, is clearest on the question of religion. While in *The Missionary*, Hinduism is a religion marred by 'super-stition' and Hindu society divided by caste, in the character of Luxima there emerges the possibility of a sublime literary orientalism. By contrast with both Owenson and her sources, Hockley's novels and *The Confessions* represent Hinduism and Islam as the sites of superstition and fanaticism and, what is more, as the sources of political unrest and criminal enter-prise. Thus, cults and practices like those of the *gosains* and the *thags*, as well as the peripatetic fakirs, the mullahs, the *pindari* militia and Hindu priests are now the confirmation of an essential moral-religious turpitude that missionary evangelicalism had long denounced, and the portentous signs of a chthonic, anarchic and often inscrutable society that poses an insidious challenge to the colonial regime and its reformist ambitions. To that extent, the autobiographical subject at once resembles the native informant/collaborator in the philological, archaeological, religious, judicial and cadastral investigations of the orientalist-surveyor, and a dual modification of that figure. First, the informant is now criminalised, as in the case of Ameer Ali, or associated with a suspiciously criminal India, as in the case of Bapoo Brahmin and Pandurang Hari. Beyond the picturesque alienness of their subjectivity and the world they inhabit, the autobiographical subjects are the source of information about the social and political conditions of the newly conquered western and central India. Second, the collaboration between the informer/autobiographical subject and the British (police) officer and editor are expressive of a new articulation of colonial power and knowledge. The native not merely collaborates under forensic duress but may now, as Bapoo Brahmin writes, 'thanks to the liberality of an enlightened government . . . defy the malice of my caste, and hurl back upon them their poisoned arrows of hatred'.[82]

While these fictions of native self-representation constitute a new mode of representation that draws upon yet effectively modifies orientalist sympathies and reformist antipathies, another representational emphasis surfaces in the autobiographical novel, *Oakfield, or Fellowship in the East* (1853) by William Delafield Arnold (1828–59).[83] Arnold was the youngest son of Thomas Arnold, the reforming headmaster of Rugby (1828–42), and the brother of Matthew Arnold. He first arrived in India in 1848, joined the 58th regiment of the Bengal Native Infantry at Danapur, served in the Company's war against the Sikh kingdom later that year, was promoted to lieutenant in 1850 and went back to England soon after on sick-leave. Then, on the invitation of the government, Arnold returned to India in 1854 as the Director of Public Instruction. Beyond these bare outlines of a brief career in India, three things stand out. First, Arnold's letters, as Kenneth Allott shows, reveal his sense of exile in India and his near-constant homesickness.[84] The sense of exile is exacerbated by Arnold's encounter with Anglo-Indian society, especially the regimental mess, which leads him to complain in the Dedication to the novel that there is in Anglo-India, 'a want of earnestness, a want of moral tone'.[85] Finally, the novel, together with Arnold's other writings on India that appeared in *Fraser's Magazine* between 1853 and 1858, reveals a preoccupation with reform that, in the first place, had brought him down from Oxford to India.

These themes recur in *Oakfield*, a novel about the Arnold-like Oxford undergraduate Edward Oakfield, who goes to India believing, perhaps like Arnold, that: 'was not every European in India engaged in the grand work of civilising Asia?'[86] His expectation from Anglo-India soon betrayed, Oakfield lives a misfit among fellow officers, serves in the Battle of

Chillianwalla and returns to England soon afterwards. There is little to the novel except lengthy discussions between Oakfield and his worldly and cynical friends on the state of expatriate morals and the British mission in India, and the even longer letters that Oakfield writes to his sister in England on more or less the same subjects. And for all the concern for India, there is almost nothing of India, and there are no Indian characters in the novel except the odd menial or undifferentiated masses of Indian troops; an auspicious distinction that Arnold/Oakfield shares with Winston Churchill, whose account of his Indian years in *My Early Life* (1930) suggests that he 'spent three years in India without apparently meeting any Indian other than a menial'.[87]

Despite, or perhaps because of these deficiencies and the exiguity of its deliberations, *Oakfield* is a novel of what Kaye calls the 'Progress of Englishism', and represents the self-image and the intellectual predilections of a new school of administrators for whom India was 'something of a laboratory for the creation of the liberal administrative state'.[88] In the novels by Hockley and Taylor, reform is the hidden agenda and Anglo-India an absent presence, while in *Oakfield* reform and Anglo-Indian society are the only interests. Also, the question of colonial reform, itself the extension of a metropolitan concern shared, among others, by Thomas Arnold and the soon-to-emerge Rugby–Oxford school of 'muscular fiction',[89] brings to the fore a new, more expansive, formulation of the role and responsibility of Anglo-India, and a criticism of the present state of British administration. Thus, the 'utter want of nobleness in the government of India', which 'still retains the mask of its commercial origin',[90] makes it unequal to the task of changing the 'awful *vis inertiae* of Asiaticism'. And, in order for it to reform India, Anglo-Indian society and the Company's administration must first be raised 'to a state of comparative Christian earnestness';[91] for only when: 'The spirit of philosophy, and poetry, and godliness shall move across the world, and begin to dawn even upon Englishmen in the East, – when the philosophical reformer shall become the Governor-General, – then the spirit of Mammon may tremble for its empire, but not till then.'[92] In Kaye's revisionary account of the period of reform, it is this enthusiasm among 'clever well-read secretaries'[93] that becomes one of the main causes of the rebellion. At the same time, Kaye's point is that the more radical exponents of reform were either ignorant of or inattentive to indigenous traditions and opinions, and for them the 'Progress of Englishism' meant simply the erasure of Indian traditions, practices and belief-systems.

Oakfield's rhetoric of reform and its actual indifference to India is typical of the socio-historical tendency of an emergent Anglo-India in much the same way in which *The Missionary* represents an orientalist imagination.[94] Largely a function of British ascendancy, the Anglo-Indian identity and sub-culture that emerges before and becomes more pronounced after the rebel-lion defines itself primarily through its difference from the indigenous.[95] The novel's evident lack of interest in India, its consuming, though critical, absorption with Anglo-Indian society, and its confinement to such spaces as the regimental mess, the drawing room and, significantly, the hero's let-ters home reflect the insularity that Spear traces, and set it at the other end of the scale from novels like *Pandurang Hari* and *The Confessions of a Thug*. While in these latter novels the dense representation of the indige-nous is the primary aesthetic interest, as is the interiority of the indigenous 'autobiographical' subject, *Oakfield*, like Churchill's *My Early Life* some forty years on, transforms India into a minor epiphenomenon of Anglo-India.

The contrastive interests and emphases of these autobiographical texts usually coalesce in the Mutiny novel where, schematically speaking, the nar-rative of insurgency usually turns to the Hockley–Taylor tradition, while that of counter-insurgency reintroduces Anglo-India and restores its insu-larity by turning to expatriate domesticity. While this interplay will be explored in more textual detail in the following chapters, the simultaneous locations of Anglo-India in the insular and the 'indigenist', the orientalist and the reformist complicate the separation of the metropolis from the Indian periphery, even as they raise questions about the history and char-acter of British settlement in India. The experience of exile and the modi-fications of identity that result from colonial contact are a useful heuristic. However, official Anglo-India, which, after all, comprised the majority of the British in India, must be distinguished from comparable yet radically different experiences of colonial exile in North America, Australia or New Zealand, where settlement was the norm, and where settlement also yielded a gradual dissociation from the metropolis culminating in the emergence of new nation states and identities. On the question of colonial contact, too, Anglo-India needs to be compared with its imperial predecessor, the Mughal-Timurid empire, which achieved integration and a syncretic idiom unavailable to Anglo-India, except in extremely limited areas. Finally, the class composition of the expatriates who formed and circulated opinion – the class that ran the periodicals and the government, that wrote novels and revenue reports and that unfailingly returned to Britain at the end of a career – is of not inconsiderable importance. As Douglas Peers shows in his study of the British officers in the Indian army:

Service in India catered to the needs of those who could not afford to live as gentlemen in Britain, yet considered themselves to be part of that class. India not only provided the financial means for providing such status, it also opened up the political and military avenues through which the mores and attitudes of this class could be publicly affirmed.[96]

The need to police colonial possessions and to launch further incursions meant more recruitment and more jobs, especially in the army and the navy, a correlation between colonisation and war that James Mill implicitly criticised in his article on 'Colony' for the 1834 Supplement to the *Encyclopaedia Britannica* when he wrote that were anyone to: 'examine all the wars which have afflicted this country from the time when she [Britain] first began to have colonies, [this would] show how very great a proportion of them have grown out of colony disputes'.[97]

While the Anglo-Indian experience certainly produced the inflections that Moore-Gilbert indicates, from the first quarter of the nineteenth century the commissioned/covenanted ranks of the administration and the army appeared to be on guard against a radical modification of national and cultural identity through contact with the indigenous, and, as studies of Anglo-Indian interiors, deportment and education have shown, to minimise the physical effects of exile. As Hutchins observes in his study of what he describes as the Anglo-Indian 'Middle Class Aristocracy', the 'English created for themselves in India a social world intended to be as much like life in England as possible',[98] and which ensured that the British in India remained what the Governor of Madras, William Bentinck, prophetically described in 1807 as 'strangers in the land'.[99] Insularity and exclusion functioned at once as the modalities of colonial power and as the means of articulating a differential relationship with the indigenous by a reassertion of identities, national, racial and religious. Anglo-Indian identity was as much a matter of exile from Britain as it was of a self-imposed exile from the immediacy of India, and against an experience-induced difference from the metropolis there was more fundamental distance from indigenous life forms. Put another way, despite the argot, the culinary habits and its recurrent literary or painterly tropes, Anglo-India remained more decidedly un-Indian than it was ever un-British; for the 'military and civil servants of the Company and the Crown' never ceased to function 'as the local agents for the metropolitan interests of London's commercial, financial and political elite'.[100] The dual, and often fraught, articulations of British expatriate identity in India were to a degree the consequence of what Benedict Anderson describes as 'the fundamental contradiction of English official nationalism, i.e. the inner incompatibility of empire and nation'.[101] Yet, in the case of Anglo-India this contradiction never resolved itself, as it did elsewhere, in a new national identity; and remained a double-barrelled anomaly that led Edward Oaten to observe in 1908 that: 'the British community in India is neither a colony nor a nation, but little more, relatively, than a garrison'.[102]

4

The 'Mutiny' novel and the historical archive

And, England, now avenge thy wrongs by vengeance deep and dire
Cut out this canker with the sword, and burn it out with fire;
Destroy those traitor legions, hang every pariah-hound,
And hunt them down to death, in all the cities round.

Martin Farquhar Tupper (1810–89)

BEGINNINGS, 1858–9

Fiction, poetry and drama were other contemporary vehicles for circulating and commemorating the rebellion. As a reviewer declared at the end of 1858: 'The rebellion, at least in its present stages, ere its shouts and shrieks have died away, is a fit subject for poetry.'[1] The review is of a volume of poems by Mary A. Leslie, *Sorrows, Aspirations, and Legends from India*, and an anonymous narrative poem, *The Moslem and the Hindoo; a Poem on the Sepoy Revolt*, which appeared earlier that year.[2] Of the two, it is Leslie who appears more attuned to the visceral popular mood of counter-insurgency.

Her sonnet 'Delhi' urged the destruction of a city where some fifty British officers and civilians died at the hands of the rebels in May 1857. Beyond the fact of these casualties, Delhi was the site and the sign of the counter-hegemonic claim and appeal of Islam and the Mughal empire, a city whose capture was to the British of more than military importance, and that once captured called for exemplary punishment. Hence:

> Rase her to the ground, – palace and tower
> White marble mosque and gorgeous sepulchre, –
> And let silence of the massacre
> Evermore as a cloud upon her lower,
> So that the traveller in some future hour
> May say, 'here are the whereabouts of her,
> Once India's Empress, whose high name could stir
> A thousand memories with enchantress power.

She lies a desolation, for she filled
Her houses with our slain, and took delight
In women's tortured wailings. . .'[3]

The ruins of the Mughal imperium and their historically sentient (and, presumably, European) observer invoke the topology of the Anglo-Indian picturesque that, with its fetish for ruined palaces, fortresses, temples and mosques, is a visual equivalent of orientalist nostalgia, and an Asiatic recension of the metropolitan picturesque.

In the work of Leslie, a missionary wife in India, the pleasure of ruins was however entwined with a call for chastisement, for it was now the British who would batter an imperial city into a ruin to create the artefact on which turned the aesthetic of the ruin. In the tenebrous folds of the ruin was a symbolic configuration of India's past and present shared equally by the new and the old schools of administrators, though the meanings they ascribed to that symbol deviate rather sharply. The 'fallen greatness' of the Indian polity materialised in the monument in disrepair was occasion for stylised, dignified nostalgia in narratives and paintings of a conservative, orientalist cast. But they acquired another meaning in the perception of the 'New School' where reformist-evangelical energies appeared poised to save India from its pasts, Hindu and Muslim, and where the ruined monument bore witness to irregularity, roughness, resistance and failure to ascend the progressive stages of history. The conservative version returns in the 'marble mosque and gorgeous sepulchre', though now under the aspect of a punitive vision. The (non-)memorial of an (e)rased Delhi recalled the British-led sack of Delhi from September 1857,[4] echoing commentators like Lord Ellenborough who proposed the demolition of the Mughal palace and the Jama Masjid in Delhi. And while these measures were not finally carried out, the deliberate erasure of a lived culture, the razing of an old, thriving aristocratic neighbourhood between the palace and the principal mosque, the systematic persecution of Muslims in Delhi, exiled from their city for several years and reduced to penury, recorded so poignantly by Syed Ahmad Khan, and in the diary of the court poet, Mirza Asadullah Khan 'Ghalib', came close enough to satisfy the retaliatory fantasies of Leslie and Ellenborough.[5] The ruin of Delhi Muslims, and the farcical 'trial' of the 'King of Delhi', Bahadur Shah II from January 1858, sealed forever the fate of the *ancien régime*, and of a city that for nearly eight hundred years was the real and symbolic centre of political power. As a mnemonic device, the site/sight of a demolished Delhi laid athwart the 'enchantress power' of indigenous counter-memory was the obverse of the sonnet's memorial homage to British suffering in India in 1857, an innocent poetics obscuring, yet complementing, the hard edge of colonial 'pacification'.

While the rhetoric of counter-insurgency and penality frames 'Delhi' as with the lines from Tupper cited at the head of the chapter, Tennyson's 'The Defence of Lucknow' (1879) is a retrospective commemoration of British fortitude. The narrator introduces at the outset the 'Women and children among us, God help them, our children and wives', the potent engines of a virile chivalry and national honour.[6] The siege of the Lucknow Residency fired popular imagination in Anglo-India and in Britain, for it lasted from June to November 1857, much longer than sieges elsewhere. It took moreover two protracted military campaigns to capture the city and rescue the besieged garrison, though with the fall of the capital, insurgency fanned out into the countryside. Unlike Kanpur, which left almost no survivors, the British at Lucknow held out to the last despite repeated attacks by rebel soldiers under the Begum Hazrat Mahal, the wife of the deposed Wajid Ali Shah.

Unlike historiography or the novel, the poetry of the siege excised the sequence of causes that led to the tenacious popular insurgency in Awadh, of which the events at Lucknow were only an early, dramatic crest. The elision makes for an uncomplicated story of heroism, hardship and sacrifice, embellished with figures of xenophobia and national pride. Initiated by the press, and recycled in the diaries and memoirs of survivors, the story engenders heroes like the 'saintly' Henry Lawrence, the commissioner of the newly annexed Awadh, and Henry Havelock, the 'Bayard of India'. Written two years after the Tory cabinet under Disraeli made Queen Victoria the Empress of India, the Poet Laureate's commemoration is simplistic, though characteristic of one who had defended only a few years before the brutal suppression of the Morant Bay rebellion by Governor Eyre, and 'The Defence of Lucknow' adumbrates the future uses of the rebellion in high imperial propaganda and jingoism. As the narrator, himself a member of the garrison, observes:

> Handful of men as we were, we were English in heart and in limb,
> Strong with the strength of the race to command, to obey, to endure,
> Each of us fought as if hope for the garrison hung but on him . . .[7]

Leslie's reviewer elaborated the two-part aesthetic of insurgency and counter-insurgency that Leslie and Tennyson exploited, and that rested on a skein of crucial omissions, in terms which recall the contiguity of historiography and fiction, even as they underscored the cultural and religious embellishments in British perception of the event. Thus:

India and the great rebellion are, in their present position at least, emphatically a subject for lyric poetry. They have furnished the poet with a set of circumstances, scenes and events grander than any in history, whether we look at their number, nature, causes or results. Each province in the revolted district can furnish tales of lyric value more than centuries of past history . . . Each man was a hero, each woman a man, every babe a martyr and Thermopylae and Piedmont were eclipsed, while over all Jehovah presided . . .[8]

The first work of prose fiction on the subject was perhaps Dickens's 'The Perils of Certain English Prisoners', a short novel written collaboratively with Wilkie Collins and published in the 1857 Christmas number of *Household Words*.[9] His 'wish to avoid India itself' and to commemorate, 'without any vulgar catchpenny connexion or application, some of the best qualities of the English character that have been shewn in India' led Dickens into choosing siege and captivity as the central event of his narrative. While the choice clearly gestured towards Lucknow and Kanpur, the tale is relocated in a British garrison in Central America sometime in the eighteenth century.[10] The displacement was useful, suggesting captivity narratives from the New World, and giving wider colonial amplitude to what had recently been 'shewn in India'. The displacement moreover occluded the messier details of British involvement in India, and the first-person account by the ex-Royal Marine private, Gill Davis, forms a twofold response to the news of the rebellion that filtered into Britain from June 1857. There is, on the one hand, the unmitigated villainy of Portuguese pirates, English ex-convicts, indigenous peoples, and assorted 'niggers', especially the 'Sambo', George Christian King, who betrays the garrison to the pirates; and their antithesis is in the heroism, selflessness and fortitude of Englishwomen like Miss Maryon, and English soldiers and officers such as Captain Carton. This neat opposition drew heavily on contemporary reportage of the rebellion, prefiguring the habitual characterology of fictional and personal narratives.

On the other hand, an exchange between the local British Commissioner, Pordage, and Captain Carton introduces fissures within counter-insurgency. As Carton sets out with his men to apprehend the pirates, Pordage cautions him that the 'Government requires you to treat the enemy with great delicacy, consideration, clemency, and forbearance'.[11] While this is a clear parody of the 'Clemency' Resolution, Carton's answer to Pordage reiterates the criticism of high policy in sections of the Anglo-Indian and metropolitan press, justifying indirectly the conduct of officers such as Neill, Renaud and Lieutenant William Hodson of Hodson's Horse, who shot the captive Mughal princes at Delhi in September 1857:

I am an English officer, commanding English Men, and I hope I am not likely to disappoint the Government's just expectations. But, I presume you know that these villains under their black flag have despoiled our countrymen of their property, burnt their homes, barbarously murdered them and their little children, and worse than murdered their wives and daughters . . . Believing that I hold my commission by the allowance of God . . . I shall certainly use it, with all avoidance of unnecessary suffering and with all merciful swiftness of execution, to exterminate these people from the face of the earth.[12]

As William Odie showed in his reading of 'The Perils of Certain English Prisoners', the presumed violation of 'wives and daughters' fuelled demands for punitive measures, and made the temperance of Canning suspect. Carton's statement of intent closely echoes Dickens's own call for vengeance when he wrote to Mrs Coutts on 4 October 1857:

I wish I were the Commander in Chief in India. The first thing I would do to strike that Oriental race with amazement . . . should be to proclaim to them in their language, that I considered my holding that appointment by the leave of God, to mean that I should do my utmost to exterminate the Race upon whom the stain of the late cruelties rested; and that I was there for that purpose and no other, and was now proceeding, with all convenient despatch and merciful swiftness of execution, to blot it out of mankind and raze it off the face of the Earth.[13]

While 'The Perils of Certain English Prisoners' took an indirect route to the rebellion, as did *Luxima* two years on, the first novel to treat the rebellion directly was Edward Money's *The Wife and the Ward; or, a Life's Error* (1859), a novel about the siege and massacre at Kanpur.[14] Structurally, the novel is in two parts: the first (from chapter I to chapter XIX, though the first signs of trouble appear in chapter XV) is located in Anglo-Indian society local in the civil station at the Dinapur (or Danapur) cantonment, a military station north of Calcutta where Arnold/Oakfield too had spent time, and where officers and their families attend balls, dinners, pig-sticking expeditions and a steeple-chase. In the course of these social engagements the hero, Captain Edgington, falls in love with and marries Beatrice Plane, the daughter of a Patna judge; a marriage that constitutes the 'life's error' of the subtitle. Early in 1857, Edgington's regiment is sent to Kanpur, the military and commercial town on the banks of the Ganges adjacent to the recently annexed Awadh. While he makes the move with his ward Marion Paris, a young girl fresh out of England, Beatrice, with whom his marriage has begun to go wrong because of her domineering habits, returns to live with her parents at Patna. It is from this point (chapter XX to chapter XXVI) that the novel turns to the rebellion. At Kanpur, the first intimations of revolt appear in the person of the Nana Sahib, who, while fraternising with the local British community at a ball, frightens young Marion with his sinister and sexually threatening presence; a threat refigured and underscored in Marion's premonitory dream of rebellion and siege where the Nana desires to make her his 'bride'.[15]

When the rebellion breaks out, Edgington and Marion, like the rest of the British population in the town, take refuge in the 'entrenchment'. The remainder of the novel is a close focus on the siege, as the garrison fends off rebel sorties, makes the best of its severely depleted resources, and in the course of which an Anglo-Indian love-interest emerges as Marion is wooed by Ensign Hoby between rebel assaults, and as Edgington, already estranged from his wife, finds in her a comforting companion. Finally, when the Nana Sahib sends his emissaries on 26 June to negotiate the surrender of the garrison, Marion, who fancies the Nana has designs on her, persuades Edgington to kill her rather than allow her to be taken captive. While this defence of feminine honour against a fate 'worse than death' so strenuously imagined in Mutiny literature modified the apocryphal story of Ulrica Wheeler – the daughter of General Wheeler, who allegedly killed her Muslim abductor and his family before taking her own life – it also turned on a common knowledge of the climacteric horror of the rebellion, the Bibighar massacre of 15 July.[16] At any rate, on the morning of 27 June, the survivors of the garrison are ambushed by the rebels while boarding the boats that are to take them to safety, and thus begins the Satichaura Ghat massacre, when Edgington keeps his promise and shoots Marion dead only to be sabred by the rebel cavalrymen the next instant – upon which the novel abruptly ends. A brief postscript follows, in which Money cites an anonymous report, 'lately received from India which appeared in the London papers last December [1857]' on 'the final act of the Cawnpore tragedy', the Bibighar massacre.[17]

As this summary suggests, the use of history in *The Wife and the Ward* is straightforward and transparent. The record of siege and massacre in the last six chapters resembles contemporary first-person accounts such as *The Story of Cawnpore* (1859) by Mowbray Thomson, a subaltern in the Bengal army who was among the very few survivors. As a reviewer commented, *The Wife and the Ward* is 'deficient in plot', especially in the second half of the novel where the rebellion interrupts Anglo-Indian life in the garrison town.[18] The move from the bungalow to the 'entrenchment' that Marion and Edgington make on 5 June marks the transition from an overtly fictional narrative to the narrative of history.[19] The initial interest in Edgington's marriage and his discovery of an elective affinity with Marion are now superseded by the plot of the rebellion, which suspends the plot of Anglo-Indian love and marriage, replaces domesticity with the publicity of history and truncates private destinies in the irreversible fact of the Ghat massacre.

The deficiency of plot, if that, was a result of the fact that the Anglo-Indian first half loses its way in the plot of the rebellion; and, as the death of all principal characters and the postscript attest, the end of the novel is the end too of the colonial project, and of its instrument, Anglo-India. Unmitigated by survival or revenge, Money's sense of an ending is quite unusual for the Mutiny novel. In later novels where Anglo-India rises vengefully from captivity or massacre, or in the founding template of Thomson's *Story of Cawnpore*, neither Satichaura Ghat nor Bibighar are finalities to which the Anglo-Indian plot ever succumbs. Following his escape from the Ghat with three others, Thomson survives pursuit, spends a few weeks in hiding as the guest of a 'loyal' Awadh *zamindar*, 'Raja Dirigbijah Singh, of Moorah Mhow', and meets up with a British regiment at the rear of the Allahabad Moveable Column, the first expeditionary force sent up from Allahabad to rescue the Kanpur and Lucknow garrisons. Following the advance guard led by Brigadier Neill, Thomson re-enters a deserted Kanpur with the relieving army on 17 July and resumes active service as 'commandant of Cawnpore police', a job for which his local knowledge comes in handy.[20]

Lacking such malleability and the colonial future that it ensured, *The Wife and the Ward* is innocent of the themes of masterful reconquest and punishment animating the novels and the first-person accounts that progressed from insurgency to counter-insurgency. Despite this lack, Money's novel was the first where the narrative of Anglo-Indian social life was intersected by the rebel arc to generate the typically articulated structure of the Mutiny novel. While the fact that Anglo-India does not survive insurgency is, perhaps, the reason why the reviewer deplored a plot that failed to get past history, the articulated structure opens a handy critical window on the historical, ideological and ethnographic moorings of the Mutiny novel. Though the discussion that follows is mainly prospective, the identification of the several aspects and implications of this structure will orient the reading of the novels in the following chapters.

First, the intersection of Anglo-India with the rebellion tapped into and elaborated the Oakfield–Arnold and the Hockley–Taylor representational emphases. Though in the second half of *The Wife and the Ward* the plot of the rebellion, doubling as the narrative dynamic, is manifest only in its effects on the Kanpur garrison, in later novels such as Flora Annie Steel's *On the Face of the Waters*, the engagement with expatriate society moves in tandem with representations of the world of insurgency and rebel consciousness *from the inside*, especially in the chapters where Steel reconstructs life and politics in rebel Delhi through the summer of 1857.

Second, of the two elements that constitute the articulated structure, Anglo-India and the rebellion, it is the latter that implied, when it did not expressly thematise, the contiguous context of Indian society, politics and history. As an ever-present but intermittently visible background to the rebellion, already at hand through the practices of colonial enquiry and representation, the text of India that the rebellion perforce introduced served as an explanatory meta-narrative in a manner not unlike the prefatory excursions in the histories by Martin and Ball. Put another way, the rebellion was a critical mediator between the colonial project and its instrument, Anglo-India, on the one hand, and the dense texture of a life-world that at once justified yet resisted British advance in India on the other.

Finally, the articulated structure necessarily throws open the question of history. As the *The Wife and the Ward* and the dissatisfaction of its reviewer suggests, rebel agency cuts short the progress of love, marriage, and domesticity too peremptorily. The failure to give to Anglo-India a future might have been a result of Money's nearness to the events, whereas the novels that came later made out of Kanpur a story of heroic adventure and revenge, but in either event the archive of events and interpretations sanctioned by first-person accounts and corroborated by historiography remained the horizon of fictional possibility. There were, of course, occasional modifications of the archive, as in *The End of the Nana Sahib* by Jules Verne, where the Nana returns from hiding in 1864 to foment the mother of all rebellions, when by all accounts he has died a fugitive in the Nepali Terai within two years of his fleeing Kanpur in 1857.[21] Such liberties are rare, and the usual conformity to the archive that *The Wife and the Ward* carried to a fatal extreme underscores the characteristic transvaluation of history and fiction in colonial narratives. The 'bare ungarnished story of the Rising', which Joyce Muddock celebrates in her preface to *The Great White Hand*, and which has the power to 'put fiction in the shade', now appears as a series of political and military events which overtook the narrative of marriage and colonial domesticity in Money's novel.[22]

Finally, in the large majority of the novels, history is the restorer of British future in India, in as much as the rebellion becomes the springboard to formal imperial investiture. At the narrative level, this restorative demand means that novels usually pursue the route which Thomson's account of Kanpur takes: from insurgency to counter-insurgency, from a threatened to a resurgent empire, and from martyrdom to a proactive martial heroism.

The consequences of this narrative route are important. Most Mutiny novels end with the revival of British authority and the death or capture of rebels – the point at which the histories too end. Within the fictional plot, the statist conclusion is usually configured as a safe return to those Anglo-Indian spaces that were invaded by the rebellion, or by a return to England, and by a resumption of love, marriage and domesticity, all temporarily suspended or endangered by the matter of history. Though the rebellion disturbs the stable empire of the first few chapters, the novels always end with the tranquil restorations of Crown, Parliament and a revived Anglo-India. This is not the ending of *The Wife and the Ward*, for here narratives of counter-insurgency work to restore the world that the rebellion had interrupted, a resolution that drew on the resources of the Whig version of history, transposed to prime real estate in India. Rebel agency disturbs the narrative of marriage and domesticity only to discharge a heroic narrative of counter-insurgency, which shows how by 'valour and energy India had once more been fairly conquered in the field', and how 'the triumphs of civilisation and of peace' began after the event.[23]

Though this section is titled 'Beginnings', the argument proceeds from Leslie, Dickens and Money to make several prospective theses about the uses of history in the Mutiny novel. The next section examines how narratives of the rebellion mesh with narratives of Anglo-Indian social life. The nature of this meshing, its modalities and implications, reveals the working of the articulated structure and prepares the way for later discussions of the imagining of resistance.

THE MUTINY NOVEL AND ITS NARRATIVE SEDIMENTS

The examples of Leslie, Dickens–Collins and Money show how the substrate on which the Mutiny-as-fiction rests is the *ur*-text of the Mutiny-as-history, interred within first-person accounts, the press and histories and chronicles. But this enabling archive was hardly self-contained or without wider reference to genres, disciplines and institutions that produced, systematised and disseminated British knowledge and representations of India in all the years since the *diwani*. And it is only amongst these widening ripples that a literary history of British India can convincingly serialise the mutation from *The Missionary*, to the novels by Hockley and Taylor, to *Oakfield*, to the Mutiny and the colonial adventure novel and beyond. But the reliance on history means that the novels cannot spring surprises. Quite apart from a knowledge of events – and it is a plausible assumption that the bare facts of the rebellion were common knowledge among sizeable numbers of the British reading public – the rebellion was foreclosed even as a writerly exercise.

This closure happens in several ways. While the articulated structure is formally and substantively informed by what Ball calls the 'task . . . of producing order from chaos', the matter of history appears in the course of prefatory remarks, in dialogues and in digressions that insert the archive while explaining or advancing the action of the novel. An example of the digressive mode is in Frederick P. Gibbon's *The Disputed VC: A Story of the Indian Mutiny* (1909).[24] A colonial adventure novel in the high imperial mood of Henty and others, *The Disputed VC* sprawls across the two years of the rebellion, and the boy hero, Ted Russell, takes part in all major campaigns including those at Delhi and Lucknow. Soon after the news of the Meerut uprising of 10 May arrives in the fictional frontier town of 'Aurungpore', the narrator steps in with an aside that 'most readers will know' how the 'mullahs and fakirs had been poisoning the minds of the soldiers [and] the childish, credulous, superstitious sepoys were . . . only too ready to believe all idle tales'.[25] The first hint of a resistance comes when a 'mullah who had rendered himself mad with bhang' attacks Ted in a bazaar in the native town, urging passers by with the call that 'the hundred years of the white man's *raj* are fulfilled, and the curse shall be lifted from us'.[26] A few chapters later, the news of the outbreak at Meerut prompts soldiers and the town 'mob' at Aurungpore to lay siege to the British garrison. But between the first signs of trouble and the siege, the narrator embarks on a thirteen-page essay on the causes of the rebellion and its failure.

The essay suspends the action of the novel with a document that mimics, though in an abbreviated form, the aetiological ruminations in historiography and other accounts. In Gibbon's version, the usual suspects return: British intervention in a traditional society, the declining status of the Indian officer in the regimental hierarchy, Mughal (and hence, Muslim) resentment, the annexation of Awadh, the Nana's grievances, the caste sensitivities of the Bengal soldier, the popular Indian belief that the British would rule India for only a hundred years and the 'idle tales' about a suspected British conspiracy to convert Hindus and Muslims. On the reasons for the eventual failure of resistance, the essay argues that the rebels were disorganised, and that they 'lacked the inspiration of a leader ready to sacrifice himself for their cause'. But at the end of this litany, the essay, however, cautions readers against a too-violent dislike of Indian soldiers; for, though 'in 1857 the sepoy was a madman inflamed with rage and bitter hatred against those whom he mistakenly considered his oppressors', the Indian soldier was, after all, 'simple and credulous as a child'.[27]

Gibbon's equation of the *sipahis* with children is, of course, a representation similar in pragmatic and symbolic use with the construction of the 'martial race' type, an ethnography that works equally well at the popular and the specialist levels to explain the character of the colonial small war. This equation evokes the paternalist idiom of the relation between British officers and the Indian troops, or between the peasantry and the district administrator, serving moreover to vitiate if not erase altogether the political content of resistance. As with his brisk and confident summary of causes, the narrator's moderation is a function of his distance from the event. In the fifty years between the novel and the rebellion, the Indian army began to take a shape that persists in post-independence India: from being motley bands of regional mercenaries into a professionally run institution, following a largely European model in drill, regulation and combat tactic, yet cognisant of the peculiarities of Indian ethnography in regimental formations. The army was routinely used as the instrument of British adventurism in many other theatres, and being largely untouched by the popular, radical nationalism that took shape from the first decade of the twentieth century, the army played a large if still unrecognised role in the two World Wars. Behind the caution to his young readers that 'we must not paint the sepoy in colours too black' lurks a pragmatism that recalls the insight of John Malcolm in 1823 that: 'our means of preserving and improving our possessions . . . depend on our wise and politic exercise of that military power on which the whole fabric rests'.[28] The story of insurgency may be tilted against the insurgents, and the tilt may yield a generally unkind view of natives as such, yet these must not jeopardise commitment to empire, or to those resources that empire offered.

While this historically aware essay was not the only one, for there will be more when Ted Russell campaigns at Delhi and Lucknow, its early occurrence has a prospective function. None of the military events that will engage the novel and its hero have yet occurred, and the outbreak at Meerut is off-stage. But the confident catalogue of causes, the brisk summary of 'sepoy', and, by implication, of Indian, character and finally the suggestions to the reader insert the Mutiny archive to announce, order and delimit the matter of history. These anticipatory gestures make for a horizon of expectation shared by the reader, the narrator, the colonial state and statist historiography, producing the harmonious compact such vantages share on the interpretation of resistance.

Masque of the Mutiny by C. Lestock Reid is a comparatively late novel dedicated to 'the men and women who devoted their lives, and often sacrificed their lives, to winning and holding the short-lived Indian Empire'.

Published in the year of Indian independence, Reid's somewhat belated contribution to colonial adventure is really an extended allusion to a more recent, and modally different, political resistance poised for independence from British rule. Datelined 'October 1946', a candid Foreword states how the novel aims 'to show the utter folly of handing over India . . . to the rule of Brahmins and Brahmin-controlled politicians', for – and this is a common enough wartime conservative chant most eloquent in the case of Churchill – 'to hold and rule India is absolutely essential to our continued existence not only as an Empire but even as a nation'. Like Ball blaming Hindu secret societies for the rebellion, the anti-Brahmin tirade in the novel pins the arch villain as the Brahmin 'Mahatma', Biji Rao, and a combination of caste and synecdoche explains the point of imagining a Brahmin-led rebellion: 'Gandhi, though by birth of the Vaishya Caste . . . may be said to have become the Biji Rao of today.'[29]

But the Brahmin was not the only enemy of empire. There was also the enemy within, and *Masque*, like Reid's Foreword to his east Asian novel *The Greatest Game*, fulminates at those among the British who sympathise with Indians; a treasonable 'pandering to these damned natives' – as the historical Colonel Carmichael-Smythe of the 3rd Light Infantry at Meerut puts it in the novel – that in the case of Robin Westerne caused transgressions that Owenson's *The Missionary* do not seem to mind very much: Robin falls in love with a native woman, and deserts the army to join the rebel militia.[30] In fact, the hoary tradition of intercultural love, variously explored though always eventually set aside by Owenson, Medwin, Taylor and Kipling surfaces again in Reid's novel, doubly inflected by 1857 and by the charged political atmosphere of the 1940s. As between Medwin's Seta and Major B, Shalini meanly exploits Robin's passion for her; and, like the sentimental orientalism of Major B, the 'spiritual side of Hinduism' draws Robin just 'as it has attracted better men', and the 'sensuous side of Hinduism allured him as it has allured worse men'; a confusion of identity and a blurring of the cultural boundary that make Robin naively believe that the 'blood brothers of Shalini [that is, the *sipahis*], they should be his own brothers'.[31]

The political sympathies of Robin Westerne, his willingness to cross the sexual cordon and to let the side down, is an indictment of the post-war Labour haste in the transfer of power – the 'stupidity of those politicians who, perhaps, honestly, think that Western democratic ideals are suited to the Eastern temperaments'[32] – as of liberal sympathisers with Indian nationalism such as A. O. Hume, Edward John Thompson or Malcolm Darling.[33] Viewing 1857 though the prism of the 1940s, *Masque* interpellates the rebellion with contemporary colonial policy and Indian nationalism, casting upon each the shadow of the other in a manner not unlike that of Savarkar in his *War of Indian Independence*. Though the peculiar inflection of the end games of empire is unique to *Masque*, and perversely comparable with the republican Savarkar's tactical recovery of a pre-modern resistance in 1909, the novel is nonetheless in the mould of colonial adventure, if only to show how not to capitulate to indigenous nationalism. At the end therefore the prodigal anti-hero, Robin Westerne, returns to the fold to die, and the 'Mahatma' is killed by the more sanguinely heroic Rupert Delacey and his Hindu man-Friday, Kunaji Lal; a conclusion that excises the traitor within and the enemy without with equal despatch.

Beyond such topical inflections as result from Reid's embittered rear-guard resistance, the insertion of the Mutiny archive in *Masque* was some-what more complex than in Gibbons's *Disputed VC*. The second chapter of the novel opens with the preamble that the year 1857 'was destined to prove the most terrible in all the blood-stained pageants of Indian history'; and though 'few could read portents of the coming storm . . . already behind the apparently placid surface of cantonment life, behind the dances and the gai-eties . . . the Devil's wind was beginning to blow'.[34] These premonitions are followed by a regimental dinner at Meerut late in April 1857, where officers and guests discuss the news and rumours of unrest. The curious auditor of the exchange is Robin Westerne's sister, Maud, newly arrived from England, and who though betrothed to an officer at Delhi is in love with a Rupert Delacey, whom she meets on ship to India. The conversation moves in two parallel directions. On the one hand, the references to historically verifiable names, dates and events (for example, Mangal Pandey of the 34th Native Infantry, who attacked his officers at the Barrackpur parade ground on 29 March, and was later court-martialled and executed) inserts recognis-able signposts, besides providing the backdrop for later action where Maud conceives a dislike for her betrothed, and, abducted by the rebels, she is rescued by her gallant lover Rupert, a captain in the Governor-General's bodyguard.

The undertone of the conversation suggests a familiar friction between the civil service and the army. Maud's partner at the table is the civilian Slade, who dismisses the reports the officers agitatedly debate, and assures her that the cartridge affair is simply 'one of those silly rumours that are so common in India'.[35] If the civilian will not listen to any talk of danger because he believes that India is well governed and the population at peace, others are seriously concerned. Swinging between paranoia and confidence, the group at the table discuss the Doctrine of Lapse, mention the circulating chapattis, recall the Indian belief that British rule would not survive its hundredth year, remark that Henry Lawrence, the Commissioner of the recently annexed Awadh, was 'preparing Lucknow for a siege' and suggest that the Brahmins (rather than the 'mullahs' who are Gibbons's particular phobia) are responsible for seditious propaganda. At the end of the evening, Maud, not unlike a proxy metropolitan reader, is anxious: 'A queer little shiver of apprehension shook her. If the officers of the native regiments – she felt uneasy about the whole thing. India was a horrid country, all heat and insects and unrest.'[36]

In terms of the articulated structure of the Mutiny novel, the stichomythic exchange over regimental dinner is significant. The archive is inserted through the device of conversation instead of the historical essay that Gibbon (and Reid, earlier in the chapter) employs, and the conversation reproduces post-Mutiny exhumations of the signs and symptoms of a budding resistance apparent early in 1857. The conversation is as informative as discursive excursions, but has an advantage in that often the exchange of perspectives or historical analyses contributes to an Anglo-Indian plot peopled by civilians and soldiers, sceptics and alarmists, the 'pukka' and the not-so 'pukka'. Moreover these conversations, of which the first fictional instance is chapter VI of *The Wife and the Ward*, which take place in Anglo-Indian social spaces such as the regimental mess, the veranda of a bungalow, the club, the drawing room, the ball, the dinner table or Anglo-Indian periodicals, indicate how the physical and cognitive limits of these spaces make the portents ambiguous and their reading difficult. That those who take the bazaar rumours seriously and imagine the worst are proven right, while those who do not are betrayed by the turn of events, is irrelevant here. What is germane is that both groups, and those in between, variously receive, interpret and circulate an amorphous mass of sinister but undecipherable signals that emanate from and refer to a world and a people that everywhere surround but are rigorously excluded from the social spaces of the expatriate community. The rumours of bone-dust mixed with flour and the Nana's Russian and Turkish connections, the sullen barracks, the peripatetic maulvis and *fakirs*, the 'inflammatory' articles in indigenous newspapers and posters and the unconfirmed reports of uprisings and arson in neighbouring towns and garrisons constitute a repertoire of signs that originate in the indigenous society and seep into Anglo-India; and with their polysemic discharge they prise open an insular space establishing a traffic of signs that initiated the narrative journey from Anglo-India to an insurgent India; a journey that, in terms of the topology of Anglo-Indian fiction, was from the world of Oakfield–Arnold to that of Hockley and Taylor.

The articulation of the historical with the fictional was a formal device, necessary to the novels of the rebellion in as much as they were historical novels, but it was also the machinery that enabled a rather more substantive traffic of colonial knowledge. The act of imagining the rebellion involved new appraisals of those centres and margins which constituted Anglo-Indian identity, threatened and 'taken over by the native', as Fanon argues, 'at the moment when, deciding to embody history in his own person, he surges into the forbidden quarter'.[37] The level of appraisal and awareness, or the acknowledgement of the political content of the rebellion, varied widely in the corpus of Mutiny novels. Particularly in the metropolitan adventure novel, the matter of history rested too heavily on simplification and broad strokes, with narratives usually reluctant or unable to venture beyond the expatriate world and the delights of colonial warfare. In other novels, and these are fewer, the rebellion was the occasion for a renewed observation of the Indian life-world, and where the interpretation of the rebellion stood upon a rather more dense representation of Indian politics, society and history.

With Sword and Pen (1904) by H. C. Irwin is a good example of those novels which weave the two narratives closely together without allowing either to dominate, and where the intersection of the historical and the fictional is clear and elaborate.[38] While Irwin's first novel of the rebellion, *A Man of Honour* (1896), is set in the North West Frontier, a near-hagiographical account of a Punjab School hero who comes down from his mountain fastness with a body of Irregular cavalry to capture Delhi, *With Sword and Pen* is a novel of the rebellion in Awadh and its capital, Lucknow (Irwin renames them Ghoristan and Nadirabad, respectively), where Irwin had worked in the civil administration and wrote of it in his study *The Garden of India* (1880).[39] Though otherwise a colonial adventure novel, the first quarter of the novel explores the history of the kingdom leading up to the annexation in February 1856. The witness to this history is the hero, Malcolm Mainwaring, a subaltern in the 125th Native Infantry, newly arrived from England, and posted at Nadirabad.

The second chapter is a brief detour into the history of the Company's relations with Awadh, ending with the well-publicised view that the present Nawab was 'a mere Oriental debauchee of the type with which Macaulay's Indian *Essays* are supposed to have made any schoolboy familiar'.[40] Between the canonical authority of the Whig reformer of law and education in India and the schoolboy who is also, perhaps, the implied reader of the novel, this evaluation of Awadh polity evokes and confirms a horizon of expectation where annexation and the subsequent rebellion can be forejudged, even as it occludes the processes by which Awadh was gradually transformed into a dependency of the Company. On a hunt, Malcolm meets Usman Khan, a Nadirabad courtier. Riding together, Malcolm observes that his companion seems 'a man of some mark' who 'sat his shapely Arab with easy grace'.[41] From this follows a homoerotic inter-racial bonding at the root of which lies their equestrian synergy, and the fact that they meet in the comparatively untrammelled contact-zone of sport where the two men can temporarily suspend their differences. Sometime after this, Malcolm calls on Usman at home, where their conversation turns from hunting to politics. Since the year is 1855, and Awadh still formally independent, Usman is candid about the dangerous consequences of annexation, if that were to happen. He explains the history of the Company's relations with the kingdom to Malcolm, and the imminent possibility of an event that, in his view, would spell ruin for the landed and courtly elite. For: 'Wherever the Company Bahadur rules, large estates are broken up, and the posts of the officials are abolished, and magistrates and commissioner sahibs are appointed in their stead.'[42] While this is close enough to Kaye's *post hoc* diagnosis of a 'dangerous class sullenly biding their time', Usman goes on to say that a result of the Company's direct rule of the peasantry will be that while the latter 'might escape from the class of the landholders and the local governors . . . it would only be to fall into the net of the money-lender and the lawyer'.[43]

It is remarkable that Irwin should use a citizen of a barely disguised Awadh to retail the history of Anglo-Awadh relations and to question the putative benefits of British rule. Usman Khan is better informed than his interlocutor, and the narrator does not intercede to modify, judge or refute his analysis. If Malcolm the 'griffin' stands for the metropolitan reader, like Maud Westerne in *Masque*, Usman, the native informant, represents the political elite of an Indian kingdom whose annexation figures in historical and other writings as one of the chief explanations of the rebellion. To that extent, Usman's proleptic words point to the error of a theory-driven revenue and administrative policy, combined with plain land hunger, which *The Sepoy War* ironically describes as the 'Progress of Englishism'; a mistake that cost the British the counter-terror of the rebellion. The fact that the novel begins with an account of the present state of Awadh and the controversy over annexation sets up a narrative and explanatory springboard, a social and political history elaborated in the first twelve chapters from which later action will derive plot and meaning.

Where Money, Gibbon and Reid introduce rebel agency from the vantage of the civil station or the regimental mess, the character of Usman Khan represents that agency and its motivations from within, voicing indigenous opinion on annexation, reform and intervention. Moreover, the terms of friendship between Usman and Malcolm, which enables the enunciation of this opinion, are significant too. What begins as a chance encounter develops into camaraderie made possible by the fact that Malcolm, a young newly arrived subaltern posted outside British India and equipped with some Hindustani, steps outside the usual boundaries of expatriate life to strike up a friendship with the Muslim courtier. But their friendship works too as a channel of intelligence, information and political negotiation tied to imminent political developments, and later useful during counter-insurgency campaigns.

In the third chapter Malcolm meets Donald Home, the last Resident of the Company to Ghoristan, the first Commissioner of the province following annexation, and the father of Evelyn, the girl Malcolm met on the voyage out and with whom he is in love. Impressed by Malcolm's local knowledge – a result of his conversations with Usman – Home appoints Malcolm his personal assistant, and takes him along on a tour of the kingdom to determine its affairs, preparatory to annexation.[44] From this point on Malcolm bears witness to the formulation of high policy and the negotiations between the ruling house of Ghoristan and the Company, even as both parties use him as mediator and confidante. While Home finds Malcolm's knowledge handy, the Queen Mother of Ghoristan, aware of the young subaltern's interest in the Resident's daughter, believes that if Usman can persuade Malcolm that the kingdom must not be annexed then, given his intimacy with Evelyn, Malcolm might convince Home of the same.[45] These pragmatic uses of the association between the two men by Donald Home, representing the encroaching Company, and by the Queen Mother, introduces in the friendship between the two men the conflicting trajectories of colonial expansion and indigenous resistance; and, caught between the claims of the two worlds, Usman and Malcolm stand on a threshold between the personal and the public, between Anglo-India and India, between the liberal-administrative state and 'oriental despotism' and later, between insurgency and counter-insurgency.

Malcolm's centrality to the matter of history acquires a new salience when he attends a secret meeting between the Resident and the Queen Mother, and this culminates in chapter XI when one afternoon 'it so chanced that Malcolm rode over to the Residency' to discover that the Governor General in Council has written to Home about the decision to annex Ghoristan.[46] Chance is here a device that pitchforks the Anglo-Indian hero into the theatre of history, and by which the Anglo-Indian plot weaves itself around a policy decision. As if to confirm the fortuitous elevation of the young subaltern, Donald Home sends Malcolm to the Nawab with a letter giving notice of the annexation. The letter is redundant for the decision has already arrived from Calcutta, and Home will call on the Nawab the next day to convey the decision of his government. But the ruse of sending Malcolm to a personal audience with the Nawab of Ghoristan allows the novel to ascend and occupy that cusp in the history of Anglo-Awadh relations which put an end to nearly a hundred years of the Subsidiary Alliance, signalling the usurpation of the kingdom and preparing the ground for a popular, armed resistance.

The meeting confirms the earlier suggestion that the Nawab is a 'mere Oriental debauchee', to which Malcolm now adds the caveat that 'though a worthless voluptuary', the Nawab was 'by no means ignoble or undignified'.[47] Beyond these reiterations of a statutory commonplace that indicts indigenous polity, and whose obverse is a concealment of the political economy of the Subsidiary Alliance, the visit has an additional significance. Like an earlier meeting between the Queen Mother and Evelyn where the Indian and the European woman are separated by 'a whole world of faith and feeling and civilisation', this meeting too is across an essential asymmetry that the narrator and Malcolm insist upon.[48] Notwithstanding, or perhaps because of this asymmetry, the meeting achieves some important results. Malcolm's entry into the world of the Indian political elite allows a representation of that world mediated by the perceptions and reflections of the young Englishman. The similarity between the narrator and the hero's view of this world – especially their assessment of the Nawab – sets up a continuum of reception and judgement extending from the narrator, Malcolm, and the reader, to an iconography of oriental debauchery from Macaulay to the contemporary schoolboy. Reporting from the audience chamber of the Nawab of Ghoristan, Malcolm the metropolitan subject addresses the topics of architecture and the palace decor, the Nawab's sartorial splendour and his refinements of manner and etiquette, all of which prompt in the over-awed subaltern sundry reflections on history, culture and racial character.[49]

Moreover, the insertion of Malcolm into the court, where despite his deference to the monarch, Malcolm, like Thomas Roe long ago at the court of the Mughal Emperor Jahangir, struggles to remain cool and supercilious, fulfils another significant function. During his voyage out, Malcolm has confessed to Evelyn that he has had to leave Oxford and take up an Indian career because the death of his father – the 'rector of a country parish in Cornwall'[50] – has left the family bankrupt. Measured against that provenance, the ascent is truly spectacular: from a poor undergraduate to an emissary of the Company who rides forth to inform a monarch that his kingdom no longer belongs to him, Malcolm's turn of fortune is an index of that 'making' of the English middle classes which occurs in the colonial arena. While such a leap across classes was inconceivable in England, in India as elsewhere in the colonies, transformations of status such as this are not merely demonstrations of racial and national superiority. For beyond those often strident demonstrations, beyond even the self-image of the 'New School' of administrators as the redeemers of a backward and moribund land, lies the fact of their own canny improvement. Put another way, the transformation of Malcolm reveals behind the righteous rhetoric of what empire brings to India, the unacknowledged truth of what India gave those who began without property or prospects in England.

After annexation, Malcolm leaves Nadirabad for the remote town of Imli Khera. The decision to move is partly the result of Malcolm's difficulties with Evelyn who, though she loves him, will not marry because of her reluctance to leave her widowed father. When the troops at Imli Khera rebel in the summer of 1857, Malcolm escapes with the other British and Eurasians of the town, and, after a series of adventures, reaches the town of Laluckabad (that is, Allahabad), the 'foothold . . . in the arduous task of reconquest'.[51] Somewhat in the manner of Mowbray Thomson, Malcolm next joins a body of Volunteer Horse at the rear of an army of reconquest. On their way to rescue the besieged Nadirabad Residency where, among others, Evelyn and her father wait, Malcolm's gallantry during a skirmish with a body of rebel cavalry and his local knowledge come to the notice of the general commanding, who soon appoints him aide-de-camp. With this promotion Malcolm is, once again, restored to the centre of events as a privileged witness and contributor to counter-insurgency operations, as he was earlier to the annexation. At Imli Khera and in the countryside, Malcolm's experience is mainly of flight, but from Laluckabad on he turns proactive as the rescuer of Nadirabad and Evelyn. The combination of colonial and romantic-chivalric aims in the person of Malcolm is moreover suggested by a letter from the besieged Evelyn datelined '7 June 1857, Nadirabad'. Coming from what Cave-Brown enthusiastically describes as 'the very scenes of blood',[52] such letters are among the primary texts of the Mutiny archive; and, in this case, the letter repairs a temporary rift between the lovers, and has intelligence about the state of Nadirabad that Malcolm promptly communicates to the General.

With the arrival of the army at Nadirabad and the eventual rescue of the garrison, Malcolm and Evelyn are reunited, though their marriage remains uncertain with Home's reluctance to give his daughter away. After father and daughter leave for England, Malcolm serves in counter-insurgency operations, which meanwhile have spread into the country, before returning on home leave. In the last chapter, set in London, Malcolm, a decorated officer and a deputy commissioner in the now British Ghoristan, visits Evelyn and her father, and the novel ends with the acceptance of his marriage proposal, and a suggestion that Malcolm and Evelyn will return to India after their wedding. Malcolm's historical agency is not, however, over yet. As he informs Donald Home, Malcolm is instrumental in an amnesty offer to Usman Khan and the Queen Mother; and while the latter refuses to surrender, Usman has decided 'that the Government of India was the best government going for a Musalman to live under', and that he now 'meant to be a loyal subject of the Queen'.[53] The end could not have been more appropriate, for the amnesty offer to rebels and their leaders in Awadh and elsewhere is a reference to the Proclamation of 1 November 1858 that announced, if prematurely, the end of the rebellion, with Crown and Parliament seeking gradually to restore the confidence of an expropriated and alienated landed elite and their bondsmen.[54]

Between the intermediate zone of transit, as Malcolm and Evelyn sail to India in *c.* 1855 and the terminal moment in London, the novel weaves the warp of the Anglo-Indian plot through the weft of history. The coincident conclusion of the rebellion and courtship and the postbellum just dessert ends a process that begins in earnest when Malcolm re-enlists at Laluckabad. Seen from these entwined ends of the novel, the process harmonises the public and historical with the domestic, restores the colonial state and guarantees an Anglo-Indian future. In so doing, *With Sword and Pen* employs the sense of an ending characteristic of the histories by Ball or Martin, though the novel also explores, through the agency of its mobile hero, the idioms and the ambience of the Awadh elite. The exploration is not in as great detail as in *On the Face of the Waters*, which appeared the same year, and it employs the English hero (and Donald Home, when he goes to annex the kingdom the following day) to mediate the representation of a moment where an Indian state awaits the judgement of the alien overlord. In the manner of the topology of a historical painting like Thomas Daniell's *Sir Charles Warre Malet, Bt, the British Resident at the court of Poona in 1790, concluding a treaty in Durbar with Souae Madarow, the Peshwa or Prince of the Maratha Empire* (1805), the narrative of encounter endows the European figure with a salience and an agency unavailable to an otherwise splendid and martial court.[55] It is this 'flexible positional superiority' – to use Said's felicitous phrase – which allows Malcolm and Home, distinctly foreign to the dense interiority of the chamber, to enter it and judge the state of morals and progress. As Said explains, this superiority stems from the fact that by being in the Orient 'with very little resistance on the Orient's part', the European enters 'in a whole series of possible relationships with the Orient without ever losing . . . the upper hand'.[56]

Malcolm's journey into the world of native polity is complemented, though with other emphases, in the ambiguous location of Usman Khan. The friend of Malcolm and a Nadirabad courtier, Usman turns into a rebel follower of the Queen Mother following annexation, though, curiously, he sends intelligence about rebel movements to Home during the siege, and after pardon, retails 'the mutiny from the mutineer's point of view' to Malcolm, as earlier he had represented the cause of the people of Ghoristan.[57] Braided into these multiple, and even contradictory, roles is a little history of Indian Muslims of the landed elite and the ex-Mughal higher service class, in the decades between the rebellion and the novel. Usman's decision to be a 'loyal subject' of the British empire, and his new-found faith that the British government was 'the best government going' for Indian Muslims suggests the end of any compact that may have been forged between Hindus and Muslims during the rebellion, and the beginning of an identity politics that led eventually to Muslim separatism and the Partition. Irwin's representation of the reformed, 'loyalist' Muslim is not unlike Sir Syed's attempt to exonerate Muslims in the *Causes*, and to urge the community to integrate with the new dispensation; for, as he observed in the early 1880s: 'If the Muslims do not take to the system of education introduced by the British, they will not only remain a backward community, but will sink lower and lower until there will be no hope of recovery for them'.[58] This view was in part a response to William Hunter's polemical essay, *The Indian Mussalmans: Are They Bound in Conscience to Rebel Against the Queen?* (1871), a pamphlet which argued that Islam and the memory of their former power in India were fated to make Muslims forever rebellious, a charge answered by Sir Syed Ahmad Khan's rebuttal in his *Review* of 1872. An ethno-historian and statistician of 'lower Bengal', Hunter's distrust of Muslims should be read alongside that other body of opinion best represented by the philathletic, muscular Christian and anti-orientalist 'Punjab school', whose fondness for the 'masculine' Muslim (or the Sikh) of the plains or frontier hills was the obverse of a contemptuous dislike of the western-educated Hindu Bengali.[59] In terms of this debate over acculturation, ethnographies and, indeed, the practicalities of colonial government, Irwin's position was clearly on the side of the Punjab administrators. The bonding between Usman and Malcolm is similar to the bonding between

Jim Douglas, the hero of Irwin's earlier novel, *A Man of Honour*, and his Sikh and Pathan troops, but forms a notable counterpoint to the narrator and Malcolm's casual contempt for the altogether loyal, but timorous and 'baboo', English-speaking Bengali Residency clerk, Hari Mohan Chatterji.

Furthermore, Usman Khan's successive location as a Nadirabad courtier, a rebel and, finally, a 'loyal subject' is a metonymic compression of the historical sequence comprising the annexation, the rebellion and the return of British power. These mutations of identity and political location confirm the larger comic and restorative design informing the novel as a whole; for the evolution of the loyal subject of the Queen Mother of Ghoristan into a loyal subject of the British Queen obliquely transforms the rebellion into a cathartic interlude that promises a more comprehensive incorporation of the indigenous into British India. Not only does the political trajectory of Usman Khan commemorate the successful annexation of a Shiaite kingdom but it offers a benign hope that Indian Muslims will renounce their memories and ambitions to enter an empire of consent. In this, the evolution of Usman Khan resembles the reformation of such characters as Bapoo Brahmin and Ameer Ali. Like those men, Usman mediates a narrative journey into the world of the native, at the end of which waits the baptismal drama wherein the native disowns his patrimony and proceeds to transform and reconstitute himself into a willing colonial subject. And like Ameer Ali, the former *thag* turned police informer whose 'confessions' allow the frame-narrator/auditor a privileged access into the gothic interior of *thagi*, Usman, the native aristocrat and former rebel, now translates the 'mutineer's point of view' for his new master's pleasure and profit.

5

Counter-insurgency and heroism

[D]uring the Mutiny, it was not so much the force of numbers as the dreaded calm white face, with avenging sword in hand, that made its presence terrible whenever and wherever it appeared before the mutineers.

John Tulloch Nash, *Volunteering in India* (1893)

It is against this self-worship I would raise my voice, however feebly, against this shameless self-praise, this painting in every gaudy color of the imperial idol in which Englishmen, each day of the week, behold the image of their own imperial faces . . . devouring peoples more beautiful and better than ourselves.

Wilfrid Scrawen Blunt, *The Shame of the Nineteenth Century* (1900)

FIRST-PERSON ACCOUNTS AND THE MUTINY NOVEL

While Mutiny novels derive the broad contour of events from comprehensive histories, they rely on first-person accounts for local incident and detail. Among the first publications on the rebellion, many of these accounts belong generically to an already considerable body of British Indian travel writing.[1] For novelists as for historians, first-person accounts were usually a veridical record of events at particular sites, detailing events and recording expatriate experience of the rebellion. The relation between the letter, diary or memoir, where the narrative is circumscribed by the horizon and knowledge of an individual, and the isochronous narration of historiography ranging over the sum of particular events, is mutually supportive. Despite Kaye's caution that eyewitnesses are not inevitably reliable, the histories by Ball and Nolan often rest their case on the evidence of personal accounts when writing about events in particular regions, cities and towns.[2] On the other hand, memoirs written some time after the rebellion often expect corroboration or seek more information from historiography, as with Amelia Bennett who, writing in 1913 of her experience at Kanpur in May 1857, pauses to observe of the Nana Sahib: 'what a record of sensuality, ferocity, cunning, treachery, and inhumanity did his subsequent acts unfold, as handed down to us by history'.[3]

The several score first-person accounts can be classed in three broad groups. The first comprises accounts of flight, siege or captivity, where the narrator is the victim of the rebels. Amelia Bennett's memoir, Julia Haldane's *The Story of Our Escape from Delhi in 1857* or William Edwards's *Personal Adventures during the Indian Rebellion* are good examples of this type.[4] The second group consists of personal accounts of counter-insurgency, such as Vivian Majendie's *Up Among the Pandies*, or *An Unrecorded Chapter of the Indian Mutiny* by Reginald Wilberforce.[5] The last group straddles these two narrative locations, a combination most clearly evident in Thomson's *Story of Cawnpore*, and J. W. Sherer's *Daily Life during the Indian Mutiny*.[6] The distinction between situations from which the rebellion was written about shows forms of expatriate everydayness usually elided from historiography. First-person accounts provide a bank of topoi – of flight, siege and reconquest, or of travel, the picturesque and cultural encounter – that are selectively reinscribed into the texture of the novels. While 'The Prose of Counter-Insurgency' by Ranajit Guha is a rare and insightful reading of the modular form of personal accounts of the rebellion, these writings are informed by idioms of representation that do not quite fit the binary of order–disorder that Guha locates in British narratives on colonial resistance.[7] First-person accounts, as much as official despatches, represent indigenous resistance as disorder, anarchy, fanaticism and madness, but the former depend on supplementary manoeuvres to render the binary recognisable, meaningful and legitimate, manoeuvres that become clear once the location of the memoir and the diary is addressed.

The first section of Guha's essay is a reading of official despatches, letters and one Mutiny memoir, Mark Thornhill's *Personal Adventures and Experiences of a Magistrate*.[8] The choice of material, a structuralist scaffolding and the interest in the language used to represent Indian resistance in official documents and historiography make a provocative analysis of a now mostly forgotten archive. The district magistrate of Mathura at the time the rebellion breaks out, Thornhill tries at first to keep British authority afloat in town and country with the assistance of local bankers and merchants and a clutch of troops but later, as the rebellion spirals out of control, he escapes to the Agra fort where the local British garrison and the government of the North-Western Province has taken refuge. Through the first half of the account, the narrator sees his bungalow, office and the government treasury attacked and burned down by armed villagers and the mutineers, flees with the rebels on his heels, and, at one point, finds refuge in the fortified mansion of a local *seth*. In representing these experiences, the memoir of 1884 reflects the 'anxieties of the local custodian of law and order' expressed in the letters Thornhill wrote (*in situ* on 5 June and 10 August 1857), which to Guha are comparable with the 'secondary discourse' of the retrospective memoir.[9] The latter text no less than the former makes the rebellion out to be a law and order problem or, as Thornhill insistently describes it, a state of 'anarchy' threatening the putative order of the colonial administration. And by superimposing 'a temporality of his own on that of his theme', Thornhill 'destroy[s] the entrophy' of his own original 'raw material', the letters of June and August 1857.[10]

But there are other aspects of first-person accounts that represent victimhood, such as the *Personal Adventures and Experiences of a Magistrate*, which demand attention. In the memoirs or diaries written by administrators such as Thornhill and William Edwards, the official voice is often muffled by a turn of events depriving the narrator of his official position, and making him (and sometimes the family) a fugitive at the mercy of a hitherto subject people. No less interesting is the fact that in these two instances, the personal account is prefaced by and appended with criticism of policies that the narrators claim to have opposed in their capacity as district administrators.[11] There is not the space here to explore in detail the mechanism and the import of such inflections in first-person accounts, or the disputes over policy so frequent in the official prose, but it must be stressed that the binary of order and anarchy that structures these narratives does not work very well with the erasure of official authority, and with threats to person and property.[12] Two examples from the *Personal Adventures* will demonstrate what lay beyond the official monotone on which turns the opposition of order and anarchy. During his flight to Agra with an armed escort, Thornhill notes how he: 'began to find something rather exhilarating in our position. It was such a pleasant change from our usual confinement indoors to be in the open air, and riding over the country at the head of a body of men seemed like acting in a part in a fairy tale. All possible adventures might be before us.'[13] Later, during the ride to safety in Agra on the night the rebel militia attacks the town, the magistrate observes from hiding a body of escaped convicts from the district jail march away in the light of the burning civil station:

The scene was that which painters and poets depict for the infernal regions. There was black gloom, the lurid glare, the phantoms, the clanking chains; and over us some of the awe of the shadow of death, for our prospect of reaching Agra appeared now but faint . . . As I half dozed the impression came upon me that we had really entered a place of punishment, that the figures passing beside me were condemned souls.[14]

These passages suggest a supplement that attends but slips past the official binary. The literary and painterly evocations, the chiaroscuro of the 'scene', the anticipation of 'adventures' and the exhilaration of travel may well be functions of the eighteen years that stretch between the event and its narrative recall. Yet, such garnishing of the official gaze constitutes a poetics of counter-insurgency supplementing the official prose, rewriting the rebellion in terms other than those of order and anarchy and recovering a heroic agency that, despite the 'shadow of death', stands 'at the head of a body of men'. What Guha calls the 'secondary discourse' of the memoir implies a 'secondary revision', to borrow the phrase Freud used in his dream-analysis to describe the texture of the dream's manifest content, which places the first-person account under the heteronomy of an official prosaics and a poetic supplementary, the mimetic and the diegetic modes, and that invests insurgency as much as counter-insurgency with textual traces derived from contiguous practices of colonial knowledge and representation, including travel writing. There is significant ambiguity in such revisions and transformations, for, more than the convicts of the British-administered judiciary, now freed by the rebellion, it is their weary and hunted observer hidden behind the wayside shrubbery who is 'condemned' at that point of time, as is the state he serves.

The surplus this poetics introduces into the memoir fleshes out the bare skeletal structure of 'rising-information-decision-order' that Guha reconstructs from the language of officialdom.[15] Seen from the perspective of the novels, the double logic shaping the prose of counter-insurgency in the personal account has two related effects. First-person accounts, histories and novels form successive moments of secondary revision, for these iterations across genres are already braided with acts of interpretation, condensation and displacement similar to Thornhill's ambiguous figure of 'condemned souls'. Moreover, the secondary revision gives flexibility to the novels with heroes sometimes occupying multiple points on the map of the rebellion; a ruse that novels often use to draw on the resources of historiography and first-person accounts to embellish the broad outlines of the rebellion with local incident and detail. While first-person accounts cannot usually go beyond the experience and location of the author without betraying the genre, the majority of the novels, like *The Story of Cawnpore* by Mowbray Thomson, choose to straddle across insurgency and counter-insurgency.

Following the uprising at Imli Khera, Malcolm, the hero of *With Sword and Pen*, along with the other local Britons and Eurasians, flees from the town to take refuge in the mud-fort of the *zamindar*, Raja Laik Singh. When the rebel militia threatens to attack the Raja for helping the enemy, he smuggles them away to a remote village of shepherds in the country-side. After a few weeks in hiding, the party makes its way to Laluckabad, and, on the final stage of their journey, sails down the Ganges on 13 June 1857 disguised as a group of high-caste Hindu women on a pilgrimage, and accompanied by the retainers of the Raja. After minor skirmishes with suspicious villagers on the riverside, the party reaches Laluckabad, where Malcolm enlists for counter-insurgency operations. The boat ride to safety has two sources: Mowbray Thomson's far more riveting escape down the Ganges, and the Fatehgarh fugitives who sailed to Kanpur believing that it was still under British control, only to be captured and put to death by the rebels. Additionally, the adventures at the Raja's fort and the uneasy loyalty of Laik Singh resemble Thomson's halt at the village of his somewhat reluc-tant host, 'Raja Dirigbijah Singh, of Moorah Mhow'. Again, the time the group of Britons spend at the village appears to rely on William Edwards's *Personal Adventures during the Indian Rebellion*. In that diary/memoir, the former magistrate of Budaon flees the district headquarters with his com-panions to seek refuge with the Awadh *zamindar*, Hardeo Baksh, who, when threatened by the rebels, sends his suppliants to Ranjpurah, a remote hamlet of shepherds. Edwards and his fellow fugitives spend nearly two months in hiding, and finally return by boat to Kanpur at the end of August, by that time under British occupation.

Edwards's account of his days at Ranjpurah is among the more abject passages of Mutiny literature. Living in a filthy cowshed on survival rations, unwashed and ill and faced with daily danger of betrayal, the British fugi-tives are at the furthest remove from their former status as members not only of the ruling race but of the higher echelons of the civil service. How-ever, in Irwin's reworking of these events, matters are more pleasant, and their exile has the ambience of a picnic. During the their time at the Raja's fort, Warburton, one of the officials at Imli Khera, writes an account of daily events in his pocket diary, and, in the manner of Anglo-Indian women travel writers such as Emily Eden or Fanny Parkes, the ladies of the party call on the Raja's *zenana*.[16] While Edwards and his friends march on foot to the village of Ranjpoorah, in *With Sword and Pen* the British party ride elephants on a picturesque moonlit night to reach their hideout. The suggestion of a hunting party or leisurely travel continues at the village. Unlike the hardship that Edwards and his companions suffer, the Raja has provided Malcolm's party with two servants and a handyman, besides such conveniences as soaps, towels and breakfasts announced by a *khidmatgar*.[17] Again, while Edwards and his companions have nowhere to go but where their often inscrutable hosts lead them, and are prepared to believe that all was over with the British in India, Malcolm assures his friends that once they reach a town under British control they might 'join one of the relieving columns that are sure to be sent up country before long'; a certainty which derives from a knowledge of history that Edwards certainly does not possess.[18] And while the former magistrate of Budaon can only wait and fear the worst, Malcolm and his friends decide that 'any risks whatever would be preferable to a continuance of this sort of thing'.[19] Finally, the boat ride down the Ganges: in first-person accounts the journey, when not fatal as in the case of the fugitives from Fatehgarh, is one of exposure and fear, or of pursuit, death, capture and serious injury. But in Irwin's novel the same event is endowed with a 'strange, unreal charm', the skirmishes with villagers on the riverside are carried out with panache and wit, and it all ends with a safe landing at Laluckabad, exactly as Malcolm has predicted.[20]

In representing the effect of the rebellion on the British, this section of *With Sword and Pen* follows closely a first-person account like Edwards's, yet cleanses those traces of 'national humiliation' or helplessness so prominent in the original. Malcolm's march from Laluckabad to Nadirabad is, however, modelled on another set of narratives. The skirmishes with roving bands of rebels and the pitched battles, the routines of march and camp, the agonies of cholera, sunstroke and battle wounds, the military tactics of the British general and the passionate desire of the hero and the troops to avenge British honour and to rescue the besieged are closely affiliated to first-person accounts of the reconquest of Kanpur and Lucknow. Not only do these events and experiences resemble the accounts by Majendie and Wilberforce, but Malcolm's appointment as aide-de camp to the General suggests proximity to the *Journal of an English Officer in India* by Havelock's aide-de-camp, a Major North.[21] The *Journal* covers nearly the same territory as Malcolm does, though with one difference. While Havelock's column marched from Allahabad to Kanpur, and then to Lucknow, *With Sword and Pen* condenses the archive to proceed directly to Nadirabad, perhaps because of a parallel commitment to the relationship between Malcolm and Evelyn. Despite the altered route, the rhetoric of reconquest is complementary. In the novel the officers and men entering Nadirabad 'had looked on sights that murdered pity, and fought with a strength . . . there was no withstanding';[22] while in the *Journal*: 'nothing could resist the impetuosity of our troops, or damp the ardour of their leaders' and 'acknowledging no obstacle, and overleaping every barrier, their impetuosity was irresistible'.[23]

The Disputed VC is more ambitious. After the rebellion begins at Aurungpore, the action bifurcates and exploits two other elements supplied by first-person accounts and the local histories. The British officers and civilians (with their wives, children and some loyal Rajput *sipahis*) take refuge in the Commissioner's house, where the rebel troops and the townsfolk promptly besiege them. Meanwhile, the hero, Ted Russell, an ensign with the 193rd Native Infantry, is sent to guard the regimental arsenal with another ensign and a few soldiers. Once the building is under attack and seems likely to fall, Ted decides to lay a mine to blow it up rather than surrender the weaponry and the ammunition. So he does and by a miracle escapes alive; and soon the town is 'saved', the siege lifted and the rebels scattered with the arrival of a company of Guides, commanded by Ted's brother Jim. The brief siege of the Aurungpore British, who bear their suffering 'without flinching or showing the least sign of weakness before the eyes of their gallant and devoted Rajputs' is, of course, a cameo performance that condenses and displaces the many siege-like situations of 1857.[24] Representing the siege from the perspective of the besieged, the novel compresses into a brief episode salient aspects from personal accounts of Lucknow such as Julia Selina Inglis's *The Siege of Lucknow*, and *An Account of the Mutinies in Oudh and the Siege of the Lucknow Residency* by Martin Gubbins.[25] At Aurungpore, senior officers debate gravely on policy, tactics and the safety of the women and children, the junior officers and the other ranks gallantly defend the building and 'great-hearted Englishwomen' nurse the sick and the wounded.[26] While the narrative of events in the Commissioner's mansion relies on a common knowledge of similar sieges elsewhere, Ted Russell's blowing up of the arsenal is clearly inspired by the destruction of the Delhi Magazine on 11 May 1857 by a Lieutenant George Willoughby and his men; and Gibbon acknowledges the debt his hero owes the original when he observes in an aside: 'The idea of blowing up the magazine had come upon him suddenly as he [Ted] remembered the news that had arrived yesterday from Delhi, – how Lieutenant Willoughby and his nine heroes had blown up the immense arsenal there and destroyed hundreds of rebels.'[27]

Like the siege or the boat ride, Willoughby's defence of the Delhi Magazine is an iconic moment common to histories, first-person accounts and novels. But unlike the two former icons, the explosion in the arsenal exemplifies proactive heroism combining personal daring and military sense with anticipatory vengeance. As Henty prefaces his description of the event in his adventure novel *In Times of Peril*: 'the sufferers of Delhi did not die wholly unavenged', and 'it was calculated that from one thousand five hundred to two thousand of the mutineers and the rabble of the town were killed' in the explosion.[28] The transformation of an event that actually preceded Willoughby's full knowledge of British casualties in Delhi (since he spent most of the day confined in the arsenal) into an act of revenge indicates the ease with which *post hoc* mythography confounds cause and consequence, though there is a notable disproportion at work here. The victorious confrontation of the 'nine heroes' against the 'hundreds' (of rebels, though it is more likely that the casualties would have included local residents, for the Magazine was in the city) is an implicit demonstration of racial superiority. However, unacknowledged by Gibbon and Henty is the fact that the retributive killing of the two thousand Indians – Henty's 'voice of the hooligan' here yielding a higher body count than Gibbon – avenges the death of some two score British killed by the rebels earlier that day.[29]

Ted next goes to Delhi with the Guides for a campaign lasting nearly three months, where he meets John Nicholson, Hodson, Baird-Smith and the other stalwarts of the Delhi Ridge. After the capture of the Mughal capital, Ted leaves for Lucknow and soon attaches himself to the army under the commander-in-chief, Colin Campbell. Later, following the 'relief' of Lucknow, Ted meets and speaks with Campbell, the *Times* correspondent William Russell and the Nepalese king Jung Bahadur, who is a British ally, and participates in an improbable chase of the Nana Sahib, who fires his pistol at Ted before disappearing for ever.[30] There are several sets of interpolated elements in the post-Aurungpore adventures of the novel. Ted's march to Delhi with the Guides – those 'fierce borderers' and the Gurkhas, 'the Irishmen of Asia' – recalls Cave-Brown's *Punjab and Delhi in 1857*, a popular account of how officers of the 'Punjab school' not only 'saved' the Punjab from the rebellion but helped in the capture of Delhi.[31] Similarly, Ted's part in the assault on Delhi has shades of Henry Harris Greathed's *Letters Written during the Siege of Delhi* and the *Chaplain's Narrative of the Siege of Delhi* by the Reverend J. E. W. Rotton.[32] Finally, Ted's post-Lucknow adventures, as he rides about the Awadh countryside and into the Terai on the trail of the Nana Sahib, resemble Russell's diary and John Nash's account of his experiences during mop-up operations in *Volunteering in India*.[33]

The point of these examples is to suggest how the articulation of the historical with the fictional plot yields a series of redactions of the former. Drawing on but also condensing and displacing narrative segments from the first-person accounts, the novels by Irwin, Reid, Gibbon and others retain such salient topoi as siege, flight, boat ride and counter-insurgency

campaigns, even as they modify or elide their original context. The specificity of the Mutiny novels as historical novels is in the differential between
fidelity to the archive and the redactions. As the example of *With Sword
and Pen* shows, Malcolm not only sees the rebellion with the eyes of a
victim such as Edwards but also as a heroic agent of the colonial state, such
as Major North, Majendie and Wilberforce, who only participate in the
counter-insurgency operations. The expansion of the novel into these two
directions overcomes the fixity of first-person accounts tied by the location and experience of the narrators, allowing the novel to approximate
the totalisation of historiography. The scope of this expansion becomes
clearer on comparing an early novel like *The Wife and the Ward* by Edward
Money with *Masque*. In the latter, Maud Westerne along with her husband,
her lover and their Indian guide, Kunaji Lal, sail past Kanpur unmolested
while the rebels capture the next boat and murder its occupants. *Masque* is
made witness to the events at the Satichaura Ghat, even as it spares itself
the massacre that terminates *The Wife and the Ward*. While that conclusion prevents Money's novel from demonstrating the revival of the Indian
empire, in *Masque* Maud and Rupert survive Kanpur to reach Lucknow,
take part in its 'defence', return to England and after their marriage read
together Tennyson's memorial homage, 'The Defence of Lucknow'.[34]

But there is one more area of expansion. The *Disputed VC*, a boy's
adventure novel with traces of the picaresque, exploits almost all the iconic
moments of the rebellion. Descending from Aurungpore to, first, Delhi
and then Lucknow to, finally, the Awadh countryside, the novel and its
hero tour the principal sites on the map of the rebellion, while ranging
in time from the first signs of 'disaffection', when Ted is attacked by a
mullah in the Aurungpur bazaar, to the manhunt for the Nana Sahib on the
Nepal border two years on. These redactions work in tandem with another
strategy. As Malcolm's time as a fugitive shows, *With Sword and Pen* relies
on and closely follows Edwards's *Personal Adventures*. But the experience of
flight, fear and humiliation undergoes a secondary revision so that the novel
retains the topoi while draining their distinctive experiential character. If
the forms of revision suggested here yield a quantitative expansion that
allows a novel like the *Disputed VC* to map the Mutiny in the manner
of totalised historiography, the transformation of William Edwards into
Malcolm Mainwaring is qualitative in that the fictional revision endows
the latter with far greater agency than the former ever possessed.

These redactions and revisions are the means by which the matter of
history inserts itself into an expressly fictional plot. Faithful to, yet tran-
scending the historical archive, such processes enable the novels to articulate

the plot of the rebellion with the plot of Anglo-Indian love, marriage and domesticity, thus ensuring that unlike the *Wife and the Ward*, the latter always contains and survives the former. The official or judicial binary of order–disorder that Guha detects in the prose of counter-insurgency is inflected and overdetermined by a supplementary poetics that draws on ideologies and idioms of colonial politics, on generic practices specific to Anglo-India and on the regimes of colonial knowledge that already consti-tute the binary. The following section explores the poetics of heroism, to show how the analysis of the order–disorder nexus that structures the prose of counter-insurgency is, in fact, incomplete without an enquiry into that conjunction of discourses of which this binary is only one facet.

THE COLONIAL SMALL WAR, HEROISM AND PROPAGANDA

The subject of heroism figured at the beginning of the last chapter, where it was suggested that the discursive production of imperialism turns on themes of expansion, conquest and transformation that appear equally in historical and literary writing. The imperial imaginary at once generates and thrives on generic mixing such that the historiography of empire construes its subject as romance, and literary writings find their topics in the archive of history. The enabling dynamic of the colonial adventure novel as it develops through the nineteenth century, this generic contiguity and affiliation, is equally evident in the applications to which historiography and the first-person accounts are put in Mutiny novels.

The articulated structure of these novels braids the plot of the rebellion with that of Anglo-Indian love, marriage and domesticity, thus easing the numerous divertissements on history, politics and ethnography. This gives the Mutiny novel a double valency: representing a particular moment in the history of the Indian empire, but also part of a larger epic of national expansion where the rebellion is only one, though privileged site. From roughly 1890 to 1910 – the years in which the majority of the Mutiny novels appeared – metropolitan politics and cultures of feeling inflect the con-struction of an imperial self-image in these novels, a self-image derived not wholly from the Indian empire, with counter-insurgency serving sometimes as the occasion for representing the politics of class, gender and ethnicity in a purely metropolitan context.

If this is a reminder that British writing on India, like the Anglo-India community, forms a diptych, the representation of heroism in the novels too stands on an interstitial ground. Mobilised against Indian resistance, and drawing on a tradition of heroic British/English masculinity in India prefigured by Macaulay's 'Lord Clive', heroism forms the staple of an increasingly strident metropolitan popular culture and national self-image from the late nineteenth century; a development that owes much to the European 'scramble for Africa' which tied intra-European conflict and competition with colonial expansion. The double orientation has implications for the methodology of colonial discourse studies. The recent readings of late Victorian and Edwardian imperial culture by, for instance, John Mackenzie or Robert MacDonald are from a European vantage, for they examine the transformation of metropolitan popular culture by empire, a culture informed by *matériel* from Africa, India, China and, indeed, from all those parts of the world where the British engaged with either indigenous peoples or with European competitors.[35] While these studies are immensely useful, the theme of heroic adventure, itself one of the favourite popular vehicles for circulating the idea of empire, and arguably driving recruitment in the navy and in the Indian services, has a local context in the Mutiny novels.

In transforming a collection of first-person accounts into the adventures of Malcolm or Ted Russell, the novels till a textual space located between such accounts and historiography. A consequence of this intermediate location is that these heroes are set free to range over a large number of places and events, unlike the immobility of Major Edgington in *The Wife and the Ward* or the narrators of most of the diaries and memoirs. This freedom makes the heroes embody an impulse most clearly present in the complete histories, as agents of the colonial state in the military, administrative and narrative closure that they help to achieve. As suggested in the last section, this closure is driven by a heroic mobility and confidence that acquires spectacular proportions in the novels written between the 1890s and the First World War, and which otherwise contributes an additional gloss to the binary of order–disorder or civilisation–savagery that colonial adventures usually foreground.

In Hume Nisbet's *Queen's Desire*, Sammy Tompkins, a picaresque rogue who anticipates Kipling's boy-hero Kimball O'Hara in *Kim*, is the twelve-year-old country-born son of Sergeant Tompkins, who runs away to Meerut with his dog two days before the uprising in that town. Attacked by four *thag*s on the way, Sammy takes on the men, 'satisfied in his own mind that if a white man is the match of ten darkies, a white boy and a bloodhound might surely manage four'.[36] At Meerut, young Sammy senses the impending revolt – 'having been brought up with the natives, [he] knew their natures a great deal better than most men'[37] – and spends the morning of 10 May disguised as a native spying on the barracks where the would-be rebels meet to discuss their plans. Discovered by the soldiers and taken prisoner, Sammy manages to escape and promptly calls on General Hewitt, the commanding officer of the Meerut garrison who is, however, altogether sceptical about Sammy's report on the planned outbreak. When the rebel soldiers attack the British lines later that day, Sammy, though he 'could do little or nothing for those who were being hunted down', kills several 'ruthless scoundrels . . . as callously as if he had been a professional murderer'.[38] If this were not enough, Sammy disguises himself once again and rides with the rebel 3rd Light Cavalry through the night of 10–11 May to Delhi. As the body of men nears the city walls in the morning, the boy-hero makes a dash for the gates 'yelling himself hoarse without avail' to warn the Commissioner Fraser of Delhi of the approaching rebel cavalry.[39]

While Nisbet was a prolific boy's novelist who had by 1900 written nearly forty adventure novels, including several set in the Australian bush, masculine heroism in the service of empire figures with quite as much enthusiasm in the work of Flora Annie Steel.[40] The wife of Henry Steel of the civil service, Steel spent a number of years in the Punjab, wrote several Indian novels and later supported the Suffragette movement and engaged in public debate with Mrs Humphrey Ward.[41] Her Mutiny novel, *On the Face of the Waters*, weaves the plot of Anglo-Indian love, marriage and domesticity with the rebellion, though her interest in metropolitan gender politics led a reviewer in *Blackwood's* to complain that 'it is the obtrusion of the sex-problem, and not the mingling of history and fiction . . . that spoils her book'.[42] The déclassé Anglo-Indian hero of the novel, Jim Douglas, is a former horse-trainer with the Nawab of Awadh. Out of work following the annexation of the kingdom and deposition of the Nawab, Douglas is recruited by the political department of the government as a spy shortly before the outbreak. He rides into Delhi from Meerut with the rebel cavalry on 11 May, '[t]oo late to be the first in Delhi' and warn the British garrison, though hoping 'to help in the struggle' of survival and reconquest.[43] Combining a moody misanthropic Byronism with the 'berserker spirit' of the 'muscular' heroes of Henty, Charles Kingsley and G. P. R. James, Douglas, who also goes under the name James Greyman, rides through the city on the morning of 11 May disguised as a rebel *sawar*. Not only does the disguise allow him to escape capture and death, he also saves his future wife Mrs Erlton from the soldiers when he carries her off as his personal booty. Leaving her in a hideout by the city gate, Douglas returns quite incredibly to the lion's den. As he nonchalantly explains to Kate Erlton before turning his horse back: 'I am off to the palace to see what has really happened; information's everything.'[44]

The significance of the information that Douglas and other Mutiny heroes variously seek, and that forms a consistent core of historical interest in the Mutiny novels, will be examined in the following chapter. However, Douglas's return allows the novel to imagine the state of the city and the palace on a day and at a time of which no British eyewitness accounts are available, and to write the history of a moment when the British in Delhi were either dead or captives in the palace, or fleeing in confusion and fright into the countryside. Not only does he return to the city, but 'he had . . . several places of concealment ready to his hand without the necessity for taking anyone into his confidence';[45] a resource that comes in handy when, by another imaginative and equally implausible move, Steel has Kate Erlton, her young son and Douglas spend two months hiding in rebel Delhi.

While their co-habitation – they set up home disguised as a Muslim family – is the occasion for the unhappily married Kate Erlton to reject her insensitive and unfaithful husband and fall in love with her saviour, the ruse not only enables the novel to explore marriage, extramarital attachment and Kate Erlton's sexuality through the displacement of a mock-Muslim domesticity, but inserts Douglas as witness into the rebel world. Assuming the persona of an Afghan horse-dealer, Kate's 'husband' makes daily forays into the streets and bazaars where, observing 'the tide of life returning to the streets, his mad desire to strike a blow and smash the sham was tempered by an almost unbearable curiosity as to what really happened'.[46] Complementing Kate's curiosity about indigenous femininity and domesticity, a form of life she mimics in rebel Delhi, and which brings her to a new reckoning with her marriage to Major Erlton and her desire for Douglas, the hero's curiosity about the affairs of the enemy, and his ability to satisfy that curiosity outdoors inserts a fantasy of surveillance into the Mughal capital between 11 May and 17 September 1857.

A similar fantasy appears in A. F. P. Harcourt's first Mutiny novel, *Jenetha's Venture*.[47] The hero of the novel and a subaltern in a Sikh regiment, Roland Ashby is deputed to the Punjab administration by the order of John Lawrence, the commissioner of the province between 1853 and 1857. In the course of the first few chapters, Ashby meets Robert Montgomery, the judicial commissioner of the province and one of the 'Punjab school' administrators, and acquires a faithful Man Friday in Juggut Singh the Sikh. When the news of the Meerut outbreak reaches Lahore by telegram on 11 May, Montgomery despatches Ashby southwards to Agra with that information, for he assumes the telegraph lines will be cut down by the rebels. Ashby agrees immediately to a three-hundred mile ride through potentially hostile territory with his faithful Sikh retainer. As the narrator explains, Ashby 'was a perfect linguist and could easily pass as a native of the country'.[48] Disguised as a Sikh, the hero begins a *Kim*-like journey with Juggut Singh through towns, villages and highways, in the course of which he saves the daughter of the Hindu trader Tagu from drowning. Though the Hindu sees through Ashby's disguise, he is also grateful, and Ashby will cash in on his gratitude later in the novel. Finally the duo reaches Agra on 31 May and reports to the Lieutenant-Governor of the North-western Provinces, John Colvin. Ashby volunteers help when Colvin informs him that the government has no intelligence on the state of the kingdoms of Rajputana, especially the (fictional) kingdom of Aurungpur where lives one Alaoodin, a leader of the rebellion and an agent of the Mughal court at Delhi. After Colvin attaches Ashby and Juggut Singh to the intelligence department of the North-Western Province, the two men disguise them-selves as Muslims, and preparatory to the espionage mission Ashby forges a Persian letter from the Mughal emperor to Alaoodin in order to con-fuse the rebel movement. Of the forgery the narrator exclaims: 'so perfect [was] the calligraphy that the most experienced Orientalist might have been deceived'.[49]

Disguised as a venerable messenger from Delhi, Ashby meets Alaoodin at Aurungpur, only to find the latter a 'fair sample of the low-class Mahommedan who was brought to the surface in the days of the Mutiny'. Ashby also meets Jenetha Wentworth, the young English governess of the children of the king of Aurungpur, a meeting that opens the possibility of romance, chivalry and Anglo-Indian domesticity. While forgery and disguise satisfy a shrewd rebel leader like Alaoodin, Ashby's Englishness reappears in the presence of Jenetha. A 'good girl' but often 'troublesome as a young panther' and 'possessed of an insatiable desire to see the world', Jenetha takes a liking to Ashby and decides to accompany him on his travels.[50] Thus, a journey of reconnaissance that began at Lahore, and that advances to Aurungpur via Agra, now turns towards Delhi with an emerg-ing romantic interest. On the way, more adventure and mischance ensue and Jenetha, realising her 'foolishness' in forcing her way into the masculine business of counter-insurgency – so she claims in her parting note to Ashby – leaves camp one night with her two retainers. Her plans are, however, more audacious. Jenetha decides to enter Delhi in disguise and to gather intelli-gence about rebel activity in the city; a proactive decision that takes her to the centre of the rebellion.

Jenetha enters Delhi disguised as an old Indian woman and rooms with a washerwoman in a house beneath the city wall, while Ashby is waylaid by villagers who release him later on the fortuitous intervention of the Hindu trader Tagu. As a merchant, Tagu is politically neutral, doing business with the Mughal court and with the British army camped on the Ridge beyond the city. Escorted by Tagu, Ashby reaches the Delhi Ridge, and there meets the historical William Hodson of Hodson's Horse, the '*beau ideal* of the irregular cavalry soldier', who immediately attaches Ashby to his own intelligence corps.[51] Urged by 'an indefinable longing to meet' Jenetha again, to rescue her from Delhi, and to gather intelligence about the state of rebel forces inside the city, Ashby combines romantic-chivalric motives with the demands of counter-insurgency. Disguised as the Hindu servant of Tagu, Ashby enters the city and follows his master through the city streets, relishing an 'atmosphere . . . impregnated with those wonderful bazaar odours', yet railing at 'a whole city given up . . . to lust and bestiality'.[52] At this point Ashby, like Jim Douglas in *On the Face of the Waters*, is an instrument of the colonial state inserted into a world from which the state was historically absent; a reconstruction similar to but more ambitious than the forensic and political investigations which inform historical narratives. More interesting, however, is the new role of Jenetha in Delhi, which modifies the trope of captivity where the colonial adventure hero typically rescues the white woman from savage natives.

Jenetha is an unusually empowered Anglo-Indian woman who is, paradoxically, more than usually lusted after by a series of rebel 'villains', including Alaoodin. This ambivalence is evident in her initial desire to escape from Aurungpur. Her desire to see the world is, she admits to Ashby, unfeminine, and makes her willing to suffer the hardships of the road without concessions to her femininity; and indeed, Jenetha demonstrates a perfect knowledge of the route out of Aurungpur, carries a pistol on her person and is attended by two faithful native men-servants. But if Jenetha overcomes the limits of an Anglo-Indian feminine identity, travelling unchaperoned with a band of men as an independent witness/participant in the male pursuits of empire, martial adventure and travel, and not as mother or daughter or wife or fiancée, her apparent freedom masks a familiar undertow. Beyond a desire to see the world, Jenetha wishes to leave Aurungpur to escape the attentions of Alaoodin who, had the rebellion been successful, would have 'taken' her; an eventuality for which Jenetha has already prepared in a manner that echoes the apocryphal story of Ulrica Wheeler as well as Marion Paris's final plea to Major Edgington in *The Wife and the Ward*. As Jenetha tells Ashby, if kidnapped by the rebel leader: 'I would have pretended to accept the inevitable, and on the first opportunity I would have killed him, and taken the consequences.'[53]

This ambivalence reappears during her time at Delhi. Living by the city wall facing the British-occupied Ridge, Jenetha steals up the ramparts each night the rebel army prepares to attack British positions to the north of the city, and lights three lamps in the hope that Ashby – to whom she had earlier confided her wish to do something of the sort – will read the sign and prepare the British forces for a counter-attack. As it turns out, Ashby does notice the signal and reads its intended meaning, with the result that British troops are forewarned of rebel sorties, and Jenetha soon acquires a legendary reputation as 'our Woman in Lal Quila'.[54] Though Jenetha transforms captivity into proactive heroism, and embodies the fantasy of surveillance like Jim Douglas in *On the Face of the Waters* or Ashby later in the novel, there are signs of recurrent lapses into an altogether feminine infirmity that support the chivalric function of Ashby.

After his arrival in the city with Tagu, she is made to move to the latter's house and is immobilised by Ashby's concern for her safety. Jenetha now spends her time indoors reading the Bible and wondering: 'What had all her cleverness and quickness of intellect brought her to?'[55] The readjustment of Jenetha within a chivalric code following Ashby's arrival is reinforced when Alaoodin reaches Delhi; for the latter now wants her as a gift to the Mughal prince, Mirza Mughal. Caught between competing male desires that are inflected by a sexually potent insurrection, an unusually passive Jenetha is twice captured by the rebels and twice 'recaptured' by Ashby, who marries her in Delhi after the rebellion and returns with her to England. Jenetha is an example of the sexual prize that chivalric conduct usually acquires at the end of the Mutiny novels, a resolution that ensures the survival of Anglo-Indian domesticity, besides restoring those gendered identities that, as 'Jenetha's venture' in Delhi shows, may have been disturbed by the ambient licence of the rebellion.

Ashby's arrival in Delhi cuts short Jenetha's newfound career as the proactive heroine of colonial adventure, and makes her a passive emblem of national-racial honour. Nonetheless, *Jenetha's Venture* is the rare Mutiny novel to introduce the Anglo-Indian woman into the male activities of empire building and the colonial small war, which take Jenetha beyond the confines of expatriate domesticity. But it is Ashby who, though otherwise stereotyped and wooden as a character, remains the true hero in the tradition of the colonial adventure novel, an authenticity reinforced by his many gifts and his near-magical invincibility, and by his simultaneous curtailment of the energies of Jenetha and rebel India. As in other novels such as *The Keepers of the Gate* (1911) by S. C. Grier or *Rung-Ho* (1914) by Talbott Mundy (Sylvia Anne Matheson), where the prospective wife resists the hero's will-to-power, or endangers herself and the project of counter-insurgency with her thoughtless insubordination, heroic counter-insurgency and its chivalric underpinnings are in Harcourt's novel structured around and directed at two distinct but complexly imbricated areas of vulnerability and insurgency.

A sense of this duality emerges when Colonel Woodburn, the commanding officer of the Aurungpore garrison in *The Disputed VC*, instructs his officers that they 'must avoid alarming the ladies or the sepoys' with the news of the Meerut outbreak.[56] Invested with a chivalric charge and a domestic function in the Anglo-Indian garrison society, and configured as an exposed and vulnerable body in the wilderness outside the garrison, the Anglo-Indian woman bears a curious resemblance to the figure of the native who ensures the safety of the garrison as a 'sepoy' loyal to the Company, but who turns lustfully upon the feminine heart of the garrison as a 'mutineer'. Besides the comparable fluidity of the *sipahi* and the *memsahib*, 'alarm' too enunciates a simultaneous duality of reception: as terror and as a signal, as threat and as a mobilisation, bearing the pandemic weight of a 'contagion' that spreads among the *sipahi*s and the people and is transmitted uncannily across north India. And poised between these overlapping areas of alarm and instability, violence and vulnerability, obedience and infraction, is the figure of the white, middle-class, male hero who as civil or military official straddles and contains the homologous unreason of the white female and the brown insurgent. Recent studies of Mutiny narratives by Jenny Sharpe, Nancy Paxton and Indira Ghosh have attended to the idiom of chivalry, which constructs British women as signifiers of national and imperial honour deployed at moments of national and imperial crisis. But these studies have not quite addressed the subtle but persistent homology between the white female who resists an obedient incorporation into the romantic-domestic repertory of roles, and the brown indigene who resists incorporation into the imperial formation, its hierarchies, expropriations and its 'language of command'. To these areas of mastered resistance one might even add other contiguous acts of colonial mastery: horse riding and the hunting party, where the male hero breaking the wilful horse or tracking or shooting or sticking the quarry enacts a poetics of puissance, usually before the eyes of the primary quarries, women and natives.

There are several aspects to the mobility and suppleness that the transformation of the first-person account grants to novels written at the turn of the century. There is, first, an endless facility with disguise, language and behind-the-lines operations that anticipates Robert Baden-Powell's *Scouting For Boys* (1908), where the trained boy scout confounds with equal ease the

Zulu, the Boer, the Sioux and the tribes of the Indian frontier. As the adventures of Ashby, Jim Douglas and young Sammy show, penetrating rebel conclaves or traversing a rebellious landscape are easy tasks for the colonial hero. The knowledge and abilities of these heroes suggest forms of culture contact from an earlier period in the social history of Anglo-India, and that continued among the British-Indian *mestizo*, the so-called Eurasians. Thus, Douglas spends two and a half months in Delhi disguised as an Afghan, miraculously eluding discovery, Ashby's Persian calligraphy can deceive a 'learned Orientalist' and he can at will disguise himself into a Muslim, a Sikh and a Hindu, while the twelve-year old Sammy Tompkins rides to Delhi with the rebel cavalry. The knowledge of languages, manners, forms of life and urban and rural topographies that these disguises, roles and actions presuppose revises the sometimes terror-ridden first-person accounts, where frightened, fumbling attempts at 'going native' are the means to escape capture and death.

Unlike the accounts by Edwards, Thornhill, Fanny Peile or *A Personal Narrative* by W. J. Shepherd, survival is a minor secondary reason for going native in the heroic Mutiny novel.[57] Guaranteed invincibility from discovery, death or serious creolisation by racial supremacy and an insuperable cultural difference, the flexible Mutiny hero of the 1890s and after is buoyed by a national confidence derived from the global extension of British arms and interest. It is a confidence that inspired Richard Burton's journey to the *kaaba* at Mecca in 1843, and the 'Hero of Mafeking' Robert Baden-Powell's *My Adventures as a Spy* (1915), apotheosised in the theatrical self-fashioning of T. E. Lawrence in the 1920s as Whitehall set about carving client-states in west Asia in the years between the world wars. In a more Indian context, the mock-indigenisation of the hero enables access to the world of the native as it draws on the resources of scholarly and administrative enquiry. But it draws moreover on the memory of an earlier period in the social history of Anglo-India, when the often indigenised lifestyles and households of British spies, scholars and explorers like Neil Edmonstone, William Moorcroft, David Ochterlony and the Fraser brothers, James and William, yielded knowledge and awareness of Indian society that the Company could put to use in times of war or crisis.

Besides *The Wife and the Ward*, another exception to these intrepid romances of heroic mobility is J. F. Fanthome's *Mariam*, a novel set around the rebellion at Shahjahanpur.[58] The novel combines first-person narrative with third person, with a sub-plot on the romantic love between a Muslim boy and girl, and includes a glossary and appendices explaining linguistic and cultural details. The main interests of this novel are the experiences during the rebellion of the Anglo-Indian (or Eurasian) Mrs Mary Lavater, the daughter of a European adventurer who had served in an Indian kingdom, and her daughter. Mrs Lavater finds refuge with first a Hindu and later a Muslim family after her husband, a clerk in the District Magistrate's office, is killed in the massacre of the British at Shahjahanpur town on 31 May 1857 and her house set afire. Immobilised by the rebellion, alienated from the social world of Anglo-India and forgotten by the armies of reconquest, the Lavaters adjust to their new station in life as the adoptive family of the local rebel leader Mangal Khan. Interestingly, Mary (who takes the name Mariam during her time in Mangal Khan's *zenana*) is not eager at the prospect of leaving her home of several months after the British capture Shahjahanpur; for, as the destitute widow of a petty clerk she does not expect any social or official rejoicing at her return.

Compared with the severely circumscribed orbit of the novel and Mariam's integration within Indian domestic life, the mobility that characterises the main body of the Mutiny novels and their heroic penetration of the rebel world are truly extraordinary. While Mrs Lavater writes at the end of her travail: 'We had to forget that we were British subjects, that we had European blood running in our veins',[59] in *On the Face of the Waters*, which appeared in the same year as *Mariam*, Jim Douglas has an uncompromising sense of his origins and his identity. '[D]rinking his tea' in the house he shares with Kate Erlton in Delhi, the Afghan horse-dealer 'felt that with his eyes shut he might have dreamt himself in an English drawing-room'. The reverie posits a limit to Douglas's indigenisation, and adumbrates his later resolve as a volunteer with the army on the Ridge to 'kill them [the rebels], as I would kill a mad dog, in the quickest way handy'.[60] To that extent, 'going native' for Douglas occurs under the aspect of an imperial identity and racial difference that in fact, and despite the rhetoric to the contrary, implies not going native at all.

Steel's novel makes transparent the burden of choices involved in this traffic of assumed and essential identities. Douglas's life with Kate Erlton in Delhi recalls a similar experience earlier in his life. The novel begins at Lucknow where Douglas lives with Zora, a young dancing girl he has 'saved' from her profession eight years earlier, and who is now pregnant with his child and on her deathbed. Watching her die, Douglas muses how Zora is his 'only link to a life that had grown distasteful to him'; and, though 'brutal to dream of freedom' while she lies dying in an adjacent room, 'it was inevitable' for he can neither bring himself to 'think half-caste thoughts' nor 'rear up a tribe of half-caste children'.[61] Then follows a remarkable promontory view, as Douglas, standing on the roof of his *haveli* in the old town, reflects upon the city before and the life behind him, as the evening smoke gradually palls the city from sight, 'obscuring it hopelessly with their tale of a life he could not lead'. 'One could not help these things', the narrator explains, and in a justificatory clause belied by the earlier suggestion that while Zora has been 'a small part of his life' he had meant more to her, it now emerges that 'it was the glow and the glamour that had been the bond between them – nothing else'.[62] Annexed from view not merely by the smoke but also by the Company's breach of trust with the rulers of Awadh, the city, the kingdom and Zora's ebbing life are the three axes of a world from which the future agent of counter-insurgency now withdraws. To confirm this reorientation against a world with which he had so far co-habited, Douglas is recruited in the next chapter by a 'Political officer' to spy on the movements of the 'seditious' Syed Ahmadullah, the *maulvi* of Faizabad, on the assumption that Douglas's 'black wife' and his proximity to the royal house of Awadh make him particularly useful for espionage.[63]

While the mobility of Sammy, Douglas, Ashby and Jenetha reveals the potency of the state and its ability to penetrate the world of the rebel, other novels construct a typology of colonial heroism. *The Disputed VC* begins with a loving portrait of the teenaged hero, Ted Russell:

Our hero was a good specimen of the type of boy from whose ranks the British ensign was recruited. Rather tall for his age, he was well-built and proportioned . . . with honest eyes that could look one in the face . . . A good athlete and gymnast, he had been regarded as the strongest forward in the school fifteen . . . His intellectual attainments had perhaps been less striking, though no one had ever classed him as a 'duffer'.[64]

The physiognomy and character of Ted encodes a public school ethos that first appeared in fiction in Thomas Hughes's 'muscular' Rugby novel, *Tom Brown's Schooldays* (1857), and which, as Joseph Bristow notes, was 'connected with war, honour, and, above all, doing well on the playing field'.[65] In contrast to the anti-intellectual and philathletic hero who combines romantic-chivalric aims with colonial state building is Harry Tynan, the 'Cad of the Regiment' and an unsuitable national type. Tynan is a: 'tall, handsome lad with dark hair inclined to curl, and big brown eyes; the type of boy who from childhood is petted and spoilt by mothers and aunts. Unless such a one possess an exceptionally strong character the result is fatal, and Tynan showed a weak mouth and chin.'[66] The contrast between the types is made clear after the Aurungpore troops rebel. Ted determines to blow up the Magazine at a risk to his own life while Tynan – brought up by 'mothers and aunts', and unmoved by dreams of heroism like E. M. Forster, who satirised the energetic promotion of empire by public schools in *The Longest Journey* (1907) – makes a cowardly pact with the rebels.

Heroic physiognomy and attributes such as 'pluck', 'dash' and 'gallantry' are the vernacular of an imperial culture whose topics and commonplaces have their source not only in the rebellion or in British India. In numerous short stories and novels by Henty, Gordon Stables, F. S. Brereton and Manville Fenn among others, and in a raft of immensely popular periodicals like the *Boys' Own Paper*, *The Boys' Friend*, *Chums* and *Union Jack*, heroic romance forms the vehicle for disseminating a continuous history of national expansion, to bring home knowledge of other lands and peoples and to confirm the supremacy of the white Anglo-Saxon Protestant.[67] As Henty's range shows, the colonial adventure novel is truly global, encompassing many theatres of expansion, conquest and settlement, with exploration and the colonial small war as favourite topoi.[68] Colonial heroism turns on several clusters of ideas: muscular Christianity, which John Hobson called 'Christianity in Khaki',[69] race thinking, social Darwinism and a conceptually watered-down Whig version of national history. These ideas were energetically propagated by schools, school textbooks, sermons, newspapers, the stage and literary writing, and by evangelical associations such as the Religious Tract Society and the Society for the Propagation of Christian Knowledge, and later by the National Volunteer League.[70]

Transforming class antagonisms into militarised nationalism, the imperial culture of late-nineteenth century Britain gives ideological legitimacy to the near-constant military skirmishing in the colonial periphery, from the Afghan frontier to western Kenya, and from the South China Sea to New Zealand. Much of this activity was driven by the need to advance or guard commercial interests, but there was also an ideational element that figures as much in the pro-consular gravitas of Lord Curzon in India, or Alfred Milner in Egypt and southern Africa, as in agile heroes of the Mutiny novels. As recent studies of the popular culture of imperialism in Britain from the 1880s have shown, popular fiction of this period turns often on the compelling theme of national and imperial 'deeds of glory', where 'each new episode of bravery could be immediately classified according to type and set in a context where its full range of patriotic meanings might be apparent'.[71]

Though an Anglo-Latin imperial imaginary embroidered the Indian policies of governors-general from Cornwallis and Wellesley to Ellenborough and Dalhousie, the rising importance of colonial concerns in foreign policy and home politics in late Victorian and Edwardian Britain was coeval with the percolation of imperial ideas and attitudes into the forms and practices of popular culture.[72] These developments, which Hobson dated from 1870, and which were shared by the principal European states and the United States of America, acquired a new edge with the 'scramble' for Africa that began around the Berlin Conference of 1884. The tendency of nationalism to 'overflow its natural banks and absorb the near or distant territory of reluctant and unassimilable peoples', as Hobson defined the 'New Imperialism' inaugurated under Disraeli's second term (1874–80), was not without critics and opponents, especially the Manchester Radicals and other socialist groups.[73] In *Democracy and Reaction* (1904), John Hobhouse, the pro-Boer journalist, observed that: 'The naked fact is that we are maintaining a distinct policy of aggressive warfare on a large scale and with great persistence', and 'the only result of attempting constantly to blink the fact is to have introduced an atmosphere of self-sophistication, or in one syllable, of cant, into our politics which is perhaps more corrupting than the unblushing denial of right'.[74] The contest in metropolitan politics and public opinion between the critical fringe and the expansionist state was also over the issue of patriotism and character building. The amateur sociologist and *fin-de-siècle* pessimist Charles H. Pearson believed that European nation-states had reached a developmental plateau, but nonetheless valorised Englishness in a global hierarchy of polities, societies and cultures: 'The love of any Englishman speaking the English tongue for his country is now for a land that can give him ampler protection than his fathers ever dreamt of, that invests him with the pride of a dominant race.'[75] In reply to Pearson, Frederic Harrison, a freethinker who publicised Auguste Comte's writing on positivist sociology in Britain, argued that patriotism was incompatible with 'sham imperial vainglory'. Instead of 'sending forth millions of citizens annually to roam over the planet, the building of vast shoddy fortunes, and carrying Union Jacks and Star-Spangled Banners over new continents', patriotism meant 'a nation of real and practical local limits' that would be 'guided by a wider and dominant spirit of humanity'.[76]

Though the Mutiny novel from the 1890s to the First War does not refer openly to metropolitan debates on new imperialism, the figures of heroism and the representation of the rebellion in these texts owe much to the popularisation of an aggressive mix of nationalism and expansionism. But these narrative interests sometimes require the demonstration of an overlap between contemporary and past forms of national expansion. Thus, the continuity between the steady but ideologically unfocused territorial growth of mid nineteenth century and late Victorian imperialism that forms the core thesis of E. A. Gallagher and R. E. Robinson in their article 'The Imperialism of Free Trade' appears in the representation of the 'Punjab school' sub-culture in Talbott Mundy's *Rung Ho!*. Formulated from the late 1840s, following the fall of the Sikh kingdom, and the heraldic figure of liberal-evangelical bureaucracy, the Punjab school represents a facilitating traffic of ideas, attitudes and roles between the gentlemanly sub-culture of the reformed public school in Britain and the administration of the Punjab and the Frontier; a territory that needed military, political and adminis-trative methods other than those applied in the great acquisitions of the last hundred years – Bengal, Mysore, the Maratha lands and Awadh. The Punjab school sub-culture formed moreover the source of a network of legends, heroic actions and personalities, braiding the distinctive modali-ties of 'pacification' and government in the Punjab-Frontier region with a romantic-chivalric medievalism in taste, manners and manorial paternal-ism, and providing ready and historically verifiable material for the popular interest in overseas exploits. Published in 1914 and set in a fictional north Indian kingdom, the novel has three principal British characters: the mis-sionary Duncan MacLean and his daughter Rosemary, and Ralph Cunning-ham, a young subaltern who arrives from England a few months before May 1857 and who suppresses the uprising in the kingdom single-handedly. *Rung Ho!* begins in the fictional town of Howrah, where Mahommed Gunga, a Muslim from Rajputana and a NCO in a Company regiment and his friends and fellow soldiers discuss the rumour of an impending revolt. The discussion reveals conflicts of interest between the Hindu rulers and the Muslim subjects of the kingdom, an interesting topical detail, for the novel appeared at a time when the beginning of mass-based demands for represen-tation in government coincided with the rise of sectarian politics, leading to the carving of separate communal electorates in the Morley-Minto reform schemes of 1907–9. As Muslims, Mahommed Gunga and his friends fear that if successful the rebellion might bring about a Hindu resurgence, and they remind each other that it is to the British, and especially to the late Colonel Cunningham who led the army that first conquered them, that they owe the present peace in their otherwise fractious kingdom. 'What were we', Gunga poses to his friends, 'until Cunnigan Bahadur came?', introducing the Punjab school topos of *pax Britannia* upheld by the lone officer in the outposts of empire. Beyond that, the question suggests that as a willing collaborator in the erasure of his past the native too dates the beginning of his historical being from the arrival of the white '*bahadur*'.[77] After the meeting, Gunga rides six hundred miles to his native village to settle his affairs so that he can devote himself to the preservation of British rule, and during his journey notes the unquiet countryside where none 'seemed to be for India, except Mahommed Gunga'.[78]

There is, however, another motive for Gunga's visit home. Having heard that his ex-Colonel's son Ralph Cunningham is on his way out from England to join an Indian regiment as a subaltern, Gunga wants to take him under his wing in the belief that only the son of 'Cunnigan Bahadur' can stem the rising political disorder. To that end, Gunga raises money by mortgaging his land and begins another long journey, this time to Bombay to receive the young hero, to test his mettle, to train him for the task at hand and to bring him to the Punjab to 'save India'. If this suggests Gunga's power over his prospective ward, Gunga gives his own interpretation of the chain of command between the British empire, the white 'griffin' and the much older and experienced sergeant-major when he tells the twenty-two-year-old Ralph that, '[T]hou and I are but the servants of the peace, as he [Ralph's father] was. If I serve thee, and thou the Raj' then all shall be well with India.[79] On their way to the Punjab, Gunga and his men variously test Ralph who, being preordained a hero, is already and innately an adept, and the demonstration of his talents before the audience of loyal natives further confirms their adulation of the Cunninghams, parent and son.

Ralph, when he appears, embodies an aura first acquired by his father when he conquered Mahommed Gunga's land. If the aura descends lin-early from father to son, it is also entwined with a succession of territorial advances and military victories, from the conquest of the Punjab in 1848, to the prompt suppression of the rebellion in that province in the summer of 1857, following which the newly conquered Punjab and the Frontier became a recruiting pool for the Delhi Field Force which the British used against the Mughal capital.[80] The worshipful deference of Gunga and his men to their conquerors, and their willingness to ensure the survival of empire exploits two celebrated themes of the Punjab school. The spontaneous collabora-tion recalls the words of the Derry Orangeman and enthusiastic evangelical, Henry Lawrence, who as a pro-consul in the Punjab observed that 'Roman history shows no such instantaneous fellowship of the vanquished with the victors'.[81] The auratic presence of Ralph Cunningham, and the supreme ease with which the young subaltern contains the rebellion in Howrah, bring to mind other larger-than-life figures in the imperial pantheon. One of these was the Punjab and Mutiny hero, John Nicholson, the subject of much hagiography and many anecdotes about the Sikhs or Afghans (the legend does not clarify which, and Katherine Tidrick has recently added Hindus to the list) who worshipped him and founded, so the story goes, the sect of 'Nikkulseynites'.[82] The other and perhaps more potent hero was Charles Gordon. Gordon not only put down the Taiping rebellion for the Chinese emperor in 1860 but was apotheosised after his 'martyrdom' at Khartoum in 1886, when he was supposed single-handedly to have faced a band of 'fanatical' Mahdis with only a cane in his hand. Gordon was an auratic figure of superhuman prowess, commemorated by Tennyson as the 'Warrior of God, man's friend',[83] and by an inscription in St Paul's Cathedral which in a turn of phrase that had earlier been applied on the death of Nicholson at Delhi and Henry Lawrence at Lucknow proclaims how Lawrence 'saved an empire by his warlike genius, he ruled vast provinces with justice, wisdom and power, and . . . died in the heroic attempt to save men, women and children from imminent and deadly peril'.

Complementing this aura and providing its material context is the governmental and cultural fashioning in the Punjab, which yielded in time a moral-racial and administrative ideal type to be exported to other areas of colonial settlement. At Peshawar, where like most of British India 'High Toryism, old port and proud Prerogative' reign, Ralph chafes against the legalism of a Bengal-style district administration, and feels relieved when he is given command of a body of Irregular troops on police duty.[84] The chance to draw first blood comes when Afghan raiders challenge British 'pacification' of the Frontier. And, when Ralph sets off for the hills with his troops, the narrator exclaims:

The real thing! The real, real thing within a year! A lone command – and that is the only thing a subaltern of spunk may pray for – eighty-and-eight hawk-eyed troopers asking only for the opportunity to show their worth – lean, hungry hills to hunt in, no commissariat, fair law to the quarry, and a fight – as sure as God made the mountains, a fight at the other end.[85]

A 'lone command' at the Frontier where Ralph can 'act without first submitting a request to somebody in triplicate, on blue-form B' is, of course, the favourite site of the Punjab school as it evolved from 1848 to the rebellion; and where the myth and mystique of the frontier combines a heady mix of evangelicalism high and low, public school codes, trans-Himalayan geopolitics, an exotic topography, a collection of sedentary and nomadic tribes and, as the century progressed, the compelling argument of the carbine and the Browning machine-gun.[86]

At this point the figure of Ralph – who will soon appear to the smitten Rosemary like 'a picture she had once seen of the Duke of Wellington; there was the same mastery, the same far vision, the same poise of self-contained power'[87] – evokes the iconic officer at the Frontier, Herbert Edwardes, who was one of Henry Lawrence's administrative understudies, a pious evangelical and somewhat bloodthirsty Punjab administrator during the rebellion. Edwardes was the author of *A Year on the Punjab Frontier*, a memoir that first circulated the rousing story of the middle-class hero who single-handedly brings peace and civilisation to an obscure part of the globe.[88] As he admits in the Preface, the purpose of the book is to tell his people what he accomplished in the valley of Bunno, which lay on the border between the erstwhile Sikh kingdom and Afghanistan; how 'a barbarous people [were] peacefully brought within the pale of civilisation; and one well-intentioned Englishman accomplished in three months, without a struggle, a conquest which the fanatic Sikh nation had vainly attempted, with fire and sword, for five-and-twenty years'.[89] The myth of the frontier hero travels in two directions. On the one hand, Malcolm Mainwaring, the hero of *With Sword and Pen*, comes out to India not only because he lacks prospects at home, but also because he is inspired by Edwardes's memoir. Thus, he explains to Evelyn Home during their voyage out: 'Fancy a lieutenant of eight years' service governing a province, and raising troops, and fighting pitched battles, all off his own bat!'[90] On the other hand, the myth returns to England to be canonised in metropolitan high culture when John Ruskin writes his own hero-worshipping essay on Edwardes, *A Knight's Faith: Passages in the Life of Sir Herbert Edwardes* (1885). Anticipating Talbott Mundy's celebration of the mystical aura which makes Mahommed Gunga and his men loyal to the Cunninghams, and obscuring the violent might of the state that lay behind Edwardes's personal magic, Ruskin explains the Frontier hero's power over his Pathan subjects by claiming that 'they were attached to him only by personal regard, by their knowledge of his justice, their experience of his kindness', in short 'to the English character he represented'.[91]

As these examples show, the Mutiny summons two idioms of heroism. There is, first, the vernacular heroism where the hero penetrates the rebel world either to subvert its autonomy or to return with crucial information. This heroism is based upon mimicry of the native and it underscores the plastic power of the authoritarian colonial state to mimic its subject; a fantasy of knowledge and surveillance enacted increasingly from the 1890s. The second idiom of heroism is auratic and quasi-religious. As the mythography of the Punjab school shows, the imperial hero claims and commands a spontaneous worship from the indigene, even as he represents an ideal of Christian-chivalric honour and virtue. Unlike the vernacular idiom of heroism, common to resourceful boy scout figures such as Sammy Tompkins and Kipling's Kim, the latter type represents an ideological project most clearly developed in Irwin's first novel, *A Man of Honour*.

Like Irwin's later hero Malcolm Mainwaring, James Purefoy, the son of an impecunious Ulster Protestant, leaves Oxford without taking his degree and comes out to India in 1848. Like the hero of William Arnold's *Oakfield*, who comes out the same year, Purefoy takes a dislike to Anglo-Indian society before travelling to the frontier town of Salarkot to join his regiment. At Salarkot Purefoy meets Commissioner Maitland, who briefs him on the state of the Punjab and the administration, and his wife, who gives the young subaltern a copy of the *Imitation of Christ*. Soon afterwards, the Company's second war against the Punjab kingdom begins, and following a skirmish in which he displays gallant leadership of Indian troops, Purefoy reads the *Imitation* and reflects that: 'his ideal was to be true and honest in word and deed, kindly to all men and chivalrous to all women . . . to be ready at any moment to lead forlorn hope, and to look death in the face without blanching'.[92] This leads him to wonder if there 'was any higher law which could reconcile . . . the virtues of the cloister' with 'the ideals of the soldier, his worldly ambition with a Pietist spirituality; anything that could, in short, 'blend [the two] into a perfect whole'.[93]

Disappointed in love after his best friend marries the girl he loves, there is a third antinomy that Purefoy must harmonise in the landscape of the Frontier and through the two years of the rebellion: between friendship and erotic love. When the rebellion begins, Purefoy marches to Delhi with his worshipful band of Pathans and Sikhs, and on reaching Delhi and viewing the rebel city he 'felt a sudden tingling shiver run through his veins at the [sight of] the stronghold of the treacherous enemies of his race and country, the theatre on whose stage had to be fought out the internecine conflict of which the Empire of India was the stake, and in which he, too, had a part to play'.[94] Before the assault on Delhi that began on 14 September 1858, the narrator inserts a Homeric roll-call of the Delhi heroes where: 'the greatest of all was he who whose towering form and features of stern and massive grandeur would have stamped him as a master in any assemblage in the world where deeds of desperate valour were done, Nicholson, king of men, and chiefest among ten thousand'.[95] During the battle that follows, Purefoy takes a bullet in his shoulder while his hero, Nicholson, is fatally wounded, and his beloved friend Mowbray, the husband of Margaret, dies. While the latter death would have allowed Purefoy to marry her at last, and she has now confessed to loving him while her husband was alive, he decides to 'banish from his heart all dreams of ever calling her his wife'; for 'was it not baser, because more cowardly, to think of courting Margaret now that her husband was no longer alive to resent it'.[96]

Long before he marries Margaret, Mowbray has spoken to Purefoy of his wish that women should not marry after their husband's death, but remain monogamous through their lives. Though he has no similar condition for men, it is to this fantasy of an uninterrupted ownership of the wife through life and after death, remarkably similar to the British view of the ritual of *sati*, that Purefoy appoints himself the guardian. Consigning Margaret to England and himself to a 'solitary exploration of the loneliest roads he could find', Jim takes his troops to Lucknow and participates in the final attack on that city in March 1858.[97] After the rebellion, he visits Kanpur with a friend and imagines the capture and punishment of the Nana Sahib:

we'll have a court-martial, and when he's been thoroughly identified, we'll build a gallows a hundred feet high between Massacre Ghat and Bibighar, and hang him up on it, alive and in chains, for all the world to see. Then we'll surround the gallows with a strong cordon of British troops and leave him to starvation and the vultures . . .[98]

Striken by his 'private sorrow' for he still is in love with Margaret as she is with him, yet bound by a fretful compulsion to keep the widow chaste, Purefoy's only purpose in life 'was vengeance on the archenemies of his race and country'.[99] Thus he spends his days on the trail of the Nana Sahib, seeking distraction in the colonial small war until shot dead by fugitive rebels in another frontier near the Nepalese Terai.

A Man of Honour represents the inner life of the Punjab and Mutiny hero, a colonial adventure novel where counter-insurgency provides occasions for stylised self-fashioning. As Joseph Bristow notes, appealing to 'a romanticized tradition of medieval knights in shining armour, the aristocratic masculinity' which emerged from the Crimean war 'became the major shaping force in British imperialism. Such an ideal would feed down to the middle classes as they entered the newly founded public schools opened in the 1860s and 1870s in increasing numbers.' Thus, a middle-class and impecunious but educated hero like James Purefoy, while 'he still had the traits of his raffish forbears, in terms of "grit" and "pluck" . . . now tried to combine the fighting spirit with the even older, more honourable ideal of the polite gentleman who based his very being in what the middle classes most admired: respect'.[100] The antinomies that Purefoy creates upon reading the *Imitation* and after the Battle of Chillianwalla are no less significant for his self-fashioning. The 'cloister' that Purefoy yearns for represents the homoerotic possibilities of the public school and the Oxford college, now rediscovered in his bonding with loyal native troops, with his friend Mowbray and with his hero the bachelor Nicholson, a bond that requires a compulsive exclusion of women and wives. Moreover, the language of knight errantry is not only the martial obverse of the medieval cloister, but finds fruition in two areas of activity: in ensuring the chastity of his friend's widow and in the colonial small war: the 'theatre on whose stage' suitably medieval punishments of the 'treacherous enemies of his race and country' are imagined. Though neither Purefoy nor the narrator acknowledge this, the 'higher law' which can and does harmonise the opposed impulses is in conquering and administering the colonial periphery, where the middle class discovers a sonorous self-importance, and reinventing itself in an archaic literary idiom discovers a feudal-aristocratic identity consonant with the non-representative and authoritarian character of the government it usually represents.

The two varieties of heroism, however, need to be addressed together, for, if the boy scout hero demonstrates the plasticity of the colonial state in managing surveillance, sabotage and technology, the auratic hero embodies the ideological justification and legitimacy of the ruling mission. As Mark Girouard observes in his study of the medieval revival in late Victorian Britain, *The Return of Camelot*, the ideological combination of chivalry and imperialism provided 'a moral justification for England's rule both of newly acquired territory and of the existing empire'.[101] In the development of the adventure novel through the nineteenth century – from Frederick Marryat's naval yarns to the ironic reversal of Conrad's *Heart of Darkness* – Sammy Tompkins and James Purefoy embody two crucial aspects of the mythography of the small war. While the studies of imperial ideology by MacDonald, MacKenzie, Bristow and others have provided valuable analyses of the making and circulation of such myths and topoi, and their applications in popular culture, these studies do not perhaps sufficiently address the logic of an imagination that demands, especially in the quite substantial case of the Mutiny novel, the insertion of the hero into the rebel world. The insertion is a fantasy of mastery and colonial knowledge especially characteristic of the Mutiny novel from the 1890s, and it functions as a device for mediating the representation of rebel agency and, indeed, the representation of India as such, a project that reworks the ethnographic interests of the novels by Hockley and Taylor.

6

Imagining resistance

How little we even now know of the millions of Hindostan – their motives, their secrets, their animosities, their aspirations.

Chamber's History of the Indian Revolt (1859)

I am off to the palace to see what has really happened; information's everything.

Jim Douglas in F. A. Steel, *On the Face of the Waters* (1896)

INTELLIGENCE FAILURE AND THE VISIONS OF SUTURE

It was suggested in the last chapter that Jim Douglas's return to rebel Delhi in May 1857 to gather information, together with the fact that he lives in the city for over two months, represents a fantasy of surveillance projected on a site that otherwise lay beyond the colonial state between May and September that year. In so doing, *On the Face of the Waters* marks a significant literary-historical development. Whereas in Money's *The Wife and the Ward*, the world of the rebel beyond the all-too vulnerable walls of the Kanpur entrenchment appears only through its effect upon the garrison, in somewhat later novels such as James Grant's *First Love and Last Love* (1868), or George Chesney's *The Dilemma* (1876) that world appears *alongside* a besieged or beleaguered Anglo-India. But in the novels of the nineties and after, the two worlds are often energetically bridged by heroes such as Douglas, Sammy, Ashby and Jenetha who, as they pass unhampered between one and the other bearing information, mediate the representation of the rebel world in a manner not dissimilar to the iterological mediation of indigenous society and landscape in a fairly long tradition of British Indian travel writing.

This interest in surveillance is understandable in the light of the fact that the British empire grew by some 4,700,000 square miles between 1874 and 1902, an expansion that stretched national resources but created in the process new, extra-systemic, methods of conflict management. Situated amidst military, commercial and ideological developments that attached, governed and patrolled and that, not least, legitimised the acquisition of all those square miles of land and water, the spy-hero of the Mutiny novel from the 1890s reveals the modes of expansion and colonial administration, while at the same time recalling earlier practices of social monitoring and intelligence gathering in India. As C. A. Bayly observes, British advances from the eighteenth century owed much to the observation and penetration of Indian society, and it was by 'controlling newswriters, corralling groups of spies and runners, and placing agents at religious centres, in bazaars and among bands of military men and wanderers' that the Company had successfully 'been able to anticipate the coalitions of the Indian powers and to plot their enemies' movements and alliances'.[1]

By inserting the hero(ine) into rebel conclaves or otherwise foregrounding issues of information, the Mutiny novel of the nineties, like novels of policing such as the *Confessions of a Thug* or *Kim*, is 'located precisely on [the] cusp between British intelligence and indigenous knowledge'.[2] At once a sign of mastery and anxiety, of lack and promise, the fantasy of surveillance projected back from the 1890s on to the 1850s is important for at least two related reasons. Though there were many Indian spies, *harkaras* (messengers) and double agents who operated behind the lines in 1857–9, and like the *maulvi* Rajab Ali at Delhi provided valuable intelligence to the army of reconquest, there are no records of ethnic British spies.[3] Read against that historical absence, the novels revise the Mutiny archive with insertions that construct masterful knowledge and control, and their obverse, the transparency of native society. The demand for knowledge and transparency are significant when read alongside the concerns of the last three decades of the century, when the British state in India, faced with internal 'disaffection', sectarian conflict, border skirmishing and the Russian threat, set about reorganising and extending its intelligence apparatus. Viewed thus, Jim Douglas's remark at the Mori Gate in Delhi inscribes an institutional history that led to the enlargement of the Anti-Thagi and Dacaity Department of 1835 vintage, through the post-rebellion provincial Criminal Intelligence Departments, to the Central Criminal Intelligence Department of 1904.[4]

There is, however, a further resonance to surveillance. Projected upon the rebellion, such fantasies invite comparison with the lives and the careers of an earlier generation of scholar-explorer-'intelligencers'. As Bayly shows in his study of the interaction between the Indian public spheres and the British 'information order' between 1780 and 1870, until the 1830s Britons and Eurasians like Neil Edmonstone, William Moorcroft, James Skinner and Hyder Jung Hearsay were nodal links in the Company's access to Indian society, to its channels of social communication and to the Indo-Persian intelligentsia.[5] Company servants and linguists, but also adventurers and privateers often with a *bibi* and an Indian family, and combining orientalist interest in language and manners with empirical observation of topographies, polities and peoples, these men, and in particular Moorcroft, are historical prototypes for the plasticity of Roland Ashby and Jim Douglas. Initially a horse trainer of the Nawab of Awadh living with his 'black wife' in the Muslim quarter of Lucknow, next recruited by the Political Department to spy on the movements of the *maulvi* of Faizabad, and finally disguised as an Afghan horse-dealer in rebel Delhi, Douglas is a composite drawn from the biographical resources of 'India hands'. Moorcroft's work as a veterinary surgeon and as the Superintendent of the Company's Stud Farm at Pusa in modern-day Bihar brought him into close contact with Afghan horse-dealers, horse breeders, *zamindars*, merchants and planters – a logistical and information network on the border between the Company's territories and Nepal that Moorcroft used during the Company's war with the Himalayan kingdom (1814–16). Similarly, his travels through the western Himalayas to Central Asia were 'ostensibly scientific expeditions in search of information about sources of cavalry horses, though in truth they became espionage exercises accumulating political data and exotica'.[6]

Douglas's travelling companions and informants underscore the broad similarities between the biographical figure of the pro-consul and adventurer and the modes of counter-intelligence in Steel's novel. One of these is Tara, a Hindu widow Douglas has saved from *sati*, and her brother Soma, an infantryman from a mutinous Meerut regiment who joins the rebel army at Delhi, but remains personally faithful to Douglas. The *banjara* Tiddu is another of Douglas's associates, one of a band of travelling players and a master of disguise and hypnotism; and, for a hundred rupees Tiddu agrees to impart to Douglas an arcane skill in disguise that will help him blend into Indian society. Though sceptical about Tiddu's claims, Douglas nonetheless decides to give it a try, for 'if there was anything certain in this world it was the wisdom of forgetting Western prejudices occasionally in dealing with the East'.[7] It is a suspension of disbelief that ironically confirms and activates another body of 'Western prejudices', so that the magical/mystical knowledge the imperial hero acquires from the indigenous shaman is brought to bear on counter-insurgency operations.[8] Disguised as an Afghan, Douglas visits a brothel in the heart of the Mughal capital days before the rebellion breaks out, overhears talk of an imminent revolt, registers the rifts between the Muslims and the Hindus and, noticing a Hindu religious procession in the street outside, transforms himself in an instant into a Hindu mendicant before vanishing in the crowd.

The point of these similarities is not, however, to establish the sources of the novel. More interesting than a reduction to or comparison with probable models is the historical and ideological freight that surveillance carries, projected upon the rebellion from the 1890s, and recalling those capillaries of colonial counter-intelligence that by all accounts appear to have withered by the 1830s. As such, these novels are located between the transformation of the criminal and political intelligence apparatus that occurred in the period between 1878 and 1904, and the earlier and lived, everyday forms of information gathering wherein Company functionaries could directly tap into the channels of indigenous social communication.[9] If the romance of surveillance resourcefully inserted into the historical archive of the rebellion produces – like Moorcroft's journey through the Punjab and the Frontier – a map of the *terra incognita* of rebel Delhi and its palace politics, it underscores, moreover, a series of withdrawals that, from roughly the third decade of the nineteenth century, had resulted in a growing distance between the 'official mind' and social world of Anglo-India on the one hand, and Indian public opinion on the other.

A sense of this withdrawal is suggested in *On the Face of the Waters*. The end of Jim Douglas's earlier life as the Nawab's horse trainer and Zora's lover, his new role as spy for the Political Department, the lover of Kate Erlton and, in time, as a heroic agent of counter-insurgency, may be read as the allegory of a 'purity campaign' that, coeval with the Company's rise to paramountcy, rigorously polices the frontiers of an insular Anglo-India. Yet through these mutations of British identity and self-image in India there runs a continuous demand for knowledge, penetration and control; a demand that points at once to the lack – cited at the head of this chapter – that the *Chambers History* laments, and to the fulfilment that the romance-hero's brisk quest for 'information' achieves. Not only are the rebels eventually captured, exiled or killed, but the temporary autonomy of the rebel must be disrupted, spied upon and otherwise recorded by a fictional reconstruction that, like the British state in India, craves a panoptic knowledge of the indigenous society.

The 'cusp between British intelligence and indigenous knowledge', that according to Bayly is the epistemological field of novels such as *Kim*, appears in the Mutiny novels when the reports or rumours of 'disaffection' and revolt seep into Anglo-Indian social spaces releasing signs and symptoms – the chapattis and the lotus, the wandering *maulvis* and the random arson attacks, the whispered suggestions, the public placards and the printed newsletters and, sometimes, the odd behaviour of servants and troops – that generate alarm, controversy and administrative unease. As the uncertain response of Anglo-Indian garrisons suggest, these signs and their sudden discharge prompt a reckoning with a larger failure that otherwise besets the colonial state and historiography alike. Thus, at the end of his analysis of the causes of the rebellion in *The Sepoy War*, Kaye confesses:

We know so little of Native Indian society beyond its merest externals, the colour of the people's skins, the form of their garments, the outer aspects of their houses, that History, whilst it states broad results, can often only surmise causes . . . It is a fact, that there is a certain description of news, which travels in India, from one station to another, with a rapidity almost electric.[10]

If this admission echoes William Bentinck's view, formulated in the aftermath of the Vellore Mutiny of 1806, that the British in India were destined to remain 'strangers in the land', and obliquely suggests a limit to the 'Progress of Englishism', it is also an endorsement of Ball's view, at the end of his account of the first stages of the rebellion, that 'there existed among Asiatics an understanding and a power of co-operation, which years of experience and uninterrupted service did not enable a European to detect and guard against'.[11] Such failures operate dangerously in military administration where the problem of monitoring a mercenary army, drawn from Indian communities, and embodying loyalties stronger than those to the Company, highlights a lasting administrative problem. As Kaye writes at the end of his summary history of earlier troubles with the army:

Some said that the Native Army should be narrowly watched, and held in control by sufficient bodies of European soldiery; others contended that we could commit no more fatal mistake than that of betraying the least suspicion of the Sepoy, and suggesting even a remote possibility of one part of our Army ever being thrown into antagonism to the other. This controversy was half a century old.[12]

In the novels the breach between Indian understanding and European ignorance, however, works as occasion for a fantasy of suture. In *Terrible Times*, a boy's novel by G. P. Raines on the rebellion in the fictional town of Churzabad, near Meerut, the two sons of the British colonel overhear a conversation between their servants. Following the court-martial of the eighty-five cavalrymen who refused to use the newly issued greased cartridges at Meerut, Peer Bux, the *khansaman* of the colonel's household, returns from a meeting of the soldiers with the news that 'to-morrow night at sunset their comrades will rise, liberate them and the work of vengeance shall commence'.[13] While the colonel knows and suspects nothing of the men under his command, the overheard conversation not only gives the teenage heroes, Harry and Claude, the chance to warn the garrison but discloses, simultaneously, a current of news, opinion, association and sympathy that flows outside and around the colonial bungalow and the regimental mess. The failure to anticipate the rebellion, and the gap between official intelligence and such currents of indigenous communication are more elaborately spelled out in J. F. Fanthome's *Mariam* and a few other novels.

One of the rare novels to represent debates among the rebels with some seriousness and without the tedious stereotypes, *Mariam* views the rebellion from the perspective not of the covenanted-commissioned officers, but of an Eurasian or lower-middle-class Anglo-Indian family located between the indigenous and the Anglo-Indian social worlds, and with access to their channels of communication. A clerk in the district magistrate's office, Mr Lavater and his wife Mary know that though watchful, the administration does not expect an uprising in Shahjahanpur. To stoke their anxiety, the magistrate rides through the town one morning without noticing the otherwise evident signs of trouble. The officer's failure to read the signs is ironic since his survey follows several chapters where the town gentry and the soldiers in the barracks plan the uprising and the massacres that will ensue. Another source of information for the Lavater household is the Anglo-Indian newspaper, the *Moffusilite* – founded by John Lang, and published from Meerut at the start of 1857 – with its reports of disturbances in other towns and stations, and of the responses of the government in Calcutta.

Complementing these sources, yet bearing a wholly different import and configured in an indigenous idiom, are other signs of 'the near approach of the catastrophe' that Mary Lavater's confiding servants provide.[14] Faced with a choice between the two tiers and languages of information and knowledge, Mrs Lavater, a country-born Briton or Eurasian with fluent Urdu and Hindustani and many Indian friends, unhesitatingly favours her immediate and indigenous sources over the official and the Anglo-Indian. Her view of the administration is deeply sceptical and at one point she wonders if 'they [the British officials at Shahjahanpur] are in touch with native society', or if the district administration had 'established any system of intelligence or espionage upon which they can rely?'[15] Observing the eddying of unrest around her, Mary Lavater laments an official blindness that, in Kaye's words, can neither penetrate the 'merest externals' of Indian society, nor prevent in *Mariam* 'the fomentors and leaders of the rebellion to receive and communicate news from and to distant stations'.[16]

Mr Lavater is killed in the massacre at the Shahjahanpur church on 31 May, while Mary Lavater, her mother, and her son and daughter take refuge in the home of the rebel leader, Mangal Khan. Mrs Lavater's access to local knowledge, her easy integration into the Muslim household, her emphasis on the breach between the official and the indigenous, the novel's learned appendices and glossary and the familiarity with Hindu-Islamic customs and Hindustani language together suggest a different class and cultural provenance for *Mariam*. Entirely non-heroic, yet published in 1896 when heroism was the norm, the world of Fanthome's novel is far removed from the homoerotic knight-errantry of Irwin's *A Man of Honour*, the worshipful portraitures of heroic masculinity in Flora Steel's novel and the tiresome inanities of Muddock's *The Great White Hand* – all published in the same year, and equally devoted to the Mutiny exploits of the covenanted and commissioned officers, their friends, families and lovers.

With its dense representation of Indian life and its acute observation of the breach between official Anglo-India and India, the plot of *Mariam* recalls, more credibly than the swashbuckling career of Jim Douglas, those serviceable networks of information that the 'intelligencers' of an earlier generation had access to. Like Edmonstone, Moorcroft or the Fraser brothers at Delhi, Mary Lavater lives between Anglo-India and India, and so can see and hear what the government cannot. Yet while the lived, everyday knowledge of those men and their access to Indian public spheres and the intelligentsia was a resource that the Company drew upon in times of crisis or in order to monitor Indian society, in Fanthome's novel that resource is vestigial. Mary Lavater's confinement to the female quarters of Mangal Khan's house (without, it must be said, the least suggestion of sexual violence), the uselessness of her knowledge and her insignificance in British Shahjahanpur are pointers to the change that the Company's intelligence-gathering mechanisms had undergone through the nineteenth century. In turn, these changes are aspects of a reformulation of British policy and identity that required the slow edging-out of those Britons whose 'modification' of their 'sense of Britishness' through 'exile' or through 'contact' with the indigenous rendered them ideologically unsuitable as the representatives of a liberal administrative state.[17]

The British Other Ranks (BOR), the Anglo-Indian lower middle class, the box-wallahs (as the European merchants, traders and planters were known) and the Eurasians are quite marginal to the Mutiny novel. Such occupational groups are, in fact, anathema to a heroic-chivalric idiom in which the lives, exploits, interests and careers of the covenanted services and the commissioned ranks of the army form the enduring interests.[18]

Among the very few novels in which the other ranks prominently figure are Hume Nisbet's *The Queen's Desire*, *Begumbagh* by George Manville Fenn and Thomas Strange's *Gunner Jingo's Jubilee*.[19] In what is perhaps a nod to Fenn's own working-class origins and later career as a journalist writing on working-class subjects, the narrator of *Begumbagh* is a Private Smith. The story of an army column's march from Patna to the fictitious Begumbagh, in the course of which rebel troops attack and besiege white officers, NCOs and their families, the novel foregrounds the daily life of the other ranks, their (rather slight) understanding of the rebellion, and their shrewd but respectful observation of the officers. The Cockney jingoism of Fenn's sergeants, corporals and privates, the racy action, and (in addition to a love-triangle between the colonel's daughter and two officers) an NCO love affair leave little room for reflections on the rebellion. While *Begumbagh*, like *Gunner Jingo's Jubilee*, underscores the end-of-the-century mobilisation of sections of the working class into the enthusiastic shock-troops of empire, Nisbet's somewhat more knowledgeable and certainly more fantastic representation of the Anglo-Indian other ranks weaves several issues together.

Besides young Sammy Tompkins, whose adventures at Meerut and Delhi were described earlier, an additional representative of the other ranks in *The Queen's Desire* is Sergeant Jackson. Later the lover of Lakshmi Bai, the queen of the Maratha kingdom of Jhansi, with whom he spends a few months and who tries to seduce him with the well-worn trappings of the imperial gothic – precious jewels and a love-philtre that makes him oblivious to the call of national duty – Sergeant Jackson articulates the critique of the insular intolerance that structures Anglo-Indian behaviour with Indians as well as an administrative insensitivity to Indian opinion. Walking one evening through the palace gardens of the Red Fort where the British society in Delhi had gathered as the guests of the Mughal court, the sergeant 'saw a good deal . . . of the frivolity, heedlessness and selfishness of this society . . . their careless contempt for the natives'; an observation the narrator glosses with the remark: 'It is astonishing how quickly even the most genial of men and the gentlest of women can become tyrants when they get the unlimited chance.'[20] To corroborate these observations, British regimental officers at Delhi fail to notice or to understand 'discontented natives jabbering about their superstitious caste wrongs'; for, as Sergeant Jackson explains to Sergeant Tompkins, 'they aren't amongst the men as we are, that's the reason for their blank confidence'.[21]

The social and official withdrawal that the NCO Jackson notices, and his often critical observation of the conduct of officers and their ladies, is akin to Mary Lavater's disappointment with an administration that can neither read the portents of insurgency nor control the 'almost electric' channels of rebel communication that flow past the colonial office house, the bungalow and the regimental mess, and that with their speed challenge the efficacy of the telegraph as a tool of colonial integration and control. But such voices and locations are extremely rare. The lack that these novels draw attention to and, arguably, compensate for, is endemic to a literary tradition devoted to perpetuating images of the officer-class, and whose idiom of heroism and gentlemanliness necessarily excludes other ranks as much as the creolised box-wallah or the planter. A sense of this emerging literary turn can be found in an essay that Kaye wrote before the rebellion. The author of *Long Engagements: A Tale of the Afghan Rebellion* (1845), and a prolific reviewer of Anglo-Indian writing, Kaye suggested in the *North British Review* in 1849/50: 'now that the old race of heroes, who saved England from the grasp of Napoleon is fast dying out, it is to India that we must turn for those noble exemplars of the true military character'.[22]

Kaye's article appeared at the end of a decade of military campaigning and annexation that vastly extended the frontiers of British India to the north-east and the north-west, and that culminated with the appointment of Dalhousie as Governor-General. Kaye's recommendation to Anglo-Indian writers, and his sense of the new literary possibilities released by the dramatic extension of territory and government was not out of place. Within a year Herbert Edwardes published his celebrated account of *A Year on the Punjab Frontier*, and in 1849 appeared William Arnold's reformist novel, *Oakfield*. To place these texts in the social and political history of mid-century Anglo-India is to observe an emerging imperial identity created and cornered by the 'noble exemplars' of middle Britain who came out to India to rule vast districts, to conquer vaster kingdoms, to quell revolts, to dispense justice, to piously struggle against the 'awful *vis inertiae* of Asiaticism'[23] and not to succumb to either sentimental orientalism, or to its sexual corollary, the allures of a *bibi*.

Parallel to the mutations in Anglo-Indian poetry that Nigel Leask traces in his essay 'Towards an Anglo-Indian Poetry', this making of an identity is prompted and facilitated by the constitutional changes introduced by the Charter Act of 1833, which was instituted when Macaulay was Secretary of the Board of Control and James Mill the Examiner of Correspondence at India House. Twenty years before its dissolution in the aftermath of the rebellion, the Charter Act took away the Company's right to engage in commerce, and in so doing transformed the merchant company into a cen-tralised administrative bureaucracy, with the presidencies brought under the supreme council in Calcutta, and the whole placed under close parliamentary observation. The Act of 1833 was the culmination of a legislative history (from the Regulating Act of 1783 to the Government of India Act of 1858) by means of which Parliament had tracked the remarkable evolution of a merchant company into a state, and curbed its tendency to acquire an indigenised administrative morality.[24] In another sense, the Charter Act marks the beginning of a new orientation and new roles for British power in India: from profit to revenue, from the merchant-factor to the officer-administrator, from a commercial syndicate to an extended arm of the metropolitan state.[25] With its incipient republicanism and its reformist energy, its view of India as an administrative laboratory and assertion of racial difference, the 'Progress of Englishism' that Kaye holds responsible for the rebellion in *The Sepoy War* is as much a result of successive charters, as of the habits and bearings of the liberal-evangelical administrator represented by Arnold's *Oakfield* and by *The Man of Honour*, James Purefoy.

Well before the *de jure* transformation following the Queen's Proclamation of November 1858, the legislations of 1813 and 1833 had transformed the Company into a heavily militarised colonial state, an institution that the prescriptions and self-representations of Kaye, Edwardes and Arnold presume on. The salient registers of these texts – principally the heroic-chivalric mode, and the doctrinal core of unconventional war and administration – reappear in a literary practice that coagulates around the rebellion of 1857–9. In the Mutiny novel can be seen the persistent power of the 'true military tradition', which finds a new lease of life in the events of the rebellion and the cultural needs of the 'High' imperial years. While the hero of Irwin's *With Sword and Pen* comes out to India inspired by Edwardes's memoir of the Frontier, the hero of Irwin's novel of 1896, *A Man of Honour*, employs a language of chivalry, piety and martial heroism that echoes Edward Oakfield and Kaye's prognosis of 1850. Yet this transformation is also the source of those crucial failures of knowledge and intelligence that perplexed British historians of the rebellion. In Kaye's reconstruction of the thirty years before the rebellion in *The Sepoy War*, the Indian soldier and his British officer made a useful team through the first quarter of the nineteenth century, not least because the latter 'had subdued his habits, and very much his way of thinking, to the Orientalism by which he was surrounded'. But this working relationship fell apart in the second quarter of the century, when 'we reformed our government and we reformed ourselves. Increased facilities of intercourse with Europe gave a more European complexion to society.'[26]

There is, moreover, a remarkable harmony between British and Anglo-Indian self-representation and the representation of India. Especially with the rebellion when, as Metcalf notes in his study of the *Ideologies of the Raj*, liberal reform came to grief and was replaced by 'a revitalised conservatism' in Indian policy, the invented tradition of heroic chivalry meshes well with post-Mutiny visions of India as analogous with Britain's medieval past.[27] Metcalf traces the making and the meaning of these visions, and there is much force in his larger point that following the rebellion the project of reform was considerably modified; yet, pushed too far the idea of Indian 'difference' can obscure areas of resemblance and overlap. The representation of India as analogous with Britain's past and the emphasis on its hypostatised and hierarchical pre-modernity is in fact consonant with a ruling race/class idiom of knight-errantry, with authoritarian and non-representative government and with literary-aesthetic modes and genres such as romance and the picturesque. It is the combination of these mutually supporting idioms of representation that makes a medievalised vassal India the secret sharer of those 'noble exemplars' whose nobility thrives, in turn, upon the asymmetries of race and the seigniorial rights of empire.

In Maxwell Gray's novel, *In the Heart of the Storm: A Tale of Modern Chivalry*, Phillip Randal, the middle-class veteran of the Crimean War, and now a heroic-chivalric fugitive in rebel Awadh, looks out of the window of his Indian host's house one night to gaze upon an 'architecture [that] was like a confused dream of feudalism and Gothic Middle Ages blended fantastically with Oriental splendour and despotism, the whole touched with the peculiar glamour of the East and the deep enchantment of the days of chivalry'.[28] Nor is this 'confused dream' of recurrence and similitude merely an instance of popular metropolitan orientalism, or its learned counterpart, the 'stage-theory' of Scots historians such as William Robertson.[29] Eight years after the novel appeared, and not unlike Kaye in 1850, the Anglo-Indian administrator and historian Alfred Lyall wrote in an article on 'The Anglo-Indian Novelist' that: 'Each successive campaign in India, from the first Afghan war to the latest expedition across the Afridi frontier, has furnished the Anglo-Indian writer with a new series of striking incidents that can be used for his heroic deeds and dire catastrophes, for new landscapes and figures . . .' If this recalls the 'Romance of Indian Warfare', Lyall attaches to his end-of-the-century recommendation of a poetics of the colonial small war, a visionary homology wherein the heroic deeds of contemporary Anglo-India find a meaningful cultural-anthropological context. Thus, Lyall counsels Anglo-Indian novelists to venture outside the garrison and to observe 'the distinctive qualities of a people that have preserved many of the features which in Europe have now vanished into the dim realms of early romance'.[30]

The imagined surveillance demonstrates access to Indian society and sutures the gaps in knowledge and intelligence that stemmed from the changing role of the Company and from the changing self-representation of the Company's functionaries in India. As Kaye and Sergeant Jackson suggest, the inability to see beyond the 'merest externals' of Indian society explained not only the administrative failure to read the portents in 1857, but also the rebellion as event. But this systemic deficiency is redressed in the Mutiny novels by imagined passages into the bazaar, brothel, temple, mosque and *sarai*. The spy-hero who joins the rebels as one of them, or the boy-hero who eavesdrops on Indian servants, steps into the breach between British intelligence and indigenous knowledge, pre-emptively narrowing the distance between Anglo-India and the 'Orientalism by which [it] was surrounded'. By entering the otherwise unobserved 'hotbeds of lies and intrigue', and by blending into a crowd that in *Red Revenge* (*c.* 1911) comprises a simmering crowd of 'moolvies (travelling pilgrims), pedlars, goojurs or robbers, barbers, basket-makers, water-carriers, grass-cutters, mendicants, and nondescripts of every variety . . . quietly spreading rebellion',[31] the state and its heroic agent traverse a frontier that the Charter Act of 1833 and the subsequent self-representation of sundry 'noble exemplars' had rendered impassable.

The cultural distance that surveillance helps to traverse is evident from a comparison of the adventures of the intrepid spy-heroes with a description of the settlement patterns of the commissioned-covenanted official class – to which these characters are directly affiliated – in R. E. Forrest's novel *Eight Days* (1891). A chivalric romance based in the fictional town of Khirzabad (Delhi), its narrator remarks at the outset that '[I]n India we English people do not usually dwell within the walled cities of the land. The mode of life of natives is too different from ours to allow of it. We live *by* Agra, or Lahore – not *in* them.'[32] In the reinventions of the 1890s and thereafter, the visions of living *in* rather than living *by* Indian society reminisce over channels of communication and interaction that began to dry up with the Company's ascent to paramountcy, even as they address turn-of-the-century concerns over crime and political resistance. There is, however, divergence between the demands of surveillance and those of the chivalric code. While tapping into Indian society by a mastery of disguise, topography and language, the spy-hero is almost never clerk, merchant, planter, creolised subaltern like Mary Lavater or British Other Ranks (BOR) like Sergeant Jackson, but belongs to the administrative-military elite. The reluctance to work with characters other than those of this class suggests the persistence in the high imperial Mutiny novel of the very failures that in some versions had produced the rebellion. The social origin and ideological bearings of the class to which the spy-hero belongs forecloses the limits of the knowledge that may be gleaned from the bazaar, the temple, the palace and the highway.

But the culturally cross-dressed spy-hero in the Mutiny novel has another valency. The spy-hero's mimicry of the native subject confounds the autonomy of the latter, and is the means by which (not unlike the lamps that Jenetha lights on the ramparts of Delhi to warn the British on the Ridge) a fictional narratology translates, encrypts and transmits the inner world of the rebellion to metropolitan subject of empire. In doing so, characters such as Jim Douglas, Jenetha Wentworth, Roland Ashby and others serve as the agents of counter-insurgency, and they help to open another window into recent debates over colonial 'mimicry' and 'hybridity'.

The colonised subject's mimicry of the colonial master is 'at once resemblance and menace'.[33] As opposed to this ambivalence, which had, historically, structured the evolution of colonial modernity and its political idioms, the rebellion constitutes a pure 'menace' – an unsynthesisable antinomy that rises against the defilement of a caste-less 'resemblance' of which the 'greased cartridge' may be read as an apt synecdoche. In refusing the project of assimilation and European modernity, and by challenging the legitimacy of British rule in India, the rebellion constitutes a radical opposition to the 'Anglicism' of Macaulay's 1835 Minute on Education. Elaborated and applied by the liberal administrative state, and designed to transform India into Britain's economic periphery, it was the 'Progress of Englishism' that provided the enabling condition and opened the representational space for the mimic gesture. In opposing this project, with its many cultural and social modalities and implications, the rebel of 1857–9 – whether a supporter of Mughal-Timurid revival, of Maratha ambition, of agrarian rights or (military) service grievances, of customary practices or of an intuited patriotism – is the enemy not only of the colonial state but also of the acculturated *babus* of Bengal precisely because the latter had sought and found a separate peace in a collaborative mimesis fundamentally irreconcilable with the broad spectrum of rebel motivations.[34]

The thrust of Homi Bhabha's view is that mimicry reveals the limits of colonial authority, in as much as the 'mimic man' not only parodies the object of his mimesis and so yields a distorted and disquieting mirror-image, but that mimicry acquires an adversarial political charge when the hybridised colonial subject begins to claim the freedom and agency of the coloniser. There is, however, another aspect to what Bhabha calls the 'third space' of mimicry, and in which the High imperial Mutiny novel invests a good deal. This is the coloniser's counter-mimicry of the colonised: if the historical entelechy of the subject's mimicry points to a transformative combination of 'resemblance and menace' that eventually chips away at, at least, the political edifice of the colonial state, the mimicry that Sammy, Ashby, Jenetha, Douglas and others unleash is the device of a heroic counter-insurgency that employs the figure of the hybrid to restore the colonial state, to reveal its ubiquity and to subvert rebel autonomy.

The 'third space' of mimicry thus functions in the Mutiny novels as a fantasy of mastery. By appropriating the language, clothes, habits, manners and politics of the colonised subject, the imperial hero(ine) controls and menaces the indigene; a project whose authenticity and effective power rests upon the assurance that the forays into hybridity do not in the end hybridise the heroic agent, who, even as he/she blends into the crowd, retains an inviolate essence that disguise cannot conceal nor the orient enervate. As Jim Douglas prepares for his peregrinations with a caravan of *banjaras*, the narrator steps in with a reminder of the auratic inner core of the spy-hero. 'There was a trick in his gait, not to be orientalised, which made policemen salute gravely as he passed disguised . . . and there was ignorance of some one or other of the million shibboleths which divide men from one another in India.'[35] In the Mutiny novel, the '*double* vision' – which in Bhabha's reckoning discloses 'the ambivalence of colonial discourse' and 'disrupts its authority' – actually shores up the authority of the imperial state by disrupting the counter-mimetic agenda of the rebel.[36]

IMAGINING RESISTANCE

The cusp between British information and Indian knowledge that Bayly draws attention to in *Empire and Information* is important for understanding the form of the Mutiny novel. The Anglo-Indian plots of these novels underscore the social and cultural affiliations of the officer ranks, and are usually concerned with love, marriage, domesticity and official life. Rendered through the invented tradition of chivalry, these concerns are homologous to visions of India as representing Britain's past. Such traditions and visions grow meaningful when read in the light of the Company's evolution from a trading venture into an imperial state, for it is in the evolution of a polity with its institutions, its practices of knowledge, representation and coercion that the settlement patterns, the census and ethnographic surveys, as well as the literary idioms of Anglo-India may be brought together as collateral phenomena. Embodying an evolution that renders the British émigré more distant from an immediate India than from a distant metropolis, and of which creole separatism forms no part, the Anglo-Indian social world of the Mutiny novel is generally insular and premised on insuperable differences from indigenous life and society.[37]

Reinforced through the obliqueness of living *by*, these locations, interests and their characteristic fictional idiom are interrupted by the plot of the rebellion. In *The Wife and the Ward* the interruption is quite literal, in as much as the Satichaura Ghat massacre of 27 June abruptly terminates the Anglo-Indian plot of love, marriage and domesticity, where heroism is reactive and the rebel world beyond the Kanpur entrenchment is absent except though its effects. However, the novels published from the 1870s, especially the Anglo-Indian novels, show the presence of two additional aspects: a dense representation of India and the rebellion and, a proactive heroism. Thus, in Taylor's *Seeta* (1872) and Sterndale's *Afghan Knife* (1879), the *thagi-dacaiti* axis and the *wahabi* movement of pan-Islamic reform are respectively among the factors that contribute to the rebellion, and in the latter a number of pages are given over to political and theological debates within the Muslim community in Sasaram, a town in modern-day Bihar. Such representations of the rebellion are clearly less constricted than *The Wife and the Ward* or the metropolitan boys' novel, and they adumbrate the trajectory of future novels where the heroes will at once mediate the representation of the indigenous society and subvert rebel autonomy. At any rate, in turning to represent the rebel, the rebellion and the social world in which these are located the novels venture into the orientalism by which the Anglo-Indian plot is 'surrounded' to live *in* the world of the indigene. These ventures have, of course, variant cultural and ideological bearings in novels such as *Mariam* and *On the Face of the Waters*; yet, on the whole, the journey traverses the breach between British intelligence and indigenous knowledge, between the Anglo-Indian plot and the plot of the rebellion, between, in other words, the Arnold–Oakfield and the Hockley–Taylor templates.

Just as the *Confessions of a Thug* and *The Memoirs of a Brahmin* had surveyed the lands and the peoples of the newly conquered western and central India and thus uncovered an insidious underworld, so too in the Mutiny novel of the 1870s and thereafter, the representation of the rebellion produces a survey of lands, peoples and polities. Again, as the former novels are contemporary with the histories and ethnography by John Malcolm,

Grant Duff and James Tod, with the criminological narratives of William Sleeman[38] and the making of the Anti-Thagi and Dacaity Department, so too the emerging trend in the Mutiny novels is simultaneous with forensic and judicial accounts of the rebellion, with classifications of the subject population through census surveys and caste categories, with the controversy over the *wahabi* movement of Islamic reform, the border wars on the north-east and the north-west and, from the late 1880s, with organised nationalism.[39] At the same time, underlying these discoveries of a restive underworld and the emerging methods of containment and surveillance there lies another resemblance.

As suggested in chapter 2, the orientalist tenor of *Confessions* has a different import from that of *The Missionary*. The historical mode and antiquarian underpinnings of the latter novel yield a sublimely spiritual Hinduism – located and preserved in the timeless fixities of caste, in wondrous cave-temples, in Sanskrit incantations, religious rituals and in the metonymic person of Luxima – that draws rather heavily on the orientalist constructions of Hinduism and Islam. However, in *Confessions of a Thug* and *The Memoirs of a Brahmin*, the journey into contemporary India retains yet transfigures the typical emphases of high orientalism. The combination of religion, poetry, caste, priests, rituals and temple architecture which together produced the hermetic and edifying text of the orientalist translator-interpreter, is now placed under new interpretative demands, and in *Confessions* yields a Benthamite panopticon from where the frame-narrator observes, records and translates the testimony of his informer. Again, while Hilarion fails to convert Luxima and himself goes native in *The Missionary*, in *Pandurang Hari* and *The Memoirs of a Brahmin* the native narrator-autobiographer not only permits access to the indigenous world but willingly reconstitutes himself in the image of his Christian-European master.

These continuities and discontinuities of the orientalist text are central to the representation of the rebellion in the Mutiny novel. Retaining, yet transfiguring, the language, the vista and the habitual tropes of an embedded orientalism, the narrative journey from Anglo-India to India is commissioned with demands for knowledge that will feed administrative demands, and that are marked by post-orientalist annotations of disorder, resistance, opacity and hypostasis. This transformation is vividly demonstrated in G. P. Raines's *Terrible Times* (1899) where, in a promontory scene that prefigures the view of Chandrapur from the civil station in the first pages of *A Passage to India* (1924), the narrator remarks that viewed from the cantonment, the city of Churzabad:

had the appearance of a city out of *Arabian Nights*, with its white buildings gleaming in the sunshine, and the gilded dome and minarets of the principal temple glittering like gold; but on closer inspection the romantic mind was apt to receive a shock, for the streets were narrow and evil-smelling, and the houses were for the most part decidedly tumble-down in appearance.[40]

Such revisions and reversals of Romantic orientalism (and of the genre of the 'oriental tale', here suggested by the *Arabian Nights*) usually occur when the narrative progresses from the distance of the civil station or the cantonment to a closer reckoning with the Indian urban space. Thus, in Talbott Mundy's *Rung Ho!* (1914), the bazaar in the fictional town of Howrah presents a medley of '[D]in, glamour, stink, incessant movement, interblended poverty and riches', and leads the narrator to reflect on the 'many peopled India' that 'surged . . . changeable and unexplainable – in ever-moving flux, but more conservative in spite of it than the very rocks she stands on'.[41]

The series of oppositions in this description of the bazaar – of flux and stasis, of the visible and the opaque – are, of course, common to other genres such as historiography and travel writing. Yet in this instance the medley of images constitutes the bazaar as the site of the ferment that precedes the rebellion in the kingdom of Howrah. Similarly in *Red Revenge*, a Kanpur officer claims before the rebellion breaks out that bazaars are the 'hotbeds of lies and intrigue . . . [and] it would be all the better for our English rule if they could be stamped out'; a wish that is complicated by the remark that 'he [the officer] might well have demanded the stamping out of the religions of the natives as the stamping out of their bazaars'.[42] As this progress of observations, reflections and security assessments (taken from three novels published between 1899 and 1914) shows, the line of continuity or contiguity between the Indian city, the bazaar, political unrest and religion is clear. However, behind the relative visibility of the bazaar are other, more secret, locations of unrest and resistance: the temple, the mosque, the palace and the brothel.

Rung Ho!, a novel published at a time when organised nationalism had turned to terrorism, provides a good example of the link between religion and political subversion. Whereas the Muslims of Howrah are loyal to the British, a temple in the capital is at the centre of the rebellion; and '[T]he sepoys were the instruments of the . . . priests and others who were feeding nothing but their own ambition.' With their religious authority, which makes the priests influential as organisers of public opinion and 'pastmasters of the art by which superstitious ignorance is swayed' they 'could swing the allegiance of the mob whichever way they chose'.[43] Beyond its political charge, the temple of Siva is also the site of *sati* and bizarre but unnamed rituals, against which the missionary, Duncan Maclean, and his daughter Rosemary rail. Thus, 'each month when the full moon rose above the carved dome of Siva's temple there was a ceremony . . . that commemorated cruelty, greed, poisoning, throat-slitting, hate, and all the hell-invented infamy that suckles . . . at the breast of the stagnant treasure'.[44]

While Hinduism and the Brahmins are the source of resistance in *Rung Ho!* as in Reid's *Masque of the Mutiny*, Islam is the antagonist in other novels. *The Afghan Knife* by R. A. Sterndale was published soon after the beginning of Britain's second war (1878–80) with Afghanistan, and echoes the debate between Hunter and Syed Ahmad Khan on Indian Muslims. At the very outset is an essay on the *wahabi* movement prefaced by the remark that the *wahabi* is known to the British administration in India as 'a fanatic, a rebel, a sort of Mahomedan Fenian, one whom the police should take under special surveillance'.[45] Like a good many *maulvis* and *fakirs* who stride through the novels spreading unrest, the *maulvi* Mahboob Ali, a veteran of many skirmishes with the British on the Frontier and an earnest *mujahid*, arrives in the town of Sasaram preaching rebellion among the Muslim gentry, and 'there was no one more ready to spring to the defence of the Holy Standard than' him.[46] However, it is in *Mariam* that the religious background to the rebellion and its implications are spelled out. The *maulvi*, Sarfaraz Ali, visits Shahjahanpur in May 1857 and, at a meeting attended by Hindus, Muslims, Company soldiers and the town gentry, speaks to his audience about the abuses and expropriations that have resulted under British administration and of the threats that the government poses to caste and religion. In the following chapter (chapter 4), a Hindu mendicant, Trilokinath Baba, similarly meets with the would-be rebels of the town; and, while the *maulvi* has helped to voice a general apprehension, the Baba comes from Meerut bringing news of the outbreak in that town. A little later the Hindu and the Muslim troops visit the *fakir*, Rasul Shah, a mystic who lives on the outskirts of Shahjahanpur, to ask him if they should rebel or not, a question that Rasul Shah answers with a politic silence.

These conclaves at which Hindus, Muslims, soldiers and civilians of Shahjahanpur confer about a rebellion that has already begun in other parts of north India, and whereby they evolve a local plan of action and reflect on a post-rebellion, post-British future, are often to be found in the Mutiny novels. In representing this public debate in Indian society, but without the sneering sarcasm of Flora Annie Steel, or the ranting of most boys' novels, *Mariam* also sets up an interpretative frame through which to view the rebellion. Concerned about the putative threats to their caste and faith, seeking the counsel of clerics, mendicants and mystics, and wavering between omens, oneiric prompting and prophesies, the indigene/rebel is in the midst of a culture where political choices and actions are overdetermined by religion and religious sectarianism. The events that follow from this initial condition, the massacre of the British and the often fractious self-government of Shahjahanpur in the months following the uprising, are thus already placed under the long shadow of an ethnography that locates the rebellion in Indian pre-modernity. And out of *Mariam*'s dense representation of the debate preceding the outbreak emerges an internally coherent cultural world where indigenous social organisation, belief-systems, rebel ideology, the conduct of the rebellion and its eventual failure are so many harmonious and mutually explanatory elements that explain, as does *The Missionary–Luxima* texts, the culture that produces and informs the rebellion.

This, in a sense, is also the aetiology that *The Sepoy War* had advanced. Kaye's defence of a political view that stressed the need for continuity rather than breach with Hindu and Muslim past and present, his new-found veneration for the Hindu law of inheritance, for *talukdar*s and deposed monarchs and his view that the *sipahi*'s loyalty to his social and cultural world was far stronger than his loyalty to the Company suggest, in sum, the contours of a world forever outside European history and modernity, a view Kaye shares with the post-rebellion conservatism in British policy on India.

But in identifying the 'Progress of Englishism' as the reason for the revolt, these narratives of the *mentalité* of a changeless orient are also riddled with post-orientalist annotations. The annotations appear when the novels pause over the body, the lifestyle, the polity and the architecture of the native. In *Red Revenge*, Dick Heron the griffin is much in love with the Nana Sahib's court dancer, Adala, though her maid, Hooseini Khanum, who visits Dick in his bungalow and escorts him to a secret assignation with Adala, is more fascinating to the narrator. With lips that 'were like those of the Hindoo god Siva . . . implacable, relentless, blood-thirsty', Hooseini commands Dick to follow her, and so he does, enchanted by the 'liquid voice, the large mystic eyes, the supple body, swathed in the picturesque one garment which the Eastern woman winds about her . . . a combination of allurements difficult to withstand'. And while Hooseini's 'scarlet mouth and . . . teeth', were 'repulsive and suggestive of savagery' they yet 'had their influence in accentuating and imparting piquancy to her charms'.[47] Led by her into the Nana's palace near Kanpur where Adala waits – along with the Nana and his adviser Azimullah – to make him an ally in the rebellion, Dick is fed sweets laced with an opiate. As he waits for Adala's entry, and as the hallucinations begin, Dick remembers the stories he has heard of the Nana's 'mysterious den of infamy', and notices paintings on the walls of the chamber that depict the 'foulness of a depraved Oriental imagination'.[48] The ambivalent response to the body and the decor extends to the representation of urban space. Later in the novel Dick's brother, Phillip Heron, a veteran of the Crimea, marches up-country to the rescue of the Kanpur and the Lucknow garrisons, and passing by Benaras, one of the centres of early orientalist research in law, language and philosophy, he 'could not help being impressed by the picturesqueness, the wealth of glowing colour, the teeming life' in the city. At the same time, the sight of a native population, 'most hideous and repulsive', offsets these attractions.[49]

In *Eight Days*, a novel that claims to be based in Delhi, though the ambience of the court suggests Lucknow before the annexation of Awadh, the urban landscape and architecture prompt the construction of a historical teleology embedded in the topology of these spaces and buildings. As the Nawab of Khizrabad flies a kite from the ramparts of the Delhi fort, an amusement that is meant to indicate the trivial engagements of the Indian ruling class, the narrator surveys a vista where the picturesque orient appears in a new topology:

Beneath him lies the grand city founded by his [the Nawab's] ancestors. There are the encircling battlements which gave it their power and importance. There is the lofty mosque, with its beautiful soaring minarets. Behind him are exquisite public halls and private chambers of the magnificent palace-fortress . . . in which they had lived for so long and with such splendour. And there, right before him, stands forth clear against the evening sky the Flagstaff Tower on the ridge, from which floats forth the . . . ensign of the . . . foreign power that holds him and his kingdom in thrall.[50]

The decline of the royal house of Khizrabad and its 'licentious Court', which the narrator had earlier described in terms that recall Kaye's account of the Nawabs of Awadh, is itself part of a Whig version of Indian history, in which the 'Christian took the place of the Mahomedan . . . Malcolms and Munros of Saadut Alis and Bahadur Khans; the East India Company of the Great Mogul';[51] so that the 'ensign' of the 'foreign power' contains the fascination and circumscribes the power of a 'grand city' that was the *de jure* lord and master of the Company until 1858. So it was with the narrator's fascinated observation of the Begum of Khizrabad, the prime mover of the rebellion in *Eight Days*. Standing on a palace balcony 'with its tapering marble columns profusely adorned with inlaid work, and its exquisitely pierced marble panels', the Begum, 'with her lovely face and exquisite figure . . . would have made a charming picture'. Yet the model, 'so fair without' and 'most foul within', mars the portraiture which otherwise turns upon the idiom of the Mughal or the Rajput schools of painting. If 'she resembled the Empress Theodosia, as depicted in the pages of Gibbon, closely in face and figure, so did she in dissoluteness, in the prodigality and promiscuousness of her favours. She was cruel, cunning, lascivious, vindictive, avaricious.'[52]

As Metcalf notes in *An Imperial Vision*, unlike the paintings of Indian vistas and buildings by William Hodges and Thomas Daniell which brought to England an 'architecture of wonder, sustaining a "picturesque" vision', and which offered, along with the national gothic, an alternative to the classical orders, Indian architecture after 1860 'provided only elements for an architecture of empire within India'.[53] While British use of what came to be known as the Indo-Saracenic style was, Metcalf argues in *An Imperial Vision*, part of the conservative revision that discovers and reifies a traditional India in the wake of the rebellion,[54] in the novels, the representation of Hindu and Islamic architecture and iconography at once reveals and revises the text of the oriental picturesque. As the iconic sign and also the living space of a people who had chosen to rebel and so refused the project of European modernity, collections of buildings such as those in the Delhi fort or the royal buildings at Lucknow signify, not nostalgia or the aesthetic of ruins (as in the broken towers and battlements of Thomas Daniell's the *West Gate of Firoz Shah's Cotillah, Delhi*) but resistance, disorder, hypostasis and irrationality.[55] No longer the models for a Senzicote or a Royal Pavilion, the 'oriental splendour', the 'dream-like vistas of domes, cupolas and arches' and the 'romance and mystery' of urban Delhi conceal a simmering discontent, as soldiers and courtiers confer with messengers from Meerut, and where the 'fiery words' and the 'savage eloquence' of yet another *maulvi* gives voice to anti-colonial resistance. To that extent, the temple in *Rung Ho!*, the chambers of *Red Revenge* and the palaces in other novels are the sites of threatening opacity that underlies the visibly picturesque, and where, as in Rudyard Kipling's description of the sixteenth century Amber fort in Rajasthan, the 'cramped and darkened rooms, the narrow smooth-walled passages with recesses where a man might wait for his enemy unseen, the maze of ascending and descending stairs leading nowhither, the ever-present screens of marble tracery that may hide or reveal so much, – all these things breathe of plot and counter-plot, league and intrigue'.[56]

The equivalence between a tortuous and opaque architectural form and indigenous life and politics is also evident in *On the Face of the Waters*.

In Book two, chapter one, where the novel turns to the events in the Mughal palace at Delhi in the weeks leading up to the rebellion, the narrator ends a detailed description of the architectural layout with the remark that 'the palace-fort – shut in from all outside influence – was like some tepid, teeming breeding-place for strange forms of life unknown to purer, clearer, atmospheres'.[57] A 'native' chapter without any British presence, it is here that the novel first enters the world of the rebel-indigene and transcribes the everydayness of a people and a polity that was the epicentre of the rebellion. However, the result of this transcription is a series of parodies. The Mughal courtiers mock and jeer at the Emperor, the Empress, Zeenat Mahal, hates him and has personal ambitions, while a toy lizard frightens the Emperor, an effete poetaster. Moreover, Mughal apparel, forms of address, political conduct and even Urdu poetry are variously derided and dismissed as the elements of a culture that had dared to replace British rule. As a demonstrative exercise, the narrative journey into the 'teeming breeding-place' at the apex of the old political order discloses the culture from which the rebellion sprang, and explains the causes of its eventual failure.

The comic cast and moral failures of Mughal court and society that Steel's novel is so keen to emphasise (hardly redeemed by the Princess Newasi, who reads English newspapers and *The Mirror of Good Behaviour*[58]) have, however, another significance. 'Shut in from all outside influence', the palace and the court at Delhi are configured as an endogamic world, an anthropological curiosity suggesting a state of perennial hypostasis, in a manner that recalls the self-enclosed essences of caste, tribe and occupation in the 'biological' ethnography of H. H. Risley.[59] The representation of the Mughal court and royal family functions as a 'para-ethnography' – a term that Christopher Pinney borrows from James Clifford and applies to the Company paintings of Indian occupational groups, and to Kaye and Watson's photographic collection, *The Peoples of India*[60] – that demonstrates the deficiencies of the indigenous ruling elite, and solicits a view of a culture that is irrational, static and morally flawed, a culture that is everything that an evangelical, imperial, industrial and Whig Britain is not. Preparatory to the rebellion, and unmediated by British spies, tourists or administrators, or by native informants and collaborators, the narrative that strides into and transcribes the life, manners and habitat of the rebel soldiers or of the traditional ruling elite such as the Nana Sahib, Wajid Ali Shah or the Mughal royalty in Delhi is the fictional counterpart of what Bernard Cohn describes as the 'museological modality' of colonial knowledge.[61] Anticipating the 'participant observation' of twentieth-century social anthropology, the visceral fieldwork of

On the Face of the Waters in the Red Fort at Delhi recalls accounts by many British officers, wives and journalists who went to see the imprisoned 'King of Delhi' after the capture of the city.[62] And if Steel's novel – drawing on the tendentious and *post-hoc* resources of the victor-as-tourist – enters and annotates the Mughal museum before it turns into a forensic exhibit in the aftermath of the rebellion, in the diary-travelogue of the *Times* correspondent, William Russell, the now imprisoned and frail person of Bahadur Shah 'Zafar' provokes a last, musing annotation of the figure of the oriental despot and the imagination that required and sustained such figures:

> In a dingy, dark passage, leading from the open court or terrace in which we stood to a darker room beyond, there sat, crouched on his haunches, a diminutive attenuated old man, dressed in an ordinary and rather dirty muslin tunic, his small lean feet bare, his head covered by a small thin cambric skull-cap . . . That dim-wandering-eyed, dreamy old man . . . was he, indeed, one who had fomented the most gigantic mutiny in the history of the world, and who, from the walls of his ancient palace, had hurled defiance and shot ridicule upon the race that held every throne in India in the hollow of their palms?

Thus, an incredulous, and anti-climactic valediction lays to rest an artefactual history: from the Elizabethan Akbar and Dryden's *Aurangzebe*, through the baroque 'Grosso Mogul' Concerto in D Major (1711) by Vivaldi, to Russell's last 'descendant of Timour the Tartar', old, ill and 'retching violently' before swarms of gawking British tourists, and soon to be exiled to die in Burma.[63]

As suggested earlier, the unmaking or, at least, the containment of the oriental picturesque parallels the transformation of the British in India from poacher to gamekeeper. If the final defeat of the Maratha states in 1817–18, the Charter Act of 1833 and the conquests of Sind and the Punjab in the 1840s are among the important stages in this transformation, they are also accompanied by policies of intervention and programmes of acculturation predicated upon, and productive of, new interpretations of Indian past and present. While these are recorded in a complementary transformation of the creole merchant-factor and 'nabob' into the officer-administrator, the obverse of these mutations is evident in the uses of the Hockley–Taylor template. Always evolving as a form of ethnography, and activated whenever historical, fictional or travel narratives venture outside the garrison society, it is this template with its characteristic interest in 'fieldwork' that informs (anachronistically speaking) *The Missionary*, or the even earlier *Adventures of a Rupee* (1782), the novels by Hockley, *Confessions of a Thug* and the

Mutiny novels, as they turn to represent the world from which the rebellion sprang.[64]

Sati, *fakirs* and *maulvis*, temples, palaces and mosques, boat-rides on the Ganges, the pageantry of the court, the bazaar or the highway, bizarre rituals, picturesque vistas, eternal villages and sublime transports are among the commonplaces that the fieldwork of narrative seeks out and finds; and these topoi and icons are the registers of a discourse on indigenous society, culture and history that stretches from *The Missionary* to *Masque of the Mutiny*. To read these registers in the history of the Anglo-Indian novel as the coeval of a political and administrative history is useful in as much as it shows an underlying ethnographic practice. For the peculiar location of Anglo-Indian fiction, as of the Company and the later British state in India – between cultures, polities and languages that were separated by the asymmetries of power, location and translation – calls forth, in each literary, painterly, military and administrative venture outside the garrison society, a fieldwork that in engaging with the indigenous world necessarily occupies the 'cusp between British intelligence and Indian knowledge'.

In tilling the same field, these engagements, however, develop new, mutant strains of a familiar crop; and though the attention to religion and caste are the constants of the ethnographic mode, the progress of this mode through the nineteenth century also shows changing needs and emphases. While in late eighteenth- and early nineteenth-century orientalist scholarship, religion and especially Hinduism functions as a site of sublime reflection, of speculative historical modelling and a degree of cultural relativism, there emerges from the *The Missionary* the conflation of religion with political resistance, moral deformity and physical infection. The text of Owenson's novel displaces (and so exonerates) Indian resistance to Portuguese Goa in the seventeenth century; yet the footnote that explains the Vellore uprising of 1806 as an instance of 'the religious bigotry of the natives'[65] anticipates the fundamental and enduring fear of the novels of Hockley and Taylor and of the Mutiny novels examined so far. Modified and inflected by new needs, creeds, self-images and institutions, by the Vellore uprising of 1806, by *thagi*, the *wahabi* movement, the rebellion, by the discovery of 'criminal tribes' and the emergence of organised and sometimes violent nationalism in the last four decades of empire, the picturesque persists even as its subject and inspiration turns restive and insurgent.

The journey from Anglo-India to India is thus one of recapitulation and revision; and, exploiting the commonplaces of orientalism and the picturesque, the Mutiny novel recasts them as the signs of political threat, disorder and resistance. As a museological exercise that devotes itself to collecting, encasing and annotating specimens of indigenous polity, life, manners, customs, the Hockley–Taylor template of these novels provides a series of moral, cultural and historical evaluations that explain the events of 1857–9, and in so doing explain India. Like the ethnographic mode that informs travelogues, historiography, forensics, orientalist research, administrative decisions, caste and census-surveys, the Mutiny novels too embody a project of colonial knowledge. The 'underworld of India' – to borrow the phrase from the title of a collection of anecdotes by George MacMunn[66] – that the Mutiny novels bring to view is, of course, based upon many simplifications, much contempt, ignorance and an inability to comprehend that 'in an Asiatic race there might be a spirit of independence and a love of country, the manifestations of which were honourable in themselves, however inconvenient' to empire.[67] Yet, in all essentials, the act of imagining resistance that sends Jim Douglas into the Delhi palace in *On the Face of the Waters*, serves the same end as a 1888 government directive demanding 'a watchful control over the movements of the criminal classes, over the conditions that predispose to crime, and over important political, religious and other movements throughout Empire'.[68]

Epilogue

In *The New Zealand Wars and the Victorian Interpretation of Racial Conflict*, James Belich makes an observation that is relevant to the ways in which the rebellion was received and circulated in British opinion for, at least, ninety years. On the internal coherence of the network of meanings through which settler and metropolitan opinion perceived the war against the indigenous peoples of New Zealand between 1845 and 1872, Belich writes that the

> dominant interpretation [of the Maori war] can be understood as a system and as a framework. It was not systematic in the sense of an artifice or conspiracy; there was no collective and methodical censorship, no conscious plot to deceive. But it was systematic in the sense that it operated according to a discernible pattern which, broadly speaking, remained constant from case to case. It was also systematic in the sense that its component parts formed an integrated whole.[1]

A similar 'dominant interpretation' is visible in the case of British writing on the rebellion, too; and this book has primarily attended to the network of plots, redactions, myths, politics and cultures that contributed to and sustained the British view of the events between 1857 and 1859. Precisely for that reason, this study has not addressed the substantial body of Indian writing on the rebellion; for to have done so would have required another methodology and distracted from the reconstruction of the dominant.

There were, however, a few dissident British voices that questioned the dominant interpretation, challenged its premises and suggested other interpretations. Among the earliest of these was Edward Leckey's *Fictions Connected with the Indian Mutiny* (1859), a slim volume where close textual analysis revealed how many putatively 'eye-witness accounts' were riddled with contradictions, half-truths and untruths.[2] Leckey's scepticism was largely ignored then and in subsequent years, and it is a forgotten and obscure volume; a penalty, perhaps, for transgressing what Belich calls the 'framework'.

Another significant dissenter was Edward J. Thompson, the historian, translator, novelist and once a Wesleyan missionary, who spent some twenty-five years in Bengal, and later went to Oxford as Professor of Bengali. Thompson's critique of the dominant interpretation was in his polemical essay, *The Other Side of the Medal* (1925), which questioned the tendentious cast of British historiography and popular fiction, and concluded that it was the 'shadow of the Mutiny', exaggerated by British writing, which had embittered relations between Indians and the British. Writing in 1925, with the memory of Jallianwalla Bagh fresh in his mind, and stricken by a liberal guilt, *The Other Side of the Medal* called for and offered an act of 'atonement' (using also its Sanskrit equivalent: *prayaschitta*), by means of which the 'unavenged and unappeased ghost' of the rebellion could at last be laid to rest.[3]

However, three years before Thompson, and thirteen years after V. D. Savarkar's *The Indian War of Independence*, there appeared another essay that is by far the most radically dissenting interpretation of the rebellion, and of the constitutional questions that the use of terms such as 'rebellion' or 'mutiny' raised. This was F. W. Buckler's essay, 'The Political Theory of the Indian Mutiny'.[4] Combining religious and constitutional history with a rigour that is not distracted by realpolitik, Buckler's case is brilliantly simple. In what follows, I shall cite him extensively to show how, from the perspective that Buckler develops, the dominant interpretation that this study has so far attended to was not merely tendentious but, arguably, a lie.

The essay begins with an excursus into the Company's history through the nineteenth century, and its dual obligation: to Parliament in Britain, and to the Mughal Emperor in Delhi. If the Company's charter to trade derived from Parliament and the Crown, its authority before Indian subjects flowed from the person of the Emperor. At this point, as at several key points in his argument, Buckler closely reads certain Persian and Arabic words and phrases and metaphors to show how the Company misrepresented itself before the Mughal Emperor and before Home opinion. Aided by a propaganda machine run by its historians and publicists, the Company 'evolved a fictitious history of India, until, in the first half of the nineteenth century, side by side there existed a politically effective Empire with an accepted history of its non-existence'.[5]

At the same time, and notwithstanding its self-representation in Britain as a merchant company with territorial powers that was subordinate only to Parliament, Buckler demonstrated how, in fact, the Company's 'authority in India lay, not in the charters of the King of England, nor in the Acts of the British Parliament, not in the sword, but in the *farmans* of the Mughal

Emperor', whose vassal the Company claimed to be in its dealings with the Mughal court and with other territorial powers of the land. Yet, if the Company was the Emperor's agent in India, collecting revenue, rendering tributes and accepting robes of honour from the Emperor, in Britain the Company excised that role, and represented itself as the protector of the 'pensioner' 'King of Delhi' on behalf of the people of Britain. Given the constitutional and symbolic subservience of the Company before Mughal authority, all the 'censure and opprobrium' the Company 'levelled against him [the Emperor, Bahadur Shah II] recoils on the Company, his disloyal vassal, since his difficulties arose mainly from its intrigues and from the fact that after 1772, the Company withheld and converted to its own use, the revenues of the richest provinces of his Empire'.[6]

Compounded by omissions of translating from Persian to English, and by the commissions of the Company's schizophrenia, successive governor-generals from Wellesley 'assumed an attitude and pursued a policy towards the Mughal Emperor which to him could appear in no other light than that of high treason; and the culmination was reached when Dalhousie and Canning attempted to tamper with the succession'.[7] Given the cleverly disguised and conveniently forgotten constitutional subordination to the Emperor, there was only one interpretation of the Company's growing insubordination: 'Hence if in 1857 there were any mutineer, it was the East India Company.'[8] Buttressing this political and constitutional history with a close reading of the *Proceedings of the Trial of the King of Delhi*, Buckler's point was that in 1857 the soldiers in the Company's employ, along with the Indian ecumene and the traditional elite, on seeing how the interloping Company had reneged against and betrayed the Emperor, turned upon the 'mutineer' Company on behalf of their true lord and master. In the light of this history, 'the use of the term "Mutiny" – unless wilful, to obscure the issue is conclusive evidence of the ignorance. Kaye alone of the historians of the outbreak seems to have understood its meaning, which he labours painfully but vainly to suppress.'[9] On the state of Delhi between May and September 1857 as recorded in the text of the trial Buckler observed that: 'Much is irrelevant. Cruelties, deaths, financial and other disorders are subordinate to the main issue. Temporary administrative chaos was inevitable when the officers of the great vassal had to flee from their posts. But there is little if any evidence to show that recovery was impossible had the outbreak been successful.'[10]

Notes

INTRODUCTION

1. [Hilda Gregg], 'The Indian Mutiny in Fiction', *Blackwood's Edinburgh Magazine* (February 1897), 218.
2. See Phillip Bobbitt, *The Shield of Achilles: War, Peace, and the Course of History* (London, 2002).
3. A. P. Thornton, *The Imperial Idea and its Enemies* (London, 1959).
4. John Hobson, *The Psychology of Jingoism* (London, 1902).
5. [Gregg], 'The Indian Mutiny in Fiction', 230.
6. Grant later wrote another Mutiny romance, 'Fairer than a Fairy', serialised in *Tinsley's Magazine* in 1874.
7. The first novel of these is *Tara* (Leipzig, 1864), a novel on Maratha history set in the year 1657, and the second, *Ralph Darnell* (Edinburgh, 1865) is on the adventures of Robert Clive in 1757.
8. 'The Romance of Indian Warfare', *North British Review*, 12 (1849), 193–224. Also relevant here is Kaye's essay on 'Military Life and Adventures in the East', *Calcutta Review*, 8 (1847), 195–230.
9. 'Novels of Adventure and Manners' (1894), in Alfred C. Lyall, *Studies in Literature and History* (London, 1915). Also see T. R. Moreman, *The Army in India and the Development of Frontier Warfare, 1849–1947* (Basingstoke, 1998), chapter 5.
10. Franz Fanon, *Black Skin, White Masks*, tr. Charles Lam Markmann (New York, 1967), and *The Wretched of the Earth*, tr. Constance Farrington (London, 1961). Other anticipations, and perhaps influences, on *Orientalism* include K. M. Pannikar's *Asia and Western Dominance* (New York, 1969), and Anwar Abdel Malik, *Orientalism in Crisis* (London, 1963) and Talal Asad, *Anthropology and the Colonial Encounter* (Ithaca, 1973).
11. Nicholas Dirks, ed., *Colonialism and Culture* (Ann Arbor, 1992), 3.
12. Bernard Cohn, 'The Transformation of Objects into Artifacts, Antiquities, and Art in Nineteenth-Century India' (1982) and 'The Command of Language and the Language of Command' (1985); reprinted in Cohn, *Colonialism and its Forms of Knowledge: The British in India* (New Delhi, 1997).
13. William Odie, 'Dickens and the Indian Mutiny', *The Dickensian*, 68.366 (1972), 3–15; Hyunji Park, '"The Story of our Lives": *The Moonstone* and the

Indian Mutiny in *All the Year Round*, and Laura Peters, '"Double-dyed Traitors and Infernal Villains": *Illustrated London News, Household Words*, Charles Dickens and the Indian Rebellion', in *Negotiating India in the Nineteenth-Century Media* (eds.) David Finkelstein and Douglas Peers (Basingstoke, 2000).

14. Though it must be said that Sara Suleri's *The Rhetoric of English India* (Chicago, 1992) begins with a fine reading of the text of Warren Hasting's impeachment trial.

15. See, for instance, Margaret F. Steig, 'Indian Romances: Tracts for the Times', *Journal of Popular Culture*, 18.4 (Spring 1985), 2–15; and David Finkenstein and Douglas M. Peers (eds.), *Negotiating India in the Nineteenth-Century Media* (Basingstoke, 2000).

16. Karl Marx, 'The Future Results of British Rule in India', in *New York Daily Tribune*, no. 3840, 8 August 1853.

17. A. J. Youngson, *The Prince and the Pretender* (London, 1985).

I FROM CHRONICLE TO HISTORY

1. 'At the moment of my writing (29th June), although the whole province of Oudh has risen against him [Henry Lawrence, the commissioner of the newly-annexed kingdom of Awadh] . . . he with a handful of Europeans, holds Lucknow, the most disaffected city in India!' [G. B. Malleson], *The Mutiny of the Bengal Army: A Historical Narrative by One Who Has Served Under Sir Charles Napier* (London, 1858), part 1, 30.

2. Charles Ball, *History of the Indian Mutiny Giving a Detailed Account of the Sepoy Insurrection in India and a Concise History of the Great Military Events Which Have Tended to Consolidate British Empire in India*, 2 vols. (London, c. 1859); *Chambers History of the Indian Revolt and of the Expeditions to Persia, China and Japan, 1856–7–8. With Map, Plans and Wood Engravings* (London, 1859); E. H. Nolan, *Illustrated History of the British Empire in India and the East, from the Earliest Times to the Suppression of the Sepoy Mutiny in 1859*, 2 vols. (London, 1858–60); and Robert Montgomery Martin, *The Indian Empire with a Full Account of the Mutiny of the Bengal Army*, 3 vols. (London, 1858–61).

3. Revd John Cave-Brown, *The Punjab and Delhi in 1857*, 2 vols. (London, 1861), vol. 1, viii, ix.

4. Rosemary Seton, *The Indian 'Mutiny' 1857–58: A Guide to Source Material in the India Office Library and Records* (London, 1986), xii.

5. *Trial of Muhammad Bahadur Shah, Titular King of Delhi, and of Mogul Beg, and Hajee, all of Delhi, for Rebellion Against the British Government, and Murder of Europeans during 1857* (n.p. 1870). For district accounts see *Narrative of Events Attending the Outbreak of Disturbances and the Restoration of Authority in all the Districts of the North-West Provinces in 1857–8* (Calcutta, n.d.), and G. W. Forrest, *The Indian Mutiny: Selections from the Letters, Despatches and Other State Papers Preserved in the Military Department of the Government of India, 1857–1858*, 4 vols. (Calcutta, 1893–1912).

6. Martin, *The Indian Empire*, vol. II, 124.

7. Herbert Butterfield, *The Whig Interpretation of History* (New York, 1965). Northrop Frye makes a similar but more tropologically sensitive point when he detects in nineteenth-century historiography the presence of certain 'comic myths of progress through evolution or revolution'. See 'New Directions from Old', in Henry A. Murray (ed.), *Myth and Mythmaking* (Boston, 1960), 117. For an interesting gloss on the tropological classification of historical narratives by Frye and others see Hayden White, *Tropics of Discourse* (Baltimore, 1978), 51–80.

8. Nolan, *Illustrated History*, vol. I, Introduction, vi, xii.

9. Ball, *History of the Indian Mutiny*, vol. II, 644.

10. See S. B. Chaudhuri, *Civil Disturbances During British Rule in India, 1765–1857* (Calcutta, 1955), and Ranajit Guha, *Elementary Aspects of Peasant Insurgency in Colonial India* (New Delhi, 1983) for studies of popular and other forms of resistance during the colonial period.

11. 'The Indian Crisis of 1857', *Calcutta Review* (December 1857), 377.

12. As T. R. Holmes claimed in his *History of the Indian Mutiny* (1883 5th edn London, 1898): 'just as a general mutiny of the London police would be followed by a violent outburst of crime on the part of the London thieves and rough, so the talukdars, and the dispossessed landholders, the Gujars, and the budmashees of India welcomed the first signs of governmental weakness as a signal for gratifying their selfish interests'.

13. Charles Raikes, *Notes on the Revolt in the North-Western Provinces of India* (London, 1858), 156.

14. *Chambers History*, 14, 538.

15. [Malleson], *The Mutiny of the Bengal Army*, Part II, 53.

16. *Ibid.*, Part II, 27, 28.

17. Ball, *History of the Indian Mutiny*, Introduction, vol. I, 1.

18. Martin, *The Indian Empire*, Introduction, vol. I, 1.

19. Cited in George Bennett (ed.), *The Concept of Empire from Burke to Attlee, 1774–1947* (London, 1953), 165.

20. 'The India Question: Its Present Aspects and Teachings', *Calcutta Review* (June 1858), 356. Similarly on 10 October 1857 *The Times* observed 'that an Indian question continued to be the "dinner-bell" of the House of Commons . . . until the massacres of Meerut and Cawnpore showed that the government of India' was at stake.

21. Martin, *The Indian Empire*, 5.

22. Ball, *History of the Indian Mutiny*, vol. I, 1.

23. John William Kaye, *The Administration of the East India Company* (London, 1853), 7.

24. James Mill, *History of British India*, 10 vols. (1817, rpt. London, 1997).

25. Martin, *The Indian Empire*, vol. I, 508.

26. Sent out by Parliament to reform the administration, Charles Cornwallis was Commander-in-Chief of the Company's army when Mysore under Tipu

Sultan was defeated in the Battle of Seringapatam (1791), and he instituted the Permanent Settlement of revenue and land ownership in Bengal in 1793.

27. Martin, *The Indian Empire*, vol. 1, 459.
28. Buchanan's first survey was published as *A Journey from Madras through the Countries of Mysore, Canara and Malabar* (London, 1807); a journey he undertook on government orders less than a decade after the defeat of Tipu Sultan. Buchanan's subsequent writing on the province of Bengal includes *An Account of the Districts of Bihar and Patna in 1811–12* (Patna, 1936). Among other early survey-histories are *Historical Sketches of South India in an Attempt to trace the History of Mysoor from the Origins of the Hindoo Government of the State to the Extinction of the Mohammedan Dynasty in 1799*, 3 vols. (London, 1810–17) by Mark Wilks; and, *A Geographical, Statistical and Historical Description of Hindostan and the Adjacent Colonies*, 2 vols. (London, *c.* 1820) by William Hamilton.
29. 'The term race was widely used in the late eighteenth and early nineteenth centuries, but its meaning was linguistic and cultural, rather than "ethnological" in the later Victorian sense, when notions of progressive evolution had emerged as a generalised theory of human racial "type".' Susan Bayly, 'Caste and "Race" in the Colonial Ethnography of India', in Peter Robb (ed.), *The Concept of Race in South Asia* (Delhi, 1997), 172.
30. Ball, *History of the Indian Mutiny*, vol. 1, 13. Also see Montstuart Elphinstone, *The History of India: Hindu and the Mahometan Periods* (London, 1841), for a similar insistence on the primacy of caste.
31. Cohn, *Colonialism and Its Forms of Knowledge*, 8.
32. Martin, *The Indian Empire*, vol. 1, 503.
33. *Ibid.*, vol. 1, 507. In the *Oriental Memoirs* James Forbes, who travelled extensively in western and central India between 1765–82, noted that differences between Hindu castes were so vast as to make them 'different nations', 4 vols. (London, 1813), vol. 1, 6.
34. See, for instance, J. Comaroff and J. Comaroff, *Ethnography and the Historical Imagination* (Oxford, 1992), and two excellent studies by George W. Stocking Jr., *Colonial Situations: Essays on the Contextualization of Ethnographic Knowledge* (Madison, 1991), and, *Victorian Anthropology* (New York, 1987).
35. Ball, *History of the Indian Mutiny*, vol. 1, 34.
36. Nolan, *Illustrated History*, Introduction, vol. 1, iii, ix.
37. *Chambers History*, Preface, iii.
38. Martin, *The Indian Empire*, vol. 1, 507.
39. George Birdwood's remark on Indian arts and crafts; cited in Thomas R. Metcalf, *Ideologies of the Raj* (Cambridge, 1997), 91.
40. *Ibid.*, 43.
41. *Ibid.*, 90.
42. See, for instance, John M. Mackenzie (ed.), *Propaganda and Empire* (Manchester, 1984); Chandrika Kaul, 'Imperial Communications, Fleet Street and the Indian Empire: *c.* 1850–1920', in Michael Bromley and Tom O'Malley (eds.),

A Journalism Reader (London, 1997); and David Finkelstein and Douglas Peers (eds.), *Negotiating India in the Nineteenth-Century Media* (Basingstoke, 2000).

43. Richard Altick, *The English Common Reader* (Chicago, 1957); and, Joanne Shattock and Michael Wolff (eds.), *The Victorian Periodical Press: Samplings and Soundings* (Leicester, 1982).

44. Linda Colley, *Britons: Forging the Nation, 1707–1837* (London, 1992), 371.

45. See, for example, the *Expansion of England* (London, 1883) by the Cambridge historian John Seeley, an important statement of the idea of a global federation of English-speaking people.

46. From Goldwin Smith, *The Empire* (1863), cited in Bennett, *The Concept of Empire*, 221, 222. Lord Russell, Speech in the House of Commons, 8 February 1850. *The Times*, 9 February 1850.

47. See Bernard Semmell, *The Governor Eyre Controversy* (London, 1962). The rebellion broke out at Morant Bay on 11 October 1865. On 13 October, Eyre suspended the government, imposed martial law, and in the course of the following month some 608 blacks were killed. In the summer of 1866 the 'Jamaica Committee' was formed with J. S. Mill as chairman, and filed criminal charges against Eyre. The trial dragged on for several years and Eyre was finally acquitted of all charges brought against him.

48. *The Times*, 15 February 1895.

49. Letter to Lord Rosebery (27 September 1897); cited in Bennett, *The Concept of Empire*, 309.

50. Ball, *History of the Indian Mutiny*, vol. II, 425.

51. Our tenure in India must . . . be a military one. If we do not hold it by the exercise of our arms, at least we do it by the impression of them . . . The most fearful of all disasters that we can dread, therefore, is disaffection among our native troops. When it does occur, and occur it will . . . it will be the work of some one bold, able man of themselves . . . Such a person has never yet appeared . . . but it would be a delusion for us to assume that no such person will appear . . . The event, if it ever do come, will be abrupt. It will be an explosion. It will give no warning, but will be upon us before there is time to arrest it. Sir Henry Russell, Chief Justice of the Bengal Presidency (1807–13), cited in Nolan, *Illustrated History*, vol. I, vii.

52. Cited in Martin, *The Indian Empire*, vol. II, 1.

53. For more on this controversial event see, S. N. Sen, *Eighteen Fifty-Seven* (Delhi, 1958). A popular British account of the massacre based on depositions of witnesses is George Otto Trevelyan's *Cawnpore* (London, 1865).

54. Martin, *The Indian Empire*, vol. II, 1.

55. Ball, *History of the Indian Mutiny*, vol. I, 607.

56. *The Times*, 2 November, 1857. The Earl had claimed that his source was a letter from 'the highest lady now in India', and the speech was soon published as a penny dreadful under the title, *The Earl of Shaftesbury's Great Speech on Indian Cruelties*. For the controversy surrounding the claim and its later retraction see Salahuddin Malik, 'Nineteenth-Century Approaches to the Indian "Mutiny"', *Journal of Asian History*, 7.2 (1973), 105.

57. Ball, *History of the Indian Mutiny*, vol. I, 97.

58. *Ibid.*, vol. I, 377.
59. *Ibid.*, vol. I, 252–3.
60. *Ibid.*, vol. II, 590.
61. Maxwell Gray [Mary Gleed Tuttiett], *In the Heart of the Storm: a Tale of Modern Chivalry*, 3 vols. (London, 1891), vol. I, 165–6.
62. Jenny Sharpe, *Allegories of Empire: Figure of the Woman in the Colonial Text* (Minneapolis, 1993), 67, 65–6; Nancy Paxton, 'Mobilizing Chivalry: Rape in British Indian Novels about the Indian Uprising of 1857', *Victorian Studies*, 36 (Fall 1992), 5–30.
63. Ball, *History of the Indian Mutiny*, vol. I, 298.
64. 'Our Future: Review of "The Oudh Proclamation" and "Mr. Beadon's Circular Letter"', *Calcutta Review* (June 1858), 437, 438.
65. Ball, *History of the Indian Mutiny*, vol. I, 645.
66. T. R. E. Holmes, *A History of the Indian Mutiny* (London, 1891), 109.
67. J. W. Kaye, *History of the Sepoy War in India, 1857–58*, 3 vols. (London, 1864–76), vol. II, 373.
68. William Coldstream (ed.), *Records of the Intelligence Department of the Government of the North-West Provinces of India during the Mutiny of 1857* (Edinburgh, 1902), vol. I, 369.
69. Ball, *History of the Indian Mutiny*, vol. I, 648.
70. *Ibid.*, vol. II, 168.
71. *Ibid.*, vol. II, 427. See Edward Leckey, *Fictions Connected with the Indian Outbreak of 1857 Exposed* (Bombay, 1859) for an indignant review of contemporary journalism and the reliability of its chief source, the 'eye-witness' account. Leckey singles out for special attention popular narratives such as the *Indian Rebellion* (Calcutta, 1858) by the Reverend Alexander Duff, and *The Sepoy Revolt, its Causes and Consequences* (London, 1858) by Henry Mead.
72. *The Times*, 10 October 1857.
73. Michael Edwardes (ed.), *My Indian Mutiny Diary* (1860; rpt. London, 1957), 162.
74. *Ibid.*, 45.
75. See Frederick Henry Cooper, *Crisis in the Punjab* (Lahore, 1858).
76. Ball, *History of the Indian Mutiny*, vol. II, 427; vol. I, 648.
77. Of the Calcutta Anglo-Indians Canning wrote:

> Men, soldiers, whose authority on matters relating to the Army and the Sepoys is readily credited, and whose words are caught up by Newspaper caterers, are spreading not reports only – in these they may have been deceived – but opinions as to present state of things present and future, which make me ashamed for Englishmen – and it is not the shame only, there is mischief in it . . . Canning to Robert Vernon Smith (President of the Board of Control), 20 May 1857; cited in Michael Maclagan, *'Clemency' Canning* (London, 1962), 86–7.

78. Among the most influential and articulate proclamations were those issued by the emperor at Delhi, by the Queen of Awadh, Begum Hazrat Mahal and the

Nana Saheb. See S. A. A. Rizvi and M. L. Bhargava (eds.), *Freedom Struggle in Uttar Pradesh*, 6 vols. (Lucknow, 1957–61), vol. 1.

79. Canning to Vernon Smith, 19 June 1857; cited in Maclagan, *'Clemency' Canning*, 103. In the same letter Canning added that: 'Such editors in such times as these and in this country need to be controlled whether they be European or Native.' *Ibid.*, 103.

80. Officially titled the 'Resolution of the Government of India, 31 July 1857', the full text of this communication to British troops and to the rebels is in *ibid.*, Appendix 11, 326.

81. *Ibid.*, 327.

82. *The Times*, 24 October 1857.

83. Drafted amid much debate and dogged by controversy, the 'Oudh Proclamation' of 14 March 1858 reflects the controversy surrounding the annexation of Awadh and the difficulty of ascertaining the causes of the rebellion, and signals a change of policy that led to the making of the traditional landed elite as the chief collaborators of the British–Indian empire in the decades after the rebellion.

84. The impossibility of a purely military containment was forcefully argued by John Lawrence, the Lieutenant-Governor of the North-West Provinces, who in a letter to the Secretary for the Colonies, Lord Stanley (16 June 1858) wrote that:

> If every insurgent, or even every mutineer, is to be put to death, or transported beyond the seas, we shall require 200,000 European soldiers, and, even then, we shall not put down all opposition in half a dozen years. Is England prepared to send out from 20,000 to 30,000 troops annually to supply casualties? . . . Our prestige is gone! Our power is literally slipping away. In attempting to encompass an impracticable policy we are endangering our very empire in the East. Cited in R. Bosworth Smith, *Life of Lord Lawrence*, 2 vols. (London, 1883), vol. 11, 303.

85. Of the British-led sack of Delhi after its capture in September 1857 the Bombay correspondent of *The Times* wrote: 'No such scene had been witnessed in the city of Shah Jehan since the day that Nadir Shah, seated in the little mosque in Chandnee Chouk, directed and superintended the massacre of its inhabitants.' Cited in Martin, *The Indian Empire*, vol. 11, 450.

86. H. L. Wesseling, *Imperialism and Colonialism: Essays on the History of European Expansion* (Westport, CT, 1997), 21.

87. See Burke's impeachment speeches of 15–19 February 1788 in the Commons in P. J. Marshall (ed.), *The Writings and Speeches of Edmund Burke*, 9 vols. vol. iv (Oxford, 1981), 264–459; and, his 'Speech on Fox's India Bill' (1783) in *ibid.*, vol. v. Richard Cobden, 'Letter on India', 16 May 1858. Cited in Bennett, *The Concept of Empire*, 174.

88. Ball, *History of the Indian Mutiny*, vol. 1, 25.

89. Kaye, *The Administration of the East India Company*, p. 8.

90. Ball, *History of the Indian Mutiny*, vol. 11, 655.

91. *Ibid.*, vol. 1, 640.

92. *Ibid.*, vol. I, 159.
93. *Ibid.*, vol. I, 610.
94. *Ibid.*, vol. I, 298.
95. *Ibid.*, vol. I, 648.
96. *Ibid.*, vol. II, 637.
97. Metcalf, *Ideologies of the Raj*, 47.

2 REFORM AND REVISION

1. For a succinct account of the Company–Parliament dispute over Indian territories, see Arthur Berridale Keith, *A Constitutional History of India, 1600–1935* (1930; rpt. New Delhi, 1996). Also, Phillip Lawson, *The East India Company. A History* (London, 1993).
2. Bennett, *The Concept of Empire*, 223.
3. Sir Syed Ahmad Khan, *Causes of the Indian Revolt*, tr. Auckland Colvin and Colonel Graham in 1873 from the Urdu original (1858; Karachi, 2000). Sir Syed's *History of the Bijnor Rebellion*, tr. Hafeez Malik and Morris Dembo (East Lansing, 1982), is forthright in accusing the people of Hindustan of ingratitude. See pp. 102–9. *Sipahi Juddher Itihash* [History of the Sipahi War] (Calcutta, 1886–1900) by Rajanikanta Gupta is a Bengali history in five volumes modelled after *Kaye and Malleson's History of the Indian Mutiny*. It raises low-keyed doubts on the legitimacy of British rule, though on the whole skirting controversy and retailing the official British version.
4. See, for instance, *The British Raj Contrasted with Its Predecessors: An Inquiry into the Disastrous Results of the Rebellion in the North-West Provinces upon the Hopes of the People of India* (London, 1858) by Dorabhoy Franjee, and S. C. Mookherjee's *The Mutinies and the People, or Statements of Native Fidelity Exhibited During the Outbreak of 1857–58* (Calcutta, 1859).
5. Sumit Sarkar, *The Swadeshi Movement in Bengal, 1903–1908* (New Delhi, 1973); A. R. Desai, *Social Background of Indian Nationalism.* (4th edn, Bombay, 1966).
6. Vinayak Damodar Savarkar, *The Indian War of Independence in 1857* (1909, Bombay, 1957).
7. High imperial histories of the rebellion include *A History of the Indian Mutiny* by T. R. E. Holmes; *Tale of the Great Mutiny* (London, 1901) by W. H. Fitchett; and G. W. Forrest, *A History of the Indian Mutiny Reviewed and Illustrated from Original Documents*, 3 vols. (Edinburgh, 1904–12).
8. [Malleson], *The Mutiny of the Bengal Army*, Part II, 53.
9. Khan, *Causes of the Indian Revolt*, 12.
10. See B. B. Mishra, *The Indian Middle Classes: Their Growth in Modern Times* (London, 1961) for a study of the professional middle class in the period between 1857 and 1947, and the social provenance of the urban-professional nationalist.
11. For more on *sharif* culture see David Lelyveld, *Aligarh's First Generation* (New Delhi, 1996), chapter 2.

12. For contrasting analytical perspectives on a complex area only just mentioned here, see Partha Chatterjee, *Nationalist Thought and the Colonial World: A Derivative Discourse?* (London, 1986); C. A. Bayly, *Origins of Nationality in South Asia: Patriotism and Ethical Government in the Making of Modern India* (New Delhi, 1998).

13. See H. V. Bowen, *Revenue and Reform: The Indian Problem in British Politics, 1757–1773* (Cambridge, 1991) for an account of the pre-*diwani* years.

14. Marshall (ed.), *The Writings and Speeches of Edmund Burke.* Vol. v, 391, 384.

15. *Ibid.*, 385.

16. For details on the overlap between Whigs and the Philosophic Radicals see William Thomas, *The Philosophic Radicals: Nine Studies in Theory and Practice, 1817–1841* (Oxford, 1979), especially chapter 2.

17. 'Impeachment of Warren Hastings', *The Writings and Speeches of Edmund Burke* (New York, 1901), vol. VII, 46.

18. See John Burrow, *A Liberal Descent: Victorian Historians and the English Past* (Cambridge, 1981) for the lineages of Whig historiography.

19. For more on the uses of the metaphor see Uday Singh Mehta, *Liberalism and Empire: A Study in Nineteenth-century British Liberal Thought* (Chicago, 1999).

20. Mill, *History of British India*, II, 107.

21. John Stuart Mill, *Considerations of Representative Government* (1861), in *Utilitarianism and Other Essays* (Oxford, 1998).

22. William Wilberforce, 'Speech on the East India Company's Charter Bill' (House of Commons, 1 July 1813), cited in Bennett, *The Concept of Empire*, 101.

23. See Jack Lively and John Rees (eds.), *Utilitarian Logic and Politics: James Mill's 'Essay on Government', Macaulay's Critique and the Ensuing Debate* (Oxford, 1978). Mill's 'Essay' was part of the debate that Bentham's *Plan* sparked between the *Edinburgh Review* and the radical *Westminster Review*.

24. 'Hallam's Constitutional History', *Edinburgh Review* (September 1828), in *Lord Macaulay's Essays and the Lays of Ancient Rome* (London, 1891), 98–9.

25. See the Letter of Indian Law Commissioners (2 May 1837), in C. D. Dharker (ed.), *Lord Macaulay's Legislative Minutes* (London, 1946), 260–1.

26. John Stuart Mill, *Principles of Political Economy* (1848), cited in Bennett, *The Concept of Empire*, 146, 147.

27. T. B. Macaulay, *Speeches*, ed. G. M. Young (Oxford, 1952), 25.

28. See Nihar Nandan Singh, *British Historiography on British Rule in India. The Life and Writings of Sir John William Kaye, 1814–76* (Patna, 1986) for more details.

29. Kaye, *The Sepoy War*, vol. I, 154–5.

30. *Ibid.*, vol. I, 69.

31. Dalhousie's Minute of 30 August 1848. Cited in Kaye, *The Sepoy War*, vol. I, 73.

32. Peshwa Baji Rao (the formal chief of the six Maratha kingdoms) of Pune, who surrendered after the Company's third war with the Marathas (1818), was granted an annual pension of 800,000 rupees and resettled in Bithoor, a

suburb of the British military station at Kanpur. The Peshwa died in 1851, on which the Nana began to press his claims to the government. Though the case of Bithoor does not quite fall in the purview of the Doctrine, the dispute over inheritance is relevant. See Pratul Chandra Gupta, *Nana Sahib and the Rising at Cawnpore* (Oxford, 1963).

33. Kaye, *The Sepoy War*, vol. i, 102.
34. *Ibid.*, vol. i, 79.
35. *Ibid.*, vol. i, 80n., 81.
36. *Ibid.*, vol. i, 70.
37. *Ibid.*, vol. i, 71.
38. See Keith, *A Constitutional History of India*, 88–92.
39. Eric Stokes, *The English Utilitarians and India* (Oxford, 1959), 9.
40. *Ibid.*, 17, 18.
41. *Ibid.*, 15.
42. For more on this debate, which Stokes describes as 'The Battle of Two Philosophies', see Metcalf, *Ideologies of the Raj*.
43. Kaye, *The Sepoy War*, vol. i, 112.
44. *Ibid.*, 113–14. The alliance had consequences for the future of the province and for British prospects. The principal recruiting ground for the Company's Bengal Army, during the latter half of the eighteenth and the early nineteenth century, Awadh served as a buffer guarding the Company's Bengal frontiers. Under the original treaty, the Governor (Nawab Wazir) of Awadh was required to maintain a garrison of the Company's troops in the state, and to grant trade and tariff privileges. In return, the British recognised the erstwhile Mughal province as *de facto* independent from Delhi; and as Mughal control over its provinces weakened, secessionist ambitions culminated in a formal declaration of independence by Ghazi-ud-Din Haidar, who became the first Padshah, or Emperor, of Awadh in 1819 under British patronage. As Michael Fisher argues, 'by privately supporting – but publicly undermining – Awadh's declaration of political independence from the Mughal empire, the Company sought to dismantle the Empire without danger to itself'. *A Clash of Cultures: Awadh, the British, and the Mughals* (New Delhi, 1987), 6.
45. Samuel Lucas, *Dacoitee in Excelsis: or, The Spoilation of Oude by the East India Company*, (*c.* 1857; Lucknow, 1971), iii.
46. Rudrangshu Mukherjee, *Awadh in Revolt, 1857–58: A Study of Popular Resistance* (New Delhi, 1984), 33.
47. Thus, under the terms of the 1801 subsidiary treaty by which Awadh's army was virtually disbanded, and half its territories annexed, the Nawab Saadat Ali was required to 'establish in his reserved dominions such a system of administration, to be carried into effect by his own officers, as shall be conducive to secure the lives and property of the inhabitants; and His Excellency will always act in conformity to, the council of the officers of the said Honourable Company'. Fisher, *A Clash of Cultures*, 99. In the event, the Company claimed that the annexation was legally valid because successive rulers had failed to secure 'the lives and the property of the inhabitants'.

48. Kaye, *The Sepoy War*, vol. 1, 114.
49. *Ibid.*, vol. 1, 132.
50. *Ibid.*, vol. 1, 143, 122.
51. *Ibid.*, vol. 1, 144.
52. *Ibid.*, vol. 1, 152. Awadh was annexed on 7 February 1856; on 8 February Dalhousie wrote in a letter that 'our gracious queen has 5,000,000 more subjects and £1,300,000 more revenue than she had yesterday'. J. G. A. Baird, *Private Letters of the Marquess of Dalhousie* (Edinburgh, 1910), 369.
53. Mukherjee, *Awadh in Revolt*, 35.
54. Kaye, *The Sepoy War*, vol. 1, 153.
55. *Ibid.*, vol. 1, 175, 158.
56. T. R. Malthus, *The Nature and Progress of Rent* (London, 1815), and David Ricardo, *Essay on the Influence of the Low Price of Corn on the Profits of Stock* (London, 1815).
57. Stokes, *The English Utilitarians and India*, 88.
58. *Ibid.*, 90.
59. Holt Mackenzie, the Secretary to the Bengal Government in the Territorial Department at Calcutta (1817–31), was the author of a memorandum on the problems of the revenue settlement of the Ceded and Conquered Provinces of north India, and his work 'became the seed-plot of the revenue systems adopted throughout northern and central India'. *Ibid.*, 94.
60. Kaye, *The Sepoy War*, vol. 1, 154, 158.
61. *Ibid.*, vol. 1, 160.
62. *Ibid.*, vol. 1, 154, 165.
63. *Ibid.*, vol. 1, 160–1, 162.
64. *Ibid.*, vol. 1, 171. Kaye's assessment of the settlement of the North Western Provinces is startlingly different in the *Administration of the East India Company*. '[W]ith progressive increase of knowledge there came a progressive improvement in the administration of our new provinces', 250. Again: 'Viewed as a whole, it is difficult not to regard the settlement . . . as a great work . . . The great experiment of Indian Government has there been pushed forward with remarkable energy and uncommon success. In no part of India are the signs of progress so great and so cheering', 266–7.
65. See Joseph Hamburger, *Macaulay and the Whig Tradition* (Chicago: 1976).
66. In his *Two Letters Addressed to a Member of the Present Parliament on the Proposals for Peace with the Regicide Directory of France* (London, 1796) Burke wrote:

> I call a commonwealth *Regicide*, which lays it down as a fixed law of nature, and a fundamental right of man, that all government, not being a democracy, is an usurpation. That all kings, as such, are usurpers; and for being kings, may and ought to be put to death . . . The commonwealth which acts uniformly upon those principles . . . and which forces all her people to observe it – this I call *Regicide by Establishment*. 97.

67. Kaye, *The Sepoy War*, vol. 1, 169, 170.
68. *Ibid.*, vol. 1, 178–9.

69. Metcalf, *Ideologies of the Raj*, 29.
70. *Ibid.*, 34.
71. Kaye, *The Administration of the East India Company*, 660.
72. Thus, Charles Wood, President of the Board of Control during the tenure of Dalhousie and in charge of the India Office following the rebellion, acknowledged in 1859 that the 'mistake we fell into, under the influence of the most benevolent principles, and according to our notion of what was right and just, was that of introducing a system foreign to the habits and wishes of the people'; and that in future 'we ought to adopt and improve what we find in existence and avail ourselves as far as possible of the existing institutions of the country'. Cited in Metcalf, *Ideologies of the Raj*, 45.
73. Kaye, *The Sepoy War*, vol. 1, 181, 183.
74. *Ibid.*, vol. 1, 184, 185.
75. *Ibid.*, vol. 1, 186, 194.
76. *Ibid.*, vol. 1, 196.
77. *Ibid.*, vol. 1, 185.
78. *Ibid.*, vol. 1, 203.
79. *Ibid.*, vol. 1, 254.
80. *Ibid.*, vol. 1, 348, 349.
81. *Ibid.*, vol. 1, xii.
82. Guha, *Elementary Aspects*, 3.

3 ROMANCES OF EMPIRE, ROMANTIC ORIENTALISM AND ANGLO-INDIA: CONTEXTS, HISTORICAL AND LITERARY

1. Lyall, *Studies in Literature and History*, 7. His other works include *Verses Written in India* (*c.* 1882, n.p.), and *The Rise and Expansion of British Dominion in India* (London, 1907).
2. Lyall, *Studies in Literature and History*, 31, 32.
3. *Ibid.*, 7.
4. *Ibid.*, 13, 8.
5. Frederic Jameson, *The Political Unconscious: Narrative as a Socially Symbolic Act* (London, 1981), 206.
6. *Nostromo*'s cross-sectional view of Iberian, British and American investment in Central and South America is a startling anticipation of the theories of 'underdevelopment' and 'dependency'. See Paul A. Baran and Paul M. Sweezy, *Monopoly Capital* (London, 1966) for more on the 'world system'. Baran provided much of the theoretical grids for later studies of inequality and underdevelopment by Immanuel Wallerstein and André Gunder Frank. See, for instance, Frank's *Dependent Accumulation and Underdevelopment* (London, 1978).
7. For more on colonial warfare see Donald Featherstone, *Colonial Small Wars, 1837–1901* (Newton Abbott, 1973).
8. William H. Prescott, *History of the Conquest of Mexico and History of the Conquest of Peru* (1843–4; New York, 1961), 9, 120–1. Similarly, on the conquest of Peru, Prescott writes that: 'It was the reality of romance. The life of the

Spanish adventurer was one chapter more – and not the least remarkable – in the chronicles of knight-errantry.' *Ibid.*, 829.

9. *Ibid.*, 9.

10. Martin Green, *Dreams of Adventure, Deeds of Empire* (London, 1980), 20. Also see Richard Helgerson, 'Camoes, Hakluyt, and the Voyages of Two Nations', in Nicholas Dirks (ed.), *Colonialism and Culture* (Ann Arbor, 1992), 27–63.

11. See David Levin, *History as Romantic Art: Bancroft, Prescott, Motley and Parkman* (Stanford, 1959), for more on Prescott's bifocal commitment to 'facts', and to a larger 'romantic' design.

12. 'Anglo-India, Social, Moral, Political', *Calcutta Review*, 1 (May 1844), 4.

13. Kaye, *The Administration of the East India Company*, 8. Stinger Lawrence, a British army captain, was the first to organise a multi-ethnic 'irregular' corps in Madras used in June 1748 to foil the French attack on Cuddalore.

14. T. B. Macaulay, 'Lord Clive', in *Critical and Historical Essays*, 2 vols. (London, 1961), vol. II, 479.

15. *Ibid.*, 507.

16. G. A. Henty, *With Clive in India: Or, the Beginnings of an Empire* (London, 1884), Preface. Other novels on Clive's career and contemporary events in India include Phillip Meadows Taylor, *Ralph Darnell*, 3 vols. (London, 1865); Allen Upward, *Athelstane Ford* (London, 1899); and two novels by Herbert Strang, *In Clive's Command* (London, 1906), and *One of Clive's Heroes. A Story of the Fight for India* (London, 1906).

17. Ball, *History of the Indian Mutiny*, vol. 1, 639.

18. In *Guerilla: A Historical and Critical Study* (London, 1977) Walter Laquer lists nearly eighty-two military campaigns during the reign of Queen Victoria, mostly of a sub-conventional type. Also see J. M. Lonsdale, 'The Politics of Conquest: The British in Western Kenya, 1894–1914,' *The Historical Journal* 20 (1977), for a list of twenty British raids in Africa during this period.

19. J. E. P. Muddock, *The Great White Hand; or, The Tiger of Cawnpore* (London, 1896), Preface, x–xi.

20. Patrick Brantlinger, *Rule of Darkness: British Literature and Imperialism, 1830–1914* (Ithaca, 1988), 49.

21. See Martha P. Conant, *The Oriental Tale in England in the Eighteenth Century* (New York, 1908).

22. Garland Cannon, *The Life and Mind of Oriental Jones: Sir William Jones, the Father of Modern Linguistics* (Cambridge, 1990), and S. N. Mukherjee, *Sir William Jones: A Study in 18th Century British Attitudes to India* (Hyderabad, 1987).

23. *The Works of Sir William Jones with the Life of the Author by Lord Teignmouth*, 13 vols. (rpt. Delhi, 1980), vol. x, 359–60.

24. Conant, *The Oriental Tale in England*, 234.

25. 'To speak of the manifestly anti-imperialist discourse in the Romantic period is thus a misnomer, for criticism of the old mercantilist system is normally accompanied by support for the new economic world system which [Bernard]

Semmel calls liberal or free-trade imperialism.' Nigel Leask, *British Romantic Writers and the East: Anxieties of Empire* (Cambridge, 1992), 94.

26. Sydney Owenson, Lady Morgan, *The Missionary: An Indian Tale*, 3 vols. (London, 1811). All subsequent references are to this edition unless otherwise noted. The novel was revised and republished by the author soon after the rebellion under the title, *Luxima, The Prophetess* (London, 1859). For a discussion of the novel's considerable influence on British Romantic orientalism, especially Shelley's ecstatic reaction on reading it, see Dennis R. Dean's Introduction to a facsimile edition of the novel (New York, 1981). Also see Leask, *British Romantic Writers and the East* for an excellent reading of the novel.

27. W. H. Dixon (ed.), *Lady Morgan's Memoirs*, 2 vols. (London, 1863), vol. I, 407.

28. Cited in Lionel Stevenson, *The Wild Irish Girl: The Life of Sydney Owenson, Lady Morgan* (London, 1936), 136.

29. *Ibid.*, 132.

30. *The Missionary*, ed. Dennis R. Dean, Introduction, n.p.

31. Recent studies of the novel include Leask, *British Romantic Writers and the East*, and Gauri Vishwanathan, *Outside the Fold: Conversion, Modernity, and Belief* (Delhi, 2001). While Leask uses *The Missionary* as the *ur*-text of Romantic orientalism, Vishwanathan reads in the novel the generic link 'between novels of sectarian conflict and novels of conversion', with missionary enterprises 'as exotic displacements of the pressing and often explosive issue of whether to admit Jews, Catholics, and Nonconformists into the English nation state' (26–7).

32. François Bernier, *History of the Late Revolution of the Empire of the Great Mogul: Together with the most considerable passages for 5 years following in that Empire* (1671–72).

33. *Minstrelsy of the Scottish Border: consisting of historical and romantic ballads, collected in the southern counties of Scotland; with a few of modern date. Compiled and edited, with an introduction by Sir Walter Scott* (Kelso, 1802–3).

34. Owenson, *The Missionary*, vol. I, 49.

35. See Lata Mani, 'The Production of an Official Discourse on *Sati* in Early 19th Century Bengal', in Francis Barker *et al.* (eds.), *Europe and its Others*, 2 vols. (Colchester, 1985), vol. I, 107–27.

36. Owenson, *The Missionary*, vol. I, 115, 104.

37. *Ibid.*, vol. III, 139.

38. *Ibid.*, vol. III, 150–1.

39. *Ibid.*, vol. III, 186, 181.

40. Leask, *British Romantic Writers and the East*, 136.

41. Owenson, *The Missionary*, II, 247.

42. Charles Grant, *Observations on the State of Society among the Asiatic Subjects of Great Britain, particularly with respect to Morals and the Means of Improving It; written chiefly in the year 1792. Parliamentary Papers* (1812–13), vol. X, Paper 282. Grant retired as a Member of the Board of Trade supervising the Company's commercial operations in Bengal, and was intermittently the Chairman of

the Company's Court of Directors between 1805 and 1815. The *Observations* was printed for Parliament in 1813 when the Company's charter came up for renewal.

43. *Ibid.*, 25, 76. 'What Grant was asking . . . the Directors of the Company to do was to take the initiative in instituting a programme of social change in India that aimed at the complete alteration of the basis on which the existing social structure existed.' Ainslee Embree, *Charles Grant and British Rule in India* (London, 1962), 150–1.

44. See Boyd Hilton, *The Age of Atonement: The Influence of Evangelicalism on Social and Economic Thought, 1785–1865* (Oxford, 1988).

45. Grant, *Observations*, 80.

46. Owenson, *The Missionary*, vol. III, 95.

47. Cited in the introduction to Abbé Dubois, *Hindu Manners, Customs, and Ceremonies* (*c.* 1805), tr. Henry K. Beauchamp (Oxford, 1906).

48. 'Speech on the Government of India', in G. M. Young (ed.), *Macaulay: Prose and Poetry* (Cambridge, 1970), 718.

49. Karl Marx, 'The British Rule in India' (1853), in *Marx and Engels: On Colonialism* (Moscow, 1960), 36.

50. Owenson, *The Missionary*, vol. III, 97.

51. *Ibid.*, vol. III, 151–2.

52. Robert Southey, *History of Brazil*, 3 vols. (London, 1810–19), vol. III, 874. Also see Prescott, *History of the Conquest of Mexico and History of the Conquest of Peru*.

53. Owenson, *The Missionary*, vol. III, 151 n.

54. The Vellore mutiny took place on the night of 8–9 July 1806 when Indian soldiers in the Company's service killed some 150 British officers and soldiers in the Vellore fort. See Maya Gupta, *Lord William Bentinck and the Vellore Mutiny* (New Delhi, 1986).

55. Editorial preface to *Luxima, the Prophetess*, vol. I, iv.

56. Cited in C. H. Philips, 'British Historical Writing on India,' *The Listener*, 54 (8 December 1955), 985.

57. Leask, *British Romantic Writers and the East*, 84.

58. *Ibid.*, 100.

59. James Mill, *History of British India* (1817), 5th edn, with notes and continuation by H. H. Wilson, 10 vols. (London, 1858); Mill's preface to the original, xxi; Wilson's preface to the 5th edn, xii, xiii.

60. Bart Moore-Gilbert (ed.), *Writing India, 1757–1990: The Literature of British India* (Manchester, 1996).

61. *Ibid.*, 'Introduction: Writing India, Reorienting Colonial Discourse Analysis', 1–29.

62. *Ibid.*, 18.

63. *Ibid.*, 19.

64. *Ibid.*, 21, 21–2.

65. 'Indian Faults and English Calumnies', *Calcutta Review* (December 1858), 433.

66. 'India in English Literature' (*Calcutta Review*, September 1859), 29–48. The article reviews several novels including Scott's *Guy Mannering* and *The Surgeon's Daughter*, Macaulay's biographies of Clive and Hastings, and *Vanity Fair, Pendennis* and *The Newcomes* by W. M. Thackeray.

67. *Ibid.*, 33, 34.

68. *Ibid.*, 36.

69. *Ibid.*, 48, 47.

70. Percival Spear, *The Nabobs: A Study of the Social Life of the English in Eighteenth-century India.* (1932; London, 1963), 129–30.

71. Spear cites the anonymous [I. Everett ?] *Observations of India* (London, 1853), describing the new Anglo-Indian family:

> Every youth, who is able to maintain a wife, marries. The conjugal pair become a bundle of English prejudices and hate the country, the natives and everything belonging to them. If the man has, by chance, a share of philosophy and reflection, the woman is sure to have none. The 'odious blacks', the 'nasty heathen wretches', the 'filthy creatures' are the shrill echoes of the 'black brutes', the 'black vermin' of the husband. The children catch up this strain. I have heard one, five years old, call the man who was taking care of him a 'black brute'. Spear, *Nabobs*, 141.

72. *Ibid.*, 138. Though true that Cornwallis had no earlier connection with India, he had nonetheless considerable experience of colonial politics and warfare from America, where as Major-General Cornwallis he commanded the British army from 1776 until his surrender at Yorktown in 1781. See Franklin B. and Mary Wickmire, *Cornwallis, the Imperial Years* (Chapel Hill, 1980).

73. For a study of the persistence of these dichotomies in official Anglo-India through the last decades of the British in India, see Clive Dewey, *Anglo-Indian Attitudes: The Mind of the Indian Civil Service* (London, 1993). Dewey offers a useful overview of 'five pendulum-like swings' of attitude, ideology and administrative practice that 'punctuate the two centuries of British rule'; see especially 14–16. On the social and occupational composition of British India and migration patterns, see P. J. Marshall, 'British Immigration into India in the Nineteenth Century', in P. C. Emmer and M. Mörner (ed.), *European Expansion and Migration: Essays on the Intercontinental Migration from Africa, Asia, and Europe* (New York, 1992), 179–196.

74. Nigel Leask, 'Towards An Anglo-Indian Poetry', in Moore-Gilbert (ed.), *Writing India*, 52–85.

75. Thus Oswald: 'Though Christian born, he followed Brahma's laws', cited in *ibid.*, 67.

76. *Ibid.*, 72, 78.

77. William Browne Hockley, *Pandurang Hari, or the Memoirs of a Hindu*, 3 vols. (London, 1826), Preface, vol. 1, xiv.

78. Hockley, *The Memoirs of a Brahmin*, 3 vols. (London, 1843), Preface, vol. 1, p. vii.

79. Javed Majeed, 'Meadows Taylor's *Confessions of a Thug*: the Anglo-Indian novel as a genre in the making', in Moore-Gilbert (ed.), *Writing India*, 86–110.

Though otherwise an interesting essay, Majeed overlooks the autobiographical mode, and seems unaware of Hockley.

80. Hockley, *The Memoirs of a Brahmin*, vol. III, 271–2.
81. C. A. Bayly, *Empire and Information: Intelligence Gathering and Social Communication in India, 1780–1870* (Cambridge, 1996), 229, 234. Also see Sisir Kumar Das, *Sahibs and Munshis: An Account of the Fort William College* (New Delhi, 1978).
82. Hockley, *Memoirs of a Brahmin*, Preface, vol. I, iv–v.
83. W. D. Arnold, *Oakfield, or Fellowship in the East. By a Punjaubee*, 2 vols. (London, 1853).
84. See Kenneth Allott's Introduction to *Oakfield* (Leicester, 1973).
85. *Ibid.*, viii.
86. Arnold, *Oakfield*, vol. I, 16.
87. Francis H. Hutchins, *The Illusion of Permanence: British Imperialism in India* (Princeton, 1967), 102.
88. Metcalf, *Ideologies of the Raj*, 29.
89. The 'Muscular School' is best represented by the boys and young men of Rugby–Oxford in Thomas Hughes's cult novel *Tom Brown's Schooldays* (1857), and in *Guy Livingstone* (1857) by G. A. Lawrence. Imbued with Carlylean hero-worship, ideas of racial purity, Christian socialism as well as a concern for social reform, the 'muscular school' of fiction has a colonial counterpart in the 'Punjab School', comprising a handful of young officers whose administrative turf was the newly conquered Punjab and the Frontier.
90. Arnold, *Oakfield*, vol. II, 223.
91. *Ibid.*, vol. I, 119.
92. *Ibid.*, vol. II, 225.
93. Kaye, *The Sepoy War*, vol. I, 169.
94. John Lang's *The Wetherbys: Father and Son* (London, 1853), which appeared in the same year as *Oakfield* is, on the other hand, a comic satire of Anglo-Indian society, and the lives of the Wetherby parent and son exemplify the 'want of moral tone' in India that Arnold regrets.
95. Reflecting on the Queen's Proclamation of 1858, the *Times* correspondent William Russell wrote that: 'The mutinies have produced too much hatred and ill-feeling between the two races to render any mere change of name of the rulers a remedy for the evils which affect India', and that 'many years must elapse before the evil passions exited by these disturbances expire; *perhaps confidence will never be restored*'. *My Indian Mutiny Diary* (1860; London, 1957), 197, 198. What Russell ignores is that the rebellion was itself the result of a polarisation of the 'two races' that predated the rebellion by a good number of years, and that was seriously exacerbated by reformist intervention and insularity.
96. Douglas M. Peers, *Between Mars and Mammon: Colonial Armies and the Garrison State in India, 1819–1835* (London, 1995), 64.
97. Cited in Bennett (ed.), *The Concept of Empire*, 81. Mill's further point in that article, true for its time but not quite for the late nineteenth century, and

in consonance with his radical politics, is that the growing military machine meant preferment for the 'few' but not the 'many'.

98. Hutchins, *The Illusion of Permanence*, 101.
99. Bentinck to the Governor in Council, 26 September 1807. Cited in John Rosselli, *Lord William Bentinck: The Making of a Liberal Imperialist, 1774–1839* (London, 1974), 146. Written to his successor at Madras as he waited for the ship home, the letter expresses a view that Bentinck possibly acquired in the aftermath of the Vellore mutiny that led to his recall. A few lines earlier he had written that 'the Europeans know little or nothing of the customs and manners of the Hindus. We are all acquainted with some prominent modes and facts, and all who run may read; but their manner of thinking, their domestic habits and ceremonies, in which circumstances a knowledge of a people consists, is, I fear, in great part wanting to us.' *Ibid.*, 146.
100. Peers, *Between Mars and Mammon*, 6.
101. Benedict Anderson, *Imagined Communities: Reflections on the Origin and Spread of Nationalism* (London, 1983), 88–9.
102. Edward Farley Oaten, *A Sketch of Anglo-Indian Literature* (London, 1908), 3.

4 THE MUTINY NOVEL AND THE HISTORICAL ARCHIVE

1. 'The Poetry of the Rebellion', *Calcutta Review* (December 1858), 349.
2. Other books of verse include the anonymous *Ex Oriente: Sonnets on the Indian Rebellion* (London, 1858), *Fallen Heroes of the Indian War* (London, 1858) by John Vaughan Williamson and *Scenes from the Late Indian Mutinies* (London, 1858) by 'D. M'. See Appendix 4, 'The Muse of the "Mutiny"', in Michael Edwardes, *The Red Year* (London, 1973), for other poems on the rebellion.
3. 'The Poetry of the Rebellion', 358.
4. A less prettifying echo of the sonnet is a letter by a British officer at Delhi who recorded how:

> There has been nothing but shooting these villains for the past three days. Some 300 or 400 were shot yesterday . . . There are several mosques in the city most beautiful to look at. But I should like to see them all destroyed. The rascally brutes desecrated our churches and graveyards, and I do not think we ought to have any regard for their stinking religion. Cited in Christopher Hibbert, *The Great Mutiny: India 1857* (Harmondsworth, 1980), 318.

5. Mirza Asadullah Khan 'Ghalib', *Dastanbuy. A Diary of the Indian Revolt of 1857*, tr. Khwaja Ahmad Faruqi (Delhi, 1970). Also see Percival Spear, *A History of Delhi under the Later Mughals* (1951; rpt. Delhi, 1995).
6. Alfred, Lord Tennyson, 'The Defence of Lucknow', Part II, *Poetical Works* (London, 1962), 482.
7. *Ibid.*, Part IV, 483.
8. 'The Poetry of the Rebellion', 355–6.

9. Charles Dickens and Wilkie Collins, 'The Perils of Certain English Prisoners', in Ruth Glancy (ed.), *Christmas Stories* (London, 1996), 171–256. The story is in three chapters, of which Dickens wrote the first and the third. In her introductory note to the story, Glancy mentions that six different versions of 'The Perils' were played at London and Brighton theatres in 1858.

10. Cited in William Odie, 'Dickens and the Indian Mutiny', 6, 7.

11. Dickens and Collins, 'The Perils of Certain English Prisoners', 190.

12. Cited in Odie, 'Dickens and the Indian Mutiny', 190–1.

13. Cited in *Ibid.*, 191.

14. Edward Money, *The Wife and the Ward; or, a Life's Error* (London, 1859). Before joining the Company's Bengal Army, Money served in the Imperial Ottoman Army as captain with the Bashi-Bazouks, an experience he recorded in *Twelve Months with the Bashi-Bazouks* (London, 1857). His other works include the travelogue, *The Truth About America* (London, 1886). In the *Novels on the Indian Mutiny* (New Delhi, 1973), Shailendra Dhari Singh suggests that Money's novel is the first novel of the rebellion; and my bibliographical enquiries have confirmed his view. Though Robert Druce claims that the first novel of the 'Mutiny' is Robert Gibney's *My Escape from the Mutinies in Oudh* (1858), like a good many 'escape' stories published in that year, Gibney's work is a first-person account rather than a novel, and lacks the typical articulation of history and fiction which, as I shall show in what follows, is characteristic of the Mutiny novel. See Druce, '"And to think that Henrietta Guise was in the hands of such human demons": Ideologies of Anglo-Indian Novels from 1859 to 1947', in C. C. Barfoot and Theo D'haen (eds.), *Shades of Empire in Colonial and Post-Colonial Literatures* (Amsterdam, 1993), 17–34.

15. Money, *The Wife and the Ward*, 294–6.

16. Margaret Frances Wheeler (who appears as Ulrica Wheeler in some accounts), the daughter of General Wheeler and his Eurasian wife, was either abducted or rescued by a *sawar* from the Satichaura Ghat. She married the man and lived in Kanpur under a different name until her death in 1907, even as her disappearance fuelled the circulation of another legend of honour and martyrdom. Amelia Bennett was other woman who survived the Satichaura Ghat and Bibighar. The daughter of a Kanpur clerk, Bennett was abducted during the massacre when she was eighteen and her account appeared under the title, 'Ten Months Captivity after the Massacre at Cawnpore' in the *Nineteenth Century* (June 1913). For more details on the survivors see Zöe Yalland, *Traders and Nabobs: The British in Cawnpore, 1765–1857* (Salisbury, 1987), 278–9, n. 6 and n. 7, and Andrew Ward, *Our Bones Are Scattered* (New York, 1996).

17. Money, *The Wife and the Ward*, 405–7.

18. 'Critical Notices of Works on India and the East', *Calcutta Review* (June 1859), xxvi.

19. It was on 4 June that the 2nd Light Cavalry, the 1st, 74th and 56th Bengal Native Infantry mutinied. On 5 June, Wheeler ordered the British to gather in the 'entrenchment', and on the following day the Nana Sahib was proclaimed

Peshwa – the hereditary Maratha title the British government had always denied him – and the soldiers began the siege.

20. Mowbray Thomson, *The Story of Cawnpore* (London, 1859), 184.

21. *The Steam-House; or the End of the Nana Sahib*, tr. A. D. Kingston (London, *c.* 1881). Like his other works, Jules Verne's Mutiny novel too is science fiction, where the 'steam-house' of the title is a futuristic vehicle in which a party of English and Frenchmen set off on the trail of the Nana.

22. J. E. Muddock, *The Great White Hand*, Preface, x–xi.

23. Charles Ball, *History of the Indian Mutiny*, vol. II, 644.

24. Frederick P. Gibbon, *The Disputed VC; A Story of the Indian Mutiny* (London, 1909). Other novels by Gibbon include the boy's adventure, *Comrades under Canvas: A Story of the Boy Brigade's Life* (London, 1907), and *With Rifle and Khukri* (London, *c.* 1910), a collection of stories about British raids on Afghan tribes in the Frontier.

25. *The Disputed VC*, 54.

26. *Ibid.*, 42.

27. *Ibid.*, 63. Gibson admits that the *sipahi* could be 'crafty and designing but suggests to his (juvenile?) reader: 'Let us try to put ourselves in his place, and see what it meant.' *Ibid.*, 63.

28. *Ibid.* John Malcolm, *The Political History of India from 1784 to 1823* (London, 1823), vol. II, 245.

29. C. Lestock Reid, *Masque of the Mutiny* (London, 1947), Foreword, unpaginated. Reid's other writings include *Trail of the Pharaoh's Treasure: A Romance of Africa* (London, 1924), which suggests the African adventures of Rider Haggard; *The Greatest Game: A Tale of Far Eastern Byways* (London, *c.* 1930) and *Dark Destiny* (London, 1936), the two latter set in east Asia during the first decades of the twentieth century. Reid also wrote a travelogue, *An Amateur in Africa* (Stuttgart, 1925).

30. So says the Colonel to Robin when he requests the former to take a lenient view of the soldiers' refusal to use the greased cartridges. Reid, *Masque*, 38. After the interview, 'Robin felt he was finished with his own damned nation; tired of their complacent stupidity, their arrogance, their complete lack of understanding of the men they professed to rule and command.' *Ibid.*, 42.

31. *Ibid.*, 42 and 18. Also see Reid, *Dark Destiny*, 51–2.

32. Reid, Foreword, *The Greatest Game*, n.p.

33. See Dewey, *Anglo-Indian Attitudes*, for a study of Darling's 'cult of friendship' with Indians through the last decades of British rule; a cult in which his friend, E. M. Forster, too came to share. In Thompson's case, sympathy prompted his critique of British historiography of the rebellion in *The Other Side of the Medal* (London, 1925).

34. Reid, *Masque*, 18.

35. *Ibid.*, 30.

36. *Ibid.*, 31.

37. Fanon, *The Wretched of the Earth*, 31.

38. H. C. Irwin, *With Sword and Pen: A Story of India in the Fifties* (London, 1904).

39. A partisan of land reform in Awadh after the rebellion, when administrative policy was generally committed to upholding the status quo, Irwin was among a 'number of officials [who] protested the denial of class antagonism in the countryside, and insisted that India's gentry, uninterested in agricultural improvement, and stripped of their former powers as rajas, no longer played any useful role in society'. Metcalf, *Ideologies of the Raj*, 192.
40. Irwin, *With Sword and Pen*, 5–6.
41. *Ibid.*, 8.
42. *Ibid.*, 10.
43. Kaye, *The Sepoy War*, vol. 1, 154; Irwin, *With Sword and Pen*, 11.
44. The character of Home is a composite of two historical figures. The first Commissioner of Awadh after annexation was Henry Lawrence, and the last Resident was William Sleeman. Home's tour of Ghoristan is modelled after Sleeman's *A Journey Through the Kingdom of Oudh in 1849–50* (London, 1858), which the latter undertook on government order to report on the state of the kingdom, and whose report was the basis for the decision to annex the kingdom.

    Though the Calcutta government used his confidential report to justify takeover, Sleeman believed that 'such doctrines [of annexation and direct intervention] are dangerous to our rule in India, and prejudicial to the best interests of the country . . . The native states I consider to be the breakwaters, and when they are swept away we shall be left to the mercy of the Native Army, which may not always be sufficiently under our control.' Sleeman to Sir James Hogg, January 1853; cited in Kaye, *The Sepoy War*, vol. 1, n., 136.
45. The model for the Queen Mother is the Begum Hazrat Mahal, wife of the Nawab Wajid Ali Shah, and mother of their minor son Birjis Qadar, who was enthroned under the guardianship of the Begum in August 1857 while the rebellion was in progress. The Begum continued to lead the rebellion in Awadh, and after the capture of Lucknow in November she took the fight into the countryside. While retaining these general outlines, the novel suggests that the Queen Mother was the mother of the Nawab.
46. Irwin, *With Sword and Pen*, 66.
47. *Ibid.*, 71.
48. *Ibid.*, 35.
49. *Ibid.*, 71.
50. *Ibid.*, 2.
51. *Ibid.*, 235.
52. Cave-Brown, *The Punjab and Delhi in 1857*, viii.
53. Irwin, *With Sword and Pen*, 307.
54. The Proclamation issued in the name of Queen Victoria was soon followed by a counter-Proclamation from the Begum Hazrat Mahal addressed to her subjects, the rebel militias, and obliquely to the British government. The argument of the counter-Proclamation was quite precise: first, that it was no good pretending that the replacement of the Company by the Crown would mean any change of affairs since laws, procedures and officials would stay unchanged.

Second, the terms announced by the British Proclamation were scarcely credible coming from an administration not especially known for its honesty, and
whose annexation of Awadh was itself a monumental breach of trust. Finally,
on the promises of improvement made in that document, the Begum contended that: 'It is worthy of a little reflection, that they have promised no
better employment for Hindostanis than making roads and digging canals. If
people cannot see clearly what this means, there is no help for them.' The full
text of the Proclamation (first translated in Foreign Political Consultations,
no. 3022, 31 December 1858) is reproduced in Michael Edwardes, *The Red Year:
The Indian Rebellion of 1857* (London, 1975), 171–3.
55. Reproduced in C. A. Bayly (ed.), *The Raj: India and the British* (London,
1990), 162.
56. Edward Said, *Orientalism: Western Conceptions of the Orient* (New York, 1975),
7.
57. Irwin, *With Sword and Pen*, 307.
58. Cited in Francis Robinson, *Separatism Among Indian Muslims: The Politics of
the United Provinces' Muslims* (Delhi, 1997), 38n.
59. Sir Syed Ahmad Khan, *Review on Dr Hunter's Indian Mussalmans* (Benares,
1872). 82.

5 COUNTER-INSURGENCY AND HEROISM

1. At a rough count, seventeen diaries, memoirs and collections of letters were
published between 1900 and 1920, sixteen between 1890 and 1899, and forty
between 1857 and 1859. These figures, based on Janice M. Ladendorf's Mutiny
bibliography, *The Revolt in India* (Zug, 1966), are suggestive but not conclusive,
for there are publications that Ladendorf does not include.
2. Kaye, *The Sepoy War*, vol. II, xii–xv. Ball's view of first-person accounts is
less sceptical than Kaye's. Not only are they a source of information but
they 'collectively exhibit, upon a foundation that cannot be questioned, the
indomitable spirit and enduring energies of the true British character, when
called into action amidst scenes of unparalleled horror and personal suffering'.
Ball, *History of the Indian Mutiny*, vol. I, 81.
3. Bennett, 'Ten Months Captivity', 436, 1216.
4. Julia Haldane, *The Story of Our Escape from Delhi in 1857* (Agra, 1888); William
Edwards, *Personal Adventures during the Indian Rebellion in Rohilcund, Futtehghur, and Oude* (London, 1858).
5. Vivian Dering Majendie, *Up Among the Pandies; or, A Year's Service in India*
(London, 1859); Reginald G. Wilberforce, *An Unrecorded Chapter of the Indian
Mutiny: Being the Personal Reminiscences of Reginald G. Wilberforce* (London,
1894).
6. J. W. Sherer, *Daily Life during the Indian Mutiny: Personal Experiences of 1857*
(London, 1898).
7. Ranajit Guha, 'The Prose of Counter-Insurgency', in Guha (ed.), *Subaltern
Studies*, 9 vols. (Delhi, 1983), vol. II, 1–42.

8. Mark Thornhill, *The Personal Adventures and Experiences of a Magistrate during the Rise, Progress, and Suppression of the Indian Mutiny* (London, 1884).

9. Guha, 'The Prose of Counter-Insurgency', 16.

10. *Ibid.*, 18.

11. While still a fugitive, William Edwards begins his diary on 27 July 1857 with the lament that: 'For more than a year previous to the outbreak, I had been publicly representing to superior authority the great abuse of power of the civil courts, and the reckless manner in which they decreed the sale of rights and interests connected with the soil . . . and the dangerous dislocation of society which was in consequence being produced'; yet: 'My warnings were unheeded and I was treated as an alarmist.' *Personal Adventures*, 14–15.

12. In the first-person accounts by British women, the gender of the narrator combines with reversals of the symbolic economy of colonial authority to make these narratives – especially when they are diaries – twice-removed from the official voice. For a study of first-person accounts of the rebellion by British women, see Indira Ghosh, *Women Travellers in Colonial India* (Delhi, 1997).

13. Thornhill, *Personal Adventures and Experiences of a Magistrate*, 48.

14. *Ibid.*, 148.

15. Guha does, however, notice the 'chinks which have allowed "comment", to worm its way into the plate armour of "fact"'. 'The Prose of Counter-Insurgency', 13. Such comments, which take the form of 'adjectives' or 'epithets', may be described as the *diegetic* elements of the primary discourse, and distinguished from the ideal minimalism of the *mimetic*.

16. Irwin, *With Sword and Pen*, 188.

17. *Ibid.*, 195–8.

18. *Ibid.*, 199.

19. *Ibid.*, 200.

20. Other novels that use the boat ride on the Ganges include *The Sword of Azrael* (London, 1903) by John Hayman, and Reid, *Masque of the Mutiny*. In the latter, the British party are disguised as Indians and escorted by the retainers of Hurdeo Buksh. While Maud Westerne along with her husband and her lover sail to safety without much ado, the following boat carrying the Fatehgarh refugees is pursued and boarded by the rebels at Kanpur, 164–5.

21. Major North, *Journal of an English Officer in India* (London, 1858). North claims that he began to write the diary soon after his arrival in India, and while the first entry is datelined 'Calcutta, May 14, 1857', later entries read suspiciously retrospective.

22. Irwin, *With Sword and Pen*, 277.

23. North, *Journal*, 53, 69.

24. *Ibid.*, 125.

25. Julia Selina Inglis, *The Siege of Lucknow, A Diary* (London, 1892), Martin R. Gubbins, *An Account of the Mutinies in Oudh and the Siege of the Lucknow Residency* (London, 1858).

26. Gibbon, *The Disputed VC*, 89.

27. *Ibid.*, 86. In Reid's *Masque*, Willoughby actually appears on-stage after he has blown up the Magazine. 95–97.

28. G. A. Henty, *In Times of Peril; a Story of India* (London, 1899), 30–31.

29. 'The Voice of the Hooligan', a review of Kipling's *Stalky and Co.* (1899) by Robert Buchanan that appeared in the *Contemporary Review*, 76 (1899), 775–89.

30. Gibbon, *The Disputed VC*, 327.

31. *Ibid.*, 146. The Guides were a hastily recruited body of mercenaries comprising Sikhs, Pathans and Gurkhas, sent down to Delhi in the summer of 1857. A Captain Spencer of the Guides explains the mystique of this British-Indian *Légion Etrangère* to an admiring Ted Russell:

   We've outlaws and dacoits, thieves and murderers; they resemble the border raiders of Scotland a hundred years ago. But every man who joins the Guides has to be strong, healthy, active, brave as a lion, able to track like a Red Indian, climb mountains, and think for himself . . . We have men of all races and creeds and men of no race or creed – mostly big, truculent Pathans, and nearly a hundred jolly little Gurkhas . . . *Ibid.*, 34–5.

32. Henry Harris Greathed, *Letters Written during the Siege of Delhi*, (London, 1858); Reverend J. E. W. Rotton, *Chaplain's Narrative of the Siege of Delhi; from the Outbreak at Meerut to the Capture of Delhi* (London, 1858).

33. John Tulloch Nash, *Volunteering in India: or, An Authentic Narrative of the Military Services of the Bengal Yeomanry Cavalry during the Indian Mutiny and Sepoy War* (London, 1893).

34. Reid, *Masque*, 238–9.

35. John Mackenzie, 'Heroic Myths of Empire', in Mackenzie (ed.), *Popular Imperialism and the Military: 1850–1950* (Manchester, 1992), pp. 109–38. Robert H. MacDonald, *The Language of Empire: Myths and Metaphors of Popular Imperialism, 1880–1918* (Manchester, 1994).

36. Hume Nisbet, *The Queen's Desire* (London, 1893), 95.

37. *Ibid.*, 112.

38. *Ibid.*, 116.

39. *Ibid.*, 133.

40. Hume Nisbet's Australian novels include *Bail-up* (London, 1890) and *A Bush Girl's Romance* (London, 1894).

41. Steel's novels and short stories include *From the Five Rivers* (London, 1893), *Miss Stuart's Legacy* (London, 1913), *The Potter's Thumb* (London, 1897), *The Curse of Eve* (London, 1929) and *The Indian Scene* (London, 1933).

42. [Gregg], 'The Indian Mutiny in Fiction', 229. Two years later, Lyall had another complaint against the novel. In his essay 'The Anglo-Indian Novelist', Lyall observes that: 'Mrs Steel not only draws too copiously, for a novelist, on history; she also undertakes to pass authoritative judgements upon disputable questions of fact and situation, with which fiction . . . has no concern.' *Edinburgh Review* (October 1899), 141.

43. Steel, *On the Face of the Waters*, 191.

44. *Ibid.*, 214.
45. *Ibid.*, 253.
46. *Ibid.*, 254.
47. A. F. P. Harcourt, *Jenetha's Venture: A Tale of the Siege of Delhi* (London, 1899). Harcourt, who was a Deputy Commissioner of the Punjab Civil Commission, also wrote *The Peril of the Sword* (London, 1903).
48. Harcourt, *Jenetha's Venture*, 10. There seems no evidence that Montgomery ever sent a British officer as messenger to Agra to inform Colvin of the rebellion. What he did do, however, was disarm the Bengal regiments stationed at neighbouring towns, warn the British stations at Ferozepur, Multan and Kangra and execute several hundred recalcitrant troops; a feat that soon earned him the reputation of 'the man who saved the Punjab'.
49. *Ibid.*, 36.
50. *Ibid.*, 72, 81.
51. *Ibid.*, 143. Lieutenant William Hodson was in charge of the British intelligence department on the Delhi Ridge that gathered information about the state of the city and ran messengers to other towns in the Punjab region. Hodson, who set up a spying network in the city, was aided by the *maulvi*, Rajab Ali.
52. *Ibid.*, 248, 279.
53. *Ibid.*, 72.
54. *Ibid.*, 140.
55. *Ibid.*, 212.
56. Gibbon, *The Disputed VC*, 52.
57. Fanny Peile, *History of the Delhi Massacre . . . By a Lady, the Wife of an Officer in the Bengal Army, and a Sufferer in the Late Tragedy* (Liverpool, 1858); W. J. Shepherd, *A Personal Narrative of the Outbreak and Massacre at Cawnpore during the Sepoy Revolt of 1857* (Lucknow, 1886).
58. J. F. Fanthome, *Mariam* (Benares, 1896).
59. *Ibid.*, 273.
60. Steel, *On the Face of the Waters*, 273, 356.
61. *Ibid.*, 32, 35.
62. *Ibid.*, 35.
63. *Ibid.*, 40.
64. Gibbon, *The Disputed VC*, 15.
65. Joseph Bristow, *Empire Boys: Adventures in a Man's World* (Manchester, 1991), 57.
66. Gibbon, *The Disputed VC*, 29–30.
67. Brereton's Mutiny novel is *A Hero of Lucknow: A Tale of the Indian Mutiny* (London, 1905). G. Manville Fenn, a prolific boys' novelist with some 140 novels to his credit, also wrote a worshipful biography of Henty, *George Alfred Henty: The Story of an Active Life* (London, 1907). Fenn's Mutiny fiction is *For the Old Flag: A Tale of the Mutiny* (London, 1899) and *Begumbagh; A Tale of the Indian Mutiny and Other Stories* (London, n.d.).
68. Besides the studies by Martin Green and Patrick Brantlinger, a well-documented reading of the imperialist/militarist slant of contemporary

juvenile literature is in Jeffrey Richards, 'Imperialism and the Image of the Army in Juvenile Literature', in Mackenzie (ed.), *Popular Imperialism and the Military*, pp. 80–108. Also see Guy Arnold, *Held Fast For England: G. A. Henty, Imperialist Boys' Writer* (London, 1980), for a study of Henty's life and writings.

69. John A. Hobson, *The Psychology of Jingoism* (London, 1901), 41–62.
70. Anne Summers, 'Edwardian Militarism', in Raphael Samuel (ed.), *Patriotism: The Making and Unmaking of British National Identity* (London, 1989), 236–56.
71. MacDonald, *The Language of Empire*, 81.
72. See J. A. Gallagher and R. E. Robinson, 'The Imperialism of Free Trade', *Economic History Review*, 2nd series, 6 (1953), 1–53, for the continuities between early nineteenth-century expansionism and late Victorian formal imperialism.
73. John A. Hobson, *Imperialism: A Study* (London, 1902), 4.
74. John Hobhouse, *Democracy and Reaction* (London, 1904), 29.
75. Charles H. Pearson, *National Life and Character: A Forecast* (London, 1893), 231.
76. Frederic Harrison, 'The Evolution of our Race: A Reply', *Fortnightly Review*, 60 (1894), 35–6, 38.
77. Talbott Mundy, *Rung Ho! A Novel of India* (London, 1914), 18.
78. *Ibid.*, 33.
79. *Ibid.*, 45.
80. Interestingly, T. E. Lawrence's own craving for a heroic pedigree led him to suggest to his American biographer, Lowell Thomas, that he was not only the descendant of a twelfth-century Crusader but also related to the Lawrence brothers who were among the 'Punjab school' and Mutiny heroes. See Mackenzie, 'Heroic Myths of Empire', 131.
81. Henry Lawrence, *Essays, Military and Political, Written in India* (London, 1859), 310.
82. Katherine Tidrick, *Empire and the English Character* (London, 1990), 19.
83. In *The Poems of Tennyson*, ed. Christopher Ricks (London, 1969),1344–5.
84. Mundy, *Rung Ho!*, 104.
85. *Ibid.*, 117.
86. *Ibid.*, 110.
87. *Ibid.*, 236.
88. Herbert Edwardes, *A Year on the Punjab Frontier in 1848–49.* 2 vols. (London, 1851).
89. *Ibid.*, Preface, viii.
90. Irwin, *With Sword and Pen*, 2.
91. Cited in Tidrick, *Empire and the English Character*, 21.
92. H. C. Irwin, *A Man of Honour* (London, 1896), 139.
93. *Ibid.*, 140.
94. *Ibid.*, 260–1.
95. *Ibid.*, 285.
96. *Ibid.*, 320–1.
97. *Ibid.*, 326.
98. *Ibid.*, 367.

99. *Ibid.*, 368.
100. Bristow, *Empire Boys*, 58.
101. Mark Girouard, *The Return to Camelot: Chivalry and the English Gentleman* (New Haven, 1981), 224.

6 IMAGINING RESISTANCE

1. Bayly, *Empire and Information*, 97.
2. *Ibid.*, 3.
3. There is the story of Thomas Kavanagh who disguised himself as an Indian, slipped out of the Lucknow Residency one night and, after eluding rebel pickets, made contact with the relieving army. But this one-off venture, which Kavanagh recounted in *How I Won the Victoria Cross* (London, 1860), is nothing like the elaborate counter-intelligence operations described in the last chapter. The other instance of intelligence gathering during the rebellion is in *A Personal Narrative of the Outbreak and Massacre at Cawnpore* by William J. Shepherd, a Eurasian clerk at Kanpur. Shepherd disguised himself and slipped out of the entrenchment to gather information about British relief forces. But having drunk rather too much rum before setting out, he was promptly discovered by the rebel militia and imprisoned.
4. See Perceval Griffiths, *To Guard My People: The History of the Indian Police* (London, 1971), 342–54, and Richard J. Popplewell, *Intelligence and Imperial Defence* (London, 1995) for an account of the security concerns and the legislation leading to the CCID and the Directorate of Intelligence, the institutional precursors of the present-day Intelligence Bureau.
5. Bayly, *Empire and Information*, 97.
6. *Ibid.*, 159. Moorcroft first travelled to Persia and Turkestan in 1813 with Abdul Qader Khan of Banaras in 1813. His second journey to Bokhara and central Asia (1820–5) was in the company of the Mughal nobleman, Izatullah Khan. See Moorcroft's *Travels in the Himalayan Provinces of Hindustan and the Punjab*, ed. H. H. Wilson (London, 1847).
7. Steel, *On the Face of the Waters*, 66.
8. Also see, Henty's *Rujjub the Juggler*, 3 vols. (London, 1893), in which Rujjub the magician – very likely named after the *maulvi* Rajab Ali who ran a spy ring for the British in rebel Delhi – employs his special skills to save the British from the Nana Sahib's men at Kanpur.
9. The process aimed at a comprehensive and centralised organisation of information and political analysis. As the viceroy Earl Lytton observed in an official communication: 'in some provinces of the Empire, there is no special officer whose duty requires him to receive, and to submit to the head of the Government confidential or secret communications on subjects of military importance. And, further, there is no recognized channel through which suspected persons can be traced from one province to another.' To redress this lack Lytton suggested the appointment of a 'special central officer, whose business it [would be] to collate such information'. Cited in Griffiths, *To Guard My People*, 343.

10. Kaye, *The Sepoy War*, vol. 1, 491.
11. Ball, *History of the Indian Mutiny*, vol. 1, 623.
12. Kaye, *The Sepoy War*, vol. 1, 340.
13. G. P. Raines, *Terrible Times; A Tale of the Sepoy Revolt* (London, *c.* 1899), 16.
14. Fanthome, *Mariam*, 131.
15. *Ibid.*, 135, 136.
16. *Ibid.*, 136.
17. Moore-Gilbert, 'Introduction', *Writing India*, 19.
18. See Douglas Peers, '"Those Noble Exemplars of True Military Tradition": Constructions of the Indian Army in the Mid-Victorian Press', *Modern Asian Studies*, 31.1 (1997), 109, 112.
19. Fenn's other Mutiny novel is *For the Old Flag: A Tale of the Mutiny*. Thomas Bland Strange, *Gunner Jingo's Jubilee* (London, 1893).
20. Nisbet, *The Queen's Desire*, 32, 33.
21. *Ibid.*, 2–3, 82.
22. J. W. Kaye, 'The Romance of Indian Warfare', review of *Papers Relating to the Punjab* (1849); *Leaves from the Journal of a Subaltern, during the Campaign in the Punjab* (1849), *North British Review*, 23 (1849/50), 222.
23. Arnold, *Oakfield*, vol. 1, 119.
24. C. H. Philips, *The East India Company, 1784–1834* (Manchester, 1940).
25. Though as L. S. S. O'Malley notes: 'The old [Company] titles of Merchants, Factors and Writers were retained . . . in the official registers till 1842, though the mercantile duties they had connoted had disappeared.' *The Indian Civil Service, 1601–1930* (London, 1965), 48.
26. Kaye, *The Sepoy War*, vol. 1, 257–8, 259.
27. This change is also evident in the replacement of the advanced liberal John Stuart Mill with John Kaye as Secretary of the Secret and Political Department in 1858. See Nihar Nandan Singh, *British Historiography*, and Lynn Zastoupil, *John Stuart Mill and India* (Stanford, CA, 1994).
28. Gray, *In the Heart of the Storm*, 282.
29. William Robertson, *A Historical Disquisition Concerning the Knowledge the Ancients had of India* (Dublin, 1791). See Jane Rendall, 'Scottish Orientalism: from Robertson to James Mill', *The Historical Journal*, 25.1 (1982), 43–69.
30. Lyall, 'The Anglo-Indian Novelist' (1899), in *Studies in Literature and History*, 153, 153–4.
31. Charles Pearce, *Red Revenge: A Romance of Cawnpore* (London, *c.* 1911), 110.
32. R. E. Forrest, *Eight Days*, 3 vols. (London, 1891), vol. 1, 11.
33. Homi Bhabha, *The Location of Culture* (London, 1994), 86.
34. The persecution of the Bengali employees of the Company by the rebel militias in towns such as Allahabad and Kanpur is recorded in Bholanath Chunder, *The Travels of a Hindoo to Various Parts of Bengal and Upper India*, 2 vols. (London, 1869), especially vol. 1, 322; and in Durgadas Bandopadhyaya (a Bengali clerk attached to a cavalry regiment at Bareilly during the rebellion), *Vidrohe Bangali; ba amar Jibon Chorit* (Calcutta, 1924). Also see *The Mutinies and the People* (Calcutta, 1859) by S. C. Mookherjee, which documents the

loyalty of the Western-educated Hindu Bengalis during the rebellion and their antipathy for the rebel cause.

35. Steel, *On the Face of the Waters*, 61–2.
36. Bhabha, *The Location of Culture*, 88.
37. For a recent feminist reading of the Anglo-Indian plot in the late-nineteenth century see Alison Sainsbury, 'Married to the Empire: The Anglo-Indian Domestic Novel', in Moore-Gilbert (ed.), *Writing India*, 163–87. Other studies of the literary construction of expatriate life include Steig, 'Indian Romances: Tracts for the Times', 2–15; Benita Parry, *Delusions and Discoveries* (1972; London, 1998); Bhupal Singh, *A Survey of Anglo-Indian Fiction* (1934; London, 1975).
38. William Sleeman, *Ramaseeana; or, a Vocabulary of the Peculiar Language used by the Thugs* (Calcutta, 1836); *Report on the Depredations Committed by the Thug Gangs of Upper and Central India, from the Cold Season of 1836–7, Down to their Gradual Suppression in the Year 1839* (Calcutta, 1840); *Report on Budhok, alias Bagree Dacoits, and other gang robbers by hereditary profession* (Calcutta, 1849).
39. See Bayly, *Empire and Information*, 352–361, for the discovery of 'little Indias' in post-rebellion ethnography.
40. Raines, *Terrible Times*, 23.
41. Mundy, *Rung Ho!* 16.
42. Pearce, *Red Revenge*, 22.
43. Mundy, *Rung Ho!* 126, 172.
44. *Ibid.*, 172.
45. R. E. Forrest, *The Afghan Knife*, 3 vols. (London, 1879), vol. I, 17. The term *wahabi* derives from Shah Wahab of Nedj, who led a militant reform movement in the Arabian peninsula in the first two decades of the nineteenth century. In India, however, the term was applied by the British administration to the followers of Ahmad Shah Barelvi, who led a revival of Islamic purism (*tariqa-i-muhamadiya*) and social reform that spread among the peasantry and the urban lower middle classes in Bihar, Bengal, the Punjab and the Frontier. Perhaps the most sustained anti-British resistance that continued from the 1820s to the late 1870s, the movement was primarily driven by an egalitarian politics, though the administration tended to view the *wahabi* as a 'fanatic'. See Qeyamuddin Ahmad, *The Wahabi Movement in India* (Calcutta, 1966) and William Hunter, *Indian Mussalmans*.
46. Forrest, *The Afghan Knife*, vol. I, 3.
47. Pearce, *Red Revenge*, 41.
48. *Ibid.*, 49.
49. *Ibid.*, p. 221. Also, see Major North's *Journal of an English Officer in India*, where a boat-ride on the Ganges and past Banaras waterfront makes North, newly arrived from England with the armies of reconquest, regret that he could not stop to see 'this wonderful city', this 'strange jumble of meanness and magnificence'. Yet without stopping by, North knows what to expect of the city: 'Banaras has been considered the chief seat of learning; it is of immense sanctity; consequently, extremely filthy.' 15, 17.

50. Forrest, *Eight Days*, 220–1.
51. *Ibid.*, 22.
52. *Ibid.*, 229.
53. Thomas Metcalf, *An Imperial Vision: Indian Architecture and Britain's Raj* (London, 1989), 22.
54. See *ibid.*, chapter 3, 'Indo-Saracenic Building Under the Raj', 55–104.
55. Reproduced in Francis W. Blagdon, *A Brief History of Ancient and Modern India. Illustrated by Thomas Daniell* (London, 1805), unpaginated. Also see Daniell's painting of a Hindu temple in *A View within the Walls of a Pagoda, Madras* in the same collection.
56. Cited in Metcalf, *An Imperial Vision*, 108.
57. Steel, *On the Face of the Waters*, 76.
58. *Ibid.*, 92.
59. H. H. Risley, *Tribes and Castes of India: Anthropometric Data*, 2 vols. (Calcutta, 1891); Christopher Pinney, 'Colonial Anthropology in the "Laboratory of Mankind"', in C. A. Bayly (ed.), *The Raj: India and the British, 1600–1947* (London, 1991), 256–9.
60. Pinney, *Colonial Anthropology*, 254 and n. 13.
61. See Cohn, Introduction, *Colonialism and its Forms of Knowledge*, for a classification of the several modalities of British knowledge of India.
62. Among others Charles Raikes, who described his visit in *Notes on the Revolt in the North-Western Provinces of India*, 81. Also see, *A Lady's Escape from Gwalior and Life in the Fort during the Mutinies of 1857* (London, 1859), where the author, Ruth Coopland, and her companions 'after gazing at the king and his son' turn to Zeenat Mahal who 'Judging by her looks . . . seemed capable of inciting the king to deeds of blood, which she was accused of having done', 276.
63. Russell, *My Indian Mutiny Diary*, 170, 171. While most British 'tourists' combined curiosity with chagrin at the ingratitude of the 'King', William Russell's account of his visit to the captured palace is tempered by an acknowledgement that British progress in India had 'depended on the bounty and favour of the lieutenants of the kings of Delhi'. *Ibid.*, 164.
64. Helenus Scott, *The Adventures of a Rupee; wherein are interspersed various anecdotes, Asiatic and European*, 3 vols (Dublin, 1782).
65. Owenson, *The Missionary*, vol. 3, 151, n.
66. George MacMunn, *The Underworld of India* (London, 1933), 16–17. Not unlike Taylor's interest in *thagi*, MacMunn's view of the 'underworld' combines the picturesque with the need to police the 'submerged tenth' of Indian population. Also see MacMunn's *Living India: Its Romance and Realities* (London, 1934).
67. Kaye, *The Sepoy War*, vol. 1, 357.
68. The Viceroy Lord Dufferin's directive of 1887 to local governments to form a Special Branch of the Police Department. Cited in Griffiths, *To Guard My People*, 344. The first two clauses of the directive reiterate the historic association of religion and political resistance. Thus, the task of the Special Branch

was to observe: '(a) all political movements and publication of seditious literature, (b) religious sects and changes in doctrine and practice having a political significance'. *Ibid.*, 344.

EPILOGUE

1. James Belich, *The New Zealand Wars and the Victorian Interpretation of Racial Conflict* (Auckland, 1986), 312.
2. Edward Leckey, *Fictions Connected with the Indian Outbreak of 1857 Exposed* (Bombay, 1859).
3. Edward J. Thompson, *The Other Side of the Medal* (London, 1925), 30.
4. F. W. Buckler, 'The Political Theory of the Indian Mutiny', in M. N. Pearson (ed.), *Legitimacy and Symbols: South Asian Writings of F. W. Buckler* (Ann Arbor, 1985), 43–73. The essay was originally published in the *Transactions of the Royal Historical Society*, 5.4. (1922), 71–100.
5. *Ibid.*, 45.
6. *Ibid.*, 45.
7. *Ibid.*, 45–6.
8. *Ibid.*, 46.
9. *Ibid.*, 46.
10. *Ibid.*, 47.

Bibliography

HISTORIES OF THE REBELLION

Ball, Charles. *History of the Indian Mutiny Giving a Detailed Account of the Sepoy Insurrection in India and a Concise History of the Great Military Events Which Have Tended to Consolidate British Empire in India.* 2 vols. London: London Printing and Publishing Company, *c.* 1859.

Buckler, F. W. 'The Political Theory of the Indian Mutiny' (1922), in M. N. Pearson (ed.), *Legitimacy and Symbols: South Asian Writings of F. W. Buckler.* Ann Arbor: Michigan University Press, 1985, 43–73.

Calcutta Review. 'The Indian Question: Its Present Aspects and Teachings', 30.60 (June 1858), 355–94.

'Our Future', 30.60 (June 1858), 423–52.

'A District during the Rebellion', 31.61 (July 1858), 54–84.

'Indian Faults and English Calumnies', 31.62 (December 1858), 443–65.

Cave-Brown, John. *The Punjab and Delhi in 1857. Being a Narrative of how the Punjab was saved and Delhi recovered during the Indian Mutiny.* 2 vols. London: Blackwood, 1861.

Chambers History of the Indian Revolt and of the Expeditions to Persia, China and Japan, 1856-7-8. With Map, Plans and Wood Engravings. London: Chambers, 1859.

Chaudhuri, S. B. *Civil Disturbances During British Rule in India, 1765–1857.* Calcutta: World Press, 1955.

Civil Rebellion in the Indian Mutinies, 1857–1859. Calcutta: World Press, 1957.

Theories of the Indian Mutiny, 1857–1859. Calcutta: World Press, 1965.

English Historical Writing on the Indian Mutiny, 1857–59. Calcutta: World Press, 1979.

Cooper, Frederick Henry. *Crisis in the Punjab from 10th May until the Fall of Delhi by a Punjab Employee.* London: Smith, Elder, 1858.

Dewar, Douglas and H. L. O. Garrett. 'Reply to Mr F. W. Buckler's Political Theory of the Indian Mutiny', *Royal Historical Society Transactions*, 7 (1924), 131–65.

Dobrulyubov, Nicolai. *The Indian National Uprising of 1857: A Contemporary Russian Account.* Tr. Harish C. Gupta. Calcutta: Nalanda, 1988.

Domin, Dolores. *India in 1857–59: A Study of the Sikhs in the People's Uprising.* Berlin: Verlag, 1977.

Duff, Alexander. *The Indian Rebellion: Its Causes and Results.* London: Nisbet, 1858.

Edwardes, Michael. *The Red Year: The Indian Rebellion of 1857.* London: Cardinal, 1975.

Embree, Ainslee T. (ed.). *1857 in India: Mutiny or War of Independence?* Boston: D. C. Heath, 1963.

English, Barbara and Rudrangshu Mukherjee. 'Debate: The Kanpur Massacres in India in the Revolt of 1857', *Past and Present*, 128 (February 1994), 169–89.

Fitchett, W. H. *Tale of the Great Mutiny.* London: Smith, Elder, 1901.

Forrest, G. W. *The Indian Mutiny: Selections from the Letters, Despatches and Other State Papers Preserved in the Military Department of the Government of India, 1857–1858.* 4 vols. Calcutta, n.p., 1893–1912.

A History of the Indian Mutiny Reviewed and Illustrated from Original Documents. 3 vols. Edinburgh: Blackwood, 1904–12.

Franjee, Dorabhoy. *The British Raj Contrasted with Its Predecessors: An Inquiry into the Disastrous Results of the Rebellion in the North-West Provinces upon the Hopes of the People of India.* London: Smith, Elder, 1858.

Frost, Thomas (ed). *A Complete Narrative of the Mutiny in India from its Commencement to the Present Time; compiled from the most authentic sources: including many very interesting letters from officers and others on the spot.* London: Reed, 1857.

Gupta, Pratul Chandra. *Nana Sahib and the Rising at Cawnpore.* Oxford: Clarendon, 1963.

Gupta, Rajanikanta. *Sipahi Juddher Itihash* (1886–1900). 5 vols. Calcutta: Nabapatra, 1981–3.

Hardikar, Srinivas Balaji. *1857 ki Chingariyan.* Kanpur: Sahitya Niketan, 1957.

Rani Lakshmibai. Delhi: National, 1968.

Nanasaheb Peshwa. Delhi: National, 1969.

Harrison, A. T. (ed.). *The Graham Indian Mutiny Papers.* Belfast: Public Records Office, 1980.

Holmes, T. R. E. *A History of the Indian Mutiny and of the Disturbances Which Accompanied it Among the Civil Population.* London: Charles Knight, 1891.

Ireland, William Witherspoon. *History of the Siege of Delhi. By an Officer who Served There: with a Sketch of the leading events in the Punjaub Connected with the Great Rebellion of 1857.* London: Adam and Charles Black, 1861.

Joshi, Puran Chand (ed.). *Rebellion 1857: A Symposium.* New Delhi: People's Publishing House, 1957.

Kaye, John W. *History of the Sepoy War in India, 1857–58.* 3 vols. London: W. H. Allen, 1864–76.

Kaye and Malleson's History of the Indian Mutiny of 1857–58. 6 vols. G. B. Malleson (ed.). London: W. H. Allen, 1889.

Keene, Henry George. *Fifty-Seven: Some Accounts of the Administration of Indian Districts During the Revolt of the Bengal Army.* London: W. H. Allen, 1883.

Khan, Syed Ahmed. *Causes of the Indian Revolt* (1858, Urdu; 1873, English). Karachi: Oxford University Press, 2000.

History of the Bijnor Rebellion. Tr. Hafeez Malik and Morris Dembo. East Lansing: Idarah-i-Adabiyat, 1982.

Ladendorf, Janice M. *The Revolt in India, 1857–58: An Annotated Bibliography of English Language Materials.* Zug: Inter Documentation, 1966.

Leckey, Edward. *Fictions Connected with the Indian Outbreak of 1857 Exposed.* Bombay: Chesson, 1859.

Lee, Joseph. *The Indian Mutiny and in Particular a Narrative of the Events at Cawnpore, June and July, 1857. By J. Lee (Now Proprietor of the Railway Hotel, Cawnpore, Formerly of the 53rd [Shropshire] Regiment of Foot. Also a Soldier of Gough's Days) Who was Present Two Hours and Ten Minutes after the Butchers completed their Sanguinary Work in the 'House of Massacre'. Supplemented by the Narrator's Travels and Visit to England and America in 1883.* Cawnpore: Victoria Press, 1893.

Lewin, Malcolm (ed.). *Causes of the Indian Revolt; by a Hindu of Bengal.* London: Edward Stanford, *c.* 1857.

Lowe, Thomas. *Central India during the Rebellion of 1857 and 1858. A Narrative of the Operations of the British Forces from the Suppression of the Mutiny in Aurangabad to the Capture of Gwalior.* London: Longman, 1860.

Ludlow, John Malcolm. *The War in Oude.* Cambridge: Macmillan, 1858.

British India: Its Races and Its History, Considered with Reference to the Mutiny of 1857: A Series of Lectures Addressed to the Students of the Working Men's College. 2 vols. Cambridge: Macmillan, 1858.

Majumdar, R. C. *The Sepoy Mutiny and the Revolt of 1857.* Calcutta: K. L. Muhkopadhyay, 1963.

Malcolm, Henry Frederick. *History of the War in India.* Philadelphia: Potter, 1859.

[Malleson, G. B.] *The Mutiny in the Bengal Army: A Historical Narrative by One Who Has Served under Sir Charles Napier.* London: Bosworth, 1858.

Malleson, G. B. *History of the Indian Mutiny, 1857–58.* London: Green, 1896.

Martin, Robert Montgomery. *The Indian Empire with a Full Account of the Mutiny of the Bengal Army.* 3 vols. London: London Printing and Publishing Company, 1858–61.

Metcalf, Thomas R. *The Aftermath of the Revolt, 1857–1870.* Princeton: Princeton University Press, 1965.

Mookherjee, Sambhu Chandra. *The Mutinies and the People, or Statements of Native Fidelity Exhibited During the Outbreak of 1857–58* (1859). Calcutta: Sanskrit Pustak Bhandar, 1969.

Muir, Sir William. *Records of the Intelligence Department of the North-West Provinces of India during the Mutiny of 1857. Including Correspondence with the Supreme Government, Delhi, Cawnpore and other Places.* 2 vols. William Coldstream (ed.). Edinburgh: Clark, 1902.

Mukherjee, Rudrangshu. *Awadh in Revolt, 1857–58: A Study of Popular Resistance.* New Delhi: Oxford University Press, 1984.

Spectre of Violence: The 1857 Kanpur Massacre. New Delhi: Viking, 1998.

Mutiny Records: Report in Two Parts. 2 vols. Lahore: Punjab Government Press, 1911.

Narrative of Events Attending the Outbreak of Disturbances and the Restoration of Authority in all the Districts of the North-West Provinces in 1857–8. Calcutta: n.p., n.d.

Narrative of Events in the North West Provinces in 1857–1858. Calcutta: n.p., n.d.

Nolan, E. H. *Illustrated History of the British Empire in India and the East, from the Earliest Times to the Suppression of the Sepoy Mutiny in 1859.* 2 vols. London: James Virtue, 1858–60.

Norton, John Bruce. *The Rebellion in India. How to Prevent Another.* London: Richardson, 1857.

Palmer, J. A. B. *The Mutiny Outbreak at Meerut in 1857.* Cambridge: Cambridge University Press, 1966.

Proceedings on the Trial of Muhammad Bahadur Shah. Titular King of Delhi, before a military commission, upon a charge of rebellion, treason, and murder . . . 1858, etc. Calcutta: n.p., 1895.

Rizvi, S. A. A. and Bhargava, M. L. (eds.). *Freedom Struggle in Uttar Pradesh.* 6 vols. Lucknow: Publications Bureau, 1957–61.

Roy, Tapati. '"Visions of the Rebels": A Study of 1857 in Bundlekhand', *Modern Asian Studies*, 27.1 (1993), 205–28.

    The Politics of a Popular Uprising: Bundlekhand in 1857. New Delhi: Oxford University Press, 1994.

Savarkar, Vinayak Damodar. *The Indian War of Independence in 1857* (1909). Bombay: Phoenix, 1957.

Scholberg, Henry. *The Indian Literature of the Great Rebellion.* New Delhi: Promilla, 1993.

Sen, Snigdha. *The Historiography of the Indian Revolt of 1857.* Calcutta: Punthi-Pustak, 1992.

Sen, Surendra Nath. *Eighteen Fifty-Seven.* Delhi: Government of India, 1958.

Seton, Rosemary. *The Indian 'Mutiny' 1857–58: A Guide to Source Material in the India Office Library and Records.* London: British Library, 1986.

Sinha, S. N. *The Revolt of 1857 in Bundlekhand.* Lucknow: Anuj, 1982.

Stokes, Eric. *The Peasant and the Raj: Studies in Agrarian Society and Peasant Rebellion in Colonial India.* Cambridge: Cambridge University Press, 1978.

    The Peasant Armed. C. A. Bayly (ed.). Oxford: Clarendon, 1986.

Taylor, P. J. O. *A Companion to the 'Indian Mutiny'.* New Delhi: Oxford University Press, 1996.

Thompson, Edward J. *The Other Side of the Medal.* London: Hogarth Press, 1925.

Thoughts of a Native of Northern India on the Rebellion, its Causes and Remedies. London: Dalton, 1858.

Trevelyan, George Otto. *Cawnpore.* London: Macmillan, 1865.

Ward, Andrew. *Our Bones are Scattered: The Cawnpore Massacres and the Indian Mutiny of 1857.* London: Murray, 1996.

FIRST-PERSON ACCOUNTS AND TRAVEL WRITING

Anderson, Robert Patrick. *A Personal Journal of the Siege of Lucknow*. Thomas Carnegie Anderson (ed.). London: Thacker, 1858.

Bartrum, Katherine. *A Widow's Reminiscence of the Siege of Lucknow*. London: James Nisbet, 1858.

Becher, Augusta. *Personal Reminiscences of India and Europe, 1830–1888*. H. G. Rawlinson (ed.). London: Constable, 1830.

Bennett, Amelia. 'Ten Months Captivity after the Massacre at Cawnpore', *Nineteenth Century*, 436 (June 1913), 1212–34, and 437 (July 1913), 78–91.

Case, Adelaide. *Day-by-day at Lucknow: A Journal of the Siege of Lucknow*. London: Richard Bentley, 1858.

Chalmers, John. *Letters from the Indian Mutiny, 1857–59*. R. Richard Terrell (ed.). Norwich: Michael Russell, 1992.

Chick, Noah. *Annals of the Indian Rebellion, 1857–58. Containing Narratives of the Outbreaks and Eventful Occurrences and Stories of Personal Adventure*. Calcutta: Sanders, 1859.

Chunder, Bholanath. *The Travels of a Hindoo to Various Parts of Bengal and Upper India*. 2 vols. London: Trübner, 1869.

Cooper, Frederick Henry. *The Crisis in the Punjab from the 10th May until the Fall of Delhi*. London: Smith, Elder, 1858.

Coopland, Ruth. *A Lady's Escape from Gwalior and Life in the Fort during the Mutinies of 1857*. London: Smith, Elder, 1859.

Duberly, Fanny. *Campaigning Experiences in Rajpootana and Central India*. London: Smith, Elder, 1859.

Eden, Emily. *Up the Country: Letters written to her Sister from the Upper Provinces of India* (1866). London: Virago, 1983.

Edwards, William. *Personal Adventures during the Indian Rebellion in Rohilcund, Futtehghur, and Oude*. London: Smith, Elder, 1858.
  Reminiscences of a Bengal Civilian. London: Smith, Elder, 1866.

Ghalib, Mirza Asadullah Khan. *Dastanbuy. A Diary of the Indian Revolt of 1857*. Tr. Khawaja Ahmad Faruqi. Delhi: University of Delhi, 1970.

Greathed, Henry Harris. *Letters Written during the Siege of Delhi*. London, 1858.

Gubbins, Martin R. *An Account of the Mutinies in Oudh and the Siege of the Lucknow Residency*. London: Richard Bentley, 1858.

Haldane, Julia. *The Story of Our Escape from Delhi in 1857*. Agra: Brown, 1888.

Halls, John James. *Two Months in Arrah in 1857*. London: Longman, 1860.

Harris, Katherine G. *A Lady's Diary of the Siege of Lucknow Written for the Perusal of Friends at Home*. London: John Murray, 1858.

Inglis, Julia Selina. *The Siege of Lucknow, A Diary*. London: Osgood, 1892.

Jivanlala, Rai Bahadur. *Short Account of the Life and family of Rai Jivan Lal Bahadur, with extracts from his diary relating to the Mutiny, 1857*. Delhi: I. M. H. Press, 1902.

Kavanagh, Thomas Henry. *How I Won the Victoria Cross*. London: Ward, 1860.

Jones, Oliver John. *Recollections of a Winter Campaign in India in 1857–58*. Saunders: n.p., 1959.

Lang, John. *Wanderings in India and other Sketches of Life in the Hindostan*. London: Routledge, 1859.

Majendie, Vivian Dering. *Up among the Pandies; or, a Year's Service in India*. London: Routledge, 1859.

Metcalfe, Charles T. *Two Native Narratives of the Mutiny in Delhi* (1898). Tr. Charles T. Metcalfe. Delhi: Seema, 1974.

North, Major. *Journal of an English Officer in India*. London: Hurst, 1858.

Paget, Mrs Leopold. *Camp and Cantonment. A Journal of Life in India in 1857–59*. London: Longman, 1865.

Parks, Fanny. *Wanderings of a Pilgrim in Search of the Picturesque* (1850). 2 vols. Karachi: Oxford University Press, 1975.

Peile, Fanny. *History of the Delhi Massacre, its supposed origin, and the means being adopted to avenge the murder of the British subjects. . . . By a Lady. the Wife of an Officer in the Bengal Army, and a Sufferer in the late Tragedy*. Liverpool: Tinling, 1858.

Pritchard, Iltudus Thomas. *The Mutinies in the Rajpootana. Being a Personal Narrative of the Mutiny at Nusseerabad, with subsequent residence at Jodpore, and a Journey across the Desert into Sind*. London: J. W. Parker, 1860.

Raikes, Charles. *Notes on the Revolt in the North-Western Provinces of India*. London: Longman, 1858.

Robertson, Henry Dundas. *District duties during the Revolt in the North-West provinces of India in 1857; with Remarks on subsequent investigations during 1858–1859*. London: Smith, Elder, 1859.

Rotton, J. W. W. *Chaplain's Narrative of the Siege of Delhi; from the Outbreak at Meerut to the Capture of Delhi*. London: Smith, Elder, 1858.

Russell, William H. *My Indian Mutiny Diary* (1860). Michael Edwardes (ed.). London: Cassell, 1957.

Shepherd, William. J. *A Personal Narrative of the Outbreak and Massacre at Cawnpore during the Sepoy Revolt of 1857*. Lucknow: Methodist Publishing House, 1886.

Sherer, J. W. *Daily Life during the Indian Mutiny: Personal Experiences of 1857*. London: Swan Sonnenschein, 1898.

Sitaram, Subahdar. *From Sepoy to Subedar. Being the Life and Adventures of a Native officer of the Bengal Army. Written and Related by Himself* (1873). Tr. James Thomas Norgate. Calcutta: Baptist Mission Press, 1911.

Thomson, Mowbray. *The Story of Cawnpore*. London: Richard Bentley, 1859.

Thornhill, Mark. *The Personal Adventures and Experiences of a Magistrate during the Rise, Progress, and Suppression of the Indian Mutiny*. London: John Murray, 1884.

Tucker, Francis (ed.). *The Memoirs of Private Henry Metcalfe*. London: Cassell, 1953.

Wilberforce, Reginald G. *An Unrecorded Chapter of the Indian Mutiny: Being the Personal Reminiscences of Reginald G. Wilberforce*. London: John Murray, 1894.

NOVELS, ETC.

Works on the rebellion are indicated by an asterisk.

*[Anon.]. *In the Company's Service: a Reminiscence*. London: W. H. Allen, 1883.

*[Anon.]. *Scenes from the Late Indian Mutinies by 'D.M.'*. London: n.p., 1858.

Arnold, William Delafield. *Oakfield, or Fellowship in the East* (1853). Leicester: Leicester University Press, 1973.

Bethell, L. A. (ed.). *Blackwood's Tales from the Outposts*. Edinburgh: Blackwood, 1942.

*Brereton, F. S. *A Hero of Lucknow: A Tale of the Indian Mutiny*. London: Blackie, 1905.

*Chesney, Sir George. *The Dilemma*. 3 vols. London: Blackwood, 1876.

*Dickens, Charles and Wilkie Collins. 'The Perils of Certain English Prisoners' (1857), *Christmas Stories*, Ruth Glancy (ed.). London: Dent, 1996, pp. 171–256.

*Doyle, Arthur Conan. *The Sign of Four* (1890). Harmondsworth: Penguin, 1982.

*Dutt, Shoshee Chunder. *Shunkur*. In *The Works of S. C. Dutt*, vol. III. London: Lovell, Reeve, 1885, 1–101.

*Fanthome, J. F. *Mariam*. Benares: Chandraprabha Press, 1896.

*Farrell, J. G. *The Siege of Krishnapur, a Novel* (1973). Harmondsworth: Penguin, 1975.

*Fenn, George Manville. *Begumbagh: A Tale of the Indian Mutiny and Other Stories*. London: Chambers, n.d.

 For the Old Flag: A Tale of the Mutiny. London: Sampson, Low, 1899.

*Forrest, R. E. *Eight Days*. 3 vols. London: Smith, Elder, 1891.

* Gibbon, Frederick P. *The Disputed VC; A Story of the Indian Mutiny*. London: Blackie, 1909.

 With Rifle and Khukri. London: Religious Tract Society, *c.* 1910.

*Grant, James. *Fairer than a Fairy; a Novel*. 3 vols. London: n.p., 1874.

 First Love and Last Love; a Tale of the Indian Mutiny. London: Routledge, 1868.

*Gray, Maxwell [Mary Gleed Tuttiett]. *In the Heart of the Storm: A Tale of Modern Chivalry*. 3 vols. London: Kegan Paul, 1891.

*Greenhow, H. M. *Brenda's Experiment*. London: Jarrold, 1896.

 The Bow of Fate. London: W. H. Allen, 1893.

Grier, S. C. [Hilda Gregg]. *Like Another Helen*. London: Blackwood, 1909.

 The Keepers of the Gate. Edinburgh: Blackwood, 1911.

*Harcourt, A. F. P. *Jenetha's Venture: A Tale of the Siege of Delhi*. London: Cassell, 1899.

 The Peril of the Sword. London: Skeffington, 1903.

*Hayman, John. *The Sword of Azrael: a Chronicle of the Great Mutiny*. London: Methuen, 1903.

Henty, G. A. *With Clive in India; Or, the Beginnings of an Empire*. London: Blackie, 1884.

 Dash for Khartoum: A Tale of the Nile Expedition. London: Blackie, 1892.

 Rujjub the Juggler. 3 vols. London: Chatto and Windus, 1893.

 In Times of Peril: A Tale of India. London: Hurst, 1899.

Hockley, William Browne. *Pandurang Hari; or the Memoirs of a Hindoo*. 3 vols. London: Whittaker, 1826.

   The English in India. 3 vols. London: Simpkin, 1828.

   The Vizier's Son; or the Adventures of a Mogul. 3 vols. London: Saunders, 1831.

   The Memoirs of a Brahmin, or the Fatal Jewels. 3 vols. London: Newby, 1843.

   Tales of the Zenana; or a Nawab's Leisure Hours (1827). 3 vols. London: Saunders, 1874.

*Irwin, H. C. *A Man of Honour*. London: Charles Black, 1896.

   With Sword and Pen: A Story of India in the Fifties. London: Fisher Unwin, 1904.

Jones, James A. *Tales of an Indian Camp*. 3 vols. London: Colburn and Bentley, 1829.

*Kaye, M. M. *Shadow of the Moon*. London: Longman, 1957.

*Kingsley, Henry. *Stretton: A Novel*. 3 vols. London: Tinsley, 1869.

Lang, John. *The Wetherbys, Father and Son; Sundry Chapters of Indian Experience*. London: Chapman and Hall, 1853.

Leslie, Mary E. *Heart Echoes from the East: Sacred Lyrics and Sonnets*. London: James Nisbet, 1861.

Lyall, Alfred C. *Verses Written in India*. London: Kegan Paul, 1896.

*Lynn, E. *A Hero of the Mutiny*. London: Chambers, *c.* 1914.

*Malet, H. P. *Lost Links in the Indian Mutiny*. London: Newby, 1867.

*Masters, John. *Nightrunners of Bengal*. London: M. Joseph, 1955.

*Merriman, H. S. *Flotsam: The Study of a Life*. London: Longmans, 1896.

Milton, C. R. *Clive*. London: Jarrolds, 1931.

*Minchin, James Innes. *Ex Oriente: Sonnets on the Indian Rebellion*. London: n.p., 1858.

*Money, Edward, *The Wife and the Ward; or, a Life's Error*. London: Routledge, 1859.

   Twelve Months with the Bashi-Bazouks. London: Chapman and Hall, 1857.

*Muddock, J. E. P. *The Great White Hand; or, the Tiger of Cawnpore*. London: Hutchinson, 1896.

*Mundy, Talbott [Sylvia Anne Matheson]. *Rung Ho! A Novel of India*. London: Cassell, 1914.

*Nisbet, Hume. *The Queen's Desire: a Romance of the Indian Mutiny*. London: F. W. White, 1893.

Owenson, Sydney, Lady Morgan. *The Missionary: An Indian Tale*. 3 vols. London: J. J. Stockdale, 1811.

   Luxima, the Prophetess. A Tale of India. 3 vols. London: Charles Westerton, 1859.

   The Missionary: An Indian Tale. Delmar: Scholars Facsimiles and Reprints, 1981.

*Partington, Norman, *And Red Flows the Ganges*. London: Collins, 1972.

*Pearce, C. E. *Love Besieged: a Romance of the Residency of Lucknow*. London: Stanley Paul, 1909.

   Red Revenge: A Romance of Cawnpore. London: Stanley Paul, *c.* 1911.

   The Star of the East: a Romance of Delhi. London: Stanley Paul, 1912.

*Phipps, Katherine C. M. *Douglas Achdale: a Tale of Lucknow*. London: Literary Society, 1885.

*Raines, G. P. *Terrible Times: a Tale of the Indian Mutiny*. London: Routledge, 1899.

Reid, C. Lestock. *The Greatest Game. A Tale of Far Eastern Byways*. London: John Lang, *c*. 1930.

  Dark Destiny. London: Phillip Allan, 1936.

  * Masque of the Mutiny. London: Temple, 1947.

Scott, Helenus. *Adventures of Rupee, wherein are interspersed various anecdotes, Asiatic and European*. 3 vols. Dublin: Whitestone, Walker, 1782.

Southey, Robert. *Thalaba, the Destroyer*. Bristol: Longman and Rees, 1801.

  The Curse of Kehama. London: Longman, Hurst, 1810.

*Stables, Gordon. *On to the Rescue: a Tale of the Indian Mutiny*. London: Shaw, 1895.

*Steel, Flora Annie. *On the Face of the Waters*. London: Heinemann, 1896.

*Sterndale, Robert A. *The Afghan Knife*. 3 vols. London: Sampson, Low, 1879.

Strang, H. *One of Clive's Heroes. A Story of the Fight for India*. London: Hodder and Stoughton, 1906.

  In Clive's Command. London: Blackie, 1906.

  * Barclay of the Guides. London: Hodder and Stroughton, 1908.

  The Air Patrol: a Story of the North-West Frontier. London: Hodder and Stoughton, 1913.

Strange, Thomas Bland. *Gunner Jingo's Jubilee*. London: Remington, 1893.

*Stuart, Alex [Violet Vivian Mann]. *The Star of Oudh*. London: Mills and Boon, 1960.

*Taylor, Lucy. *Sahib and Sepoy: or, Saving an Empire*. London: Shaw, 1897.

Taylor, Phillip Meadows. *Ralph Darnell*. 3 vols. London: Kegan Paul, 1865.

  * Seeta. 3 vols. London: Henry S. King, 1872.

  Confessions of a Thug (1839). Oxford: Oxford University Press, 1986.

Tennyson, Alfred. *Poetical Works: Including the Plays*. Oxford: Oxford University Press, 1962.

*Thomas, D. H. *The Touchstone of Peril: a Tale of the Indian Mutiny*. 2 vols. London: Fisher Unwin, 1887.

Thompson, N. F. *Intrigues of a Nabob*. London: n.p, 1780.

*Tracy, Louis. *The Red Year: a Story of the Indian Mutiny*. London: F. W. White, 1907.

Upward, Allen. *Athelstane Ford*. London: Pearson, 1899.

*Verne, Jules. *The Steam-House; or the End of the Nana Sahib*. Tr. A. D. Kingston. London: Sampson, Low, *c*. 1881.

*Wentworth, P. *The Devil's Wind*. London: Andrew Melrose, 1912.

*White, Michael. *Lachmi Bai, Rani of Jhansi. The Jeanne d'Arc of India*. New York: Taylor, 1901.

*Williamson, John Vaughan. *Fallen Heroes of the Indian War: A Poem. In Memory of Havelock and other Britons Gloriously Fallen in Defence of England's Supremacy in Asia during the Sepoy Rebellion of 1857–8*. London: Lindsey, 1858.

*Wood, J. C. *When Nicholson Kept the Border; a Tale of the Mutiny*. London: Boys' Own Paper, 1922.

HISTORICAL STUDIES, EIGHTEENTH, NINETEENTH AND TWENTIETH CENTURIES

Alavi, Seema. *Sepoys and the Company: Tradition and Transition in Northern India, 1770–1830*. New Delhi: Oxford University Press, 1995.

Anderson, David M. and David Killingray (eds.). *Policing the Empire: Government, Authority and Control, 1830–1940*. Manchester: Manchester University Press, 1991.

Anderson, George and Manilal B. Subadar. *Last Days of the Company. A Source Book of Indian History, 1818–1858*. 2 vols. London: G. Bell, 1918.

Andrews, C. F. *Maulvi Zakaullah of Delhi*. Cambridge: Heffers, 1928.

Annual Register; or a View of the History and Politics of the Year 1857. London: Rivington, 1858.

Arnold, W. D. *Short Essays on Indian and Social Subjects*. London, 1869.

Atkinson, G. F. *The Campaign in India, 1857–8: From Drawings made during the Eventful Period of the Great Mutiny*. London: Day, 1859.

Bacon, Thomas. *First Impressions and Studies from Nature in Hindostan*. 2 vols. London: W. H. Allen, 1837.

Baden-Powell, B. H. *A Short Account of the Land Revenue and its Administration in British India; with a Sketch of Land Tenures* (1907). Oxford: Clarendon, 1913.

Baden-Powell, Robert. *The Matabele Campaign, 1896. Being a Narrative of the Campaign in Suppressing the Native Rising in Matabeleland and Mashonaland*. London: Methuen, 1897.

My Adventures as a Spy. London: Pearson, 1915.

Ballhatchet, K. *Race, Sex and Class Under the Raj: Imperial Attitudes and Policies and their Critics, 1793–1905*. London: Weidenfeld and Nicholson, 1980.

Bannerjee, A. C. *Constitutional History of India*. Delhi: Macmillan, 1977–8.

Bayly, C. A. *Indian Society and the Making of the British Empire*. Cambridge: Cambridge University Press, 1988.

Empire and Information: Intelligence Gathering and Social Communication in India, 1780–1870. Cambridge: Cambridge University Press, 1996.

Origins of Nationality in South Asia: Patriotism and Ethical Government in the Making of Modern India. New Delhi: Oxford University Press, 1998.

Bayly, C. A. (ed.). *The Raj. India and the British*. London: National Portrait Gallery, 1990.

Bayly, Susan. 'Caste and "Race" in the Colonial Ethnography of India', in Peter Robb (ed.), *The Concept of Race in South Asia*. Delhi: Oxford University Press, 1997, 165–218.

Bearce, George D. *British Attitudes Towards India, 1784–1858*. Oxford: Oxford University Press, 1961.

Belich, James. *The New Zealand Wars and the Victorian Interpretation of Racial Conflict*. Auckland: Auckland University Press, 1986.

Bennett, George (ed.). *The Concept of Empire from Burke to Attlee, 1774–1947*. London: Adam and Charles Black, 1953.

Benson, A. C. and Viscount Esher (eds.). *The Letters of Queen Victoria, 1837–61*. 3 vols. London: John Murray, 1907.

Beveridge, Henry. *A Comprehensive History of India, Civil, Military and Social. From the First Landing of the British to the Sepoy Revolt*. 3 vols. London: Blackie, 1858.

Bhatnagar, G. D. *Awadh Under Wajid Ali Shah*. Varanasi: Vidya Prakashan, 1968.

Blagdon, Francis William. *A Brief History of Ancient and Modern India from the Earliest Period of Antiquity to the Termination of the Late Mahratta War. Illustrated By Thomas Daniell*. London: Edward Orme, 1805.

Blunt, Wilfred Scrawen. *The Shame of the Nineteenth Century: A Letter Addressed to the 'Times'*. London; n.p., 1900.

Bowen, H. V. *Revenue and Reform: The Indian Problem in British Politics, 1757–1773*. Cambridge: Cambridge University Press, 1991.

Bright, John. *Public Addresses*. J. E. T. Rogers (ed.). London: Macmillan, 1879.

Broome, Arthur. *History of the Rise and Progress of the Bengal Army*. Calcutta: Thacker, 1850.

Buchanan, Francis. *A Journey from Madras through the Countries of Mysore, Canara and Malabar*. London, 1807.

An Account of the Districts of Bihar and Patna in 1811–12. Patna: Bihar and Orissa Research Society, 1936.

Buckland, C. E. *Dictionary of Indian Biography*. London: Swan Sonnenschein, 1906.

Buckler, F. W. 'The Oriental Despot', *Anglican Theological Review*, 10 (1927–8), 238–49.

Burke, Edmund. *Reflections on the Revolution in France* (1790). Harmondsworth: Penguin, 1969.

Two Letters Addressed to a Member of the Present Parliament on the Proposals for Peace with the Regicide Directory of France. London: Rivington, 1796.

Burrow, John W. *A Liberal Descent: Victorian Historians and the English Past*. Cambridge: Cambridge University Press, 1981.

Butterfield, Herbert. *The Whig Interpretation of History*. New York: Norton, 1965.

Cain, P. J. and Mark Harrison (eds.). *Imperialism: Critical Concepts in Historical Studies*. 3 vols. London: Routledge, 2001.

Cain P. J. and A. G. Hopkins 'Gentlemanly Capitalism and British Imperialism: The Old Colonial System,' in P. J. Cain and Mark Harrison (eds.), *Imperialism: Critical Concepts in Historical Studies*. London: Routledge, 2001, vol. II, 301–33.

Calwell, C. E. *Small Wars: Their Principles and Practice*. London: H. M. Stationery Office, 1899.

Chatterjee, Partha. *Nationalist Thought and the Colonial World: A Derivative Discourse?* London: Zed, 1986.

Chatterji, N. 'Lawless Brigands as Soldiers of Fortune', *Journal of Indian History*, 34.2.101 (1956), 209–10.

Cheek, the Reverend Robert. *The Martyr of Allahabad. Memorials of Ensign Arthur Marcus Hill Cheek of the Sixth Native Bengal Infantry Murdered by the Sepoys at Allahabad.* James Nisbet: London, 1858.

Churchill, Winston. *My Early Years: A Roving Commission* (1930). London: Mandarin, 1989.

Cobden, Richard. *How Wars are Got up in England.* London, 1853.

Cohn, Bernard S. *An Anthropologist among Historians and Other Essays.* New Delhi: Oxford University Press, 1988.

  Colonialism and its Forms of Knowledge: The British in India. New Delhi: Oxford University Press, 1997.

Collingham, E. H. *Imperial Bodies: The Physical Experience of the Raj, 1800–1947.* Cambridge: Polity, 2001.

Comaroff, J. and J. Comaroff. *Ethnography and the Historical Imagination.* Oxford: Westview Press, 1992.

Cummerbund, Cadwallader. *From Southampton to Calcutta.* London: Saunders, Otley, 1860.

Daniell, Thomas and Daniell William. *Oriental Scenery: Containing twenty-four views of the architecture, antiquities and landscape of Hindoostan* (1795–1807). 3 vols. London: Longman, Hurst, 1815.

Das, Sisir Kumar. *Sahibs and Munshis: An Account of the Fort William College.* New Delhi: Orion, 1978.

Davies, Phillip. *Splendours of the Raj: British Architecture in India, 1660–1947.* London: Murray, 1985.

Desai, A. R. *Social Background of Indian Nationalism.* (4th edn). Bombay: Popular Prakashan, 1966.

Dewey, C. J. *Anglo-Indian Attitudes: The Mind of the Indian Civil Service.* London: Hambledon, 1993.

Dharker, C. D. (ed.). *Lord Macaulay's Legislative Minutes.* London: Oxford University Press, 1946.

Dilke, Charles Wentworth. *Greater Britain: A Record of Travels in the English-Speaking Countries during 1866 and 1867.* New York: Harper, 1869.

Dow, Alexander. *The History of Hindostan from the Earliest Account of Time to the Death of Akbar. Translated from the Persian of Mahmud Casim Ferishta of Delhi: Together with a Dissertation Concerning Religion and Philosophy of the Brahmins with an Appendix containing the History of the Mughal Empire from its Decline in the Reign of Mahummud Shaw, to the Present Time.* 2 vols. London: Becket and De Hondt, 1768.

  History of Hindostan from the Death of Akbar to the Complete Settlement of the Empire under Aurangzebe. To which are Prefixed (1) A Dissertation on the Origin and Nature of Despotism in Hindostan. (2) An Enquiry into the state of Bengal; with a Plan for restoring that kingdom to its former Prosperity and Splendour. London: Becket and De Hondt, 1772.

Dumont, Louis. *Homo Hierarchicus: The Caste System and its Implications.* Tr. Mark Sainsbury *et al.* Chicago: Chicago University Press, 1970.

Edwardes, Major Herbert M. *A Year on the Punjab Frontier in 1848–49*. 2 vols. London: Richard Bentley, 1851.

Elliott, Charles Alfred. *Chronicles of Oonao, a District in Oudh*. Allahabad: Mission Press, 1862.

Elphinstone, Montstuart. *The History of India*. 2 vols. London: John Murray, 1841.

Embree, Ainslee. *Charles Grant and British Rule in India*. London: Allen and Unwin, 1962.

Everett, I. *Observations on India. By a Resident there many years*. London: Chapman, 1853.

Farwell, Byron. *Armies of the Raj: From the Mutiny to Independence, 1858–1947*. London: Viking, 1989.

Fidler, David P. and Jennifer M. Welsh. *Empire and Community: Edmund Burke's Writings on International Relations*. Boulder, CO: Westview Press, 1999.

Finkenstein, David and Douglas M. Peers (eds.). *Negotiating India in the Nineteenth-Century Media*. Basingstoke: Macmillan, 2000.

Fisher, Michael H. *A Clash of Cultures: Awadh, the British, and the Mughals*. New Delhi: Sangam, 1987.

Forbes, James. *Oriental Memoirs*. 4 vols. London: n.p., 1813.

Gallagher, J. A. and Robinson, R. E. 'The Imperialism of Free Trade', *Economic History Review*, 2nd series, 6 (1953), 1–53.

Gopal, S. *British Policy in India, 1858–1905*. Cambridge: Cambridge University Press, 1965.

Grant, Charles. *Observations on the State of Society Among the Asiatic Subjects of Great Britain, particularly with Respect to Morals; and on the means of improving it. Written chiefly in the year 1792. Ordered by the House of Commons to be Printed, 15 June 1813*. London: n.p., 1813; *Parliamentary Papers* (1812–13), vol. x, paper 282.

Grewal, J. S. *Muslim Rule in India: The Assessment of British Historians*. Calcutta: Oxford University Press, 1970.

Griffiths, Percival. *To Guard My People: The History of the Indian Police*. London: Ernest Benn, 1971.

Guha, Ranajit. *Elementary Aspects of Peasant Insurgency in Colonial India*. New Delhi: Oxford University Press, 1983.

  'The Prose of Counter-Insurgency', in Ranajit Guha (ed.), *Subaltern Studies II*. New Delhi: Oxford University Press, 1983, 1–42.

  An Indian Historiography of India: A Nineteenth-Century Agenda and its Implications. Calcutta: Centre for Studies in Social Sciences, 1988.

Gupta, Maya. *Lord William Bentinck and the Vellore Mutiny*. New Delhi: Capital, 1986.

Gupta, Narayani. *Delhi between Two Empires, 1803–1931: Society, Government and Urban Growth*. Delhi: Oxford University Press, 1981.

Hamburger, Joseph. *Macaulay and the Whig Tradition*. Chicago: University of Chicago Press, 1976.

Hardy, Peter. *Muslims of British India*. Cambridge: Cambridge University Press, 1972.

Heesterman, J. C. 'Was There an Indian Reaction? Western Expansion in Indian Perspective', in H. L. Wesseling (ed.), *Expansion and Reaction*. Leiden: Leiden University Press, 1978, 31–58.

Hilton, Boyd. *The Age of Atonement: The Influence of Evangelicalism on Social and Economic Thought, 1785–1865*. Oxford: Clarendon, 1988.

Hilton, Edward H. *The Tourist's Guide to Lucknow. By One of the Beleaguered Garrison*. (8th edn). Lucknow: Methodist Publishing House, 1916.

Hunter, William Wilson. *The Indian Mussalmans: Are They Bound in Conscience to Rebel Against the Queen?* (1871). (3rd edn). London: n.p., 1876.

The Imperial Gazetteer of India. 9 vols. London: Trübner, 1881.

Johnson, George W. *Stranger in India; or, three years in Calcutta*. Calcutta: Henry Coburn, 1843.

Jones, Sir William. *Works*. 13 vols. Lady Anna Maria Jones (ed.). London: J. Stockdale, 1799.

Kaye, John W. *The Administration of the East India Company*. London: Richard Bentley, 1853.

Lives of Indian Officers: Illustrative of the Civil and Military Services of India (1867). 2 vols. London: W. H. Allen, 1889.

Keith, Arthur Berridale. *A Constitutional History of India, 1600–1935*. 1930; rpt. New Delhi: D. K. Publishers, 1996.

Khan, Syed Ahmad. *Review on Dr Hunter's Indian Mussalmans: Are They Bound in Conscience to Rebel Against the Queen?* Benares: Medical Hall Press, 1872.

Kidwai, S. R. *Gilchrist and the 'Language of Hindostan'*. Delhi: Rachna, 1972.

Knighton, William. *The Private Life of an Eastern King. Compiled for a member of the household of his late Majesty, Nussir-u-Deen, King of Oude*. London: Hope, 1855.

Kolff, D. H. A. *Naukar, Rajput and Sepoy*. Cambridge: Cambridge University Press, 1990.

Laird, M. A. *Missionaries and Education in Bengal. 1793–1837*. Oxford: Clarendon, 1972.

Lal, K. 'The Sack of Delhi as Witnessed by Ghalib', *Bengal Past and Present*, 74.138 (1955), 102–12.

Lawrence, Henry. *Essays, Military and Political. Written in India*. London: Allen, 1859.

Lawson, Phillip. *The East India Company. A History*. London: Longman, 1993.

Lively, Jack and John Rees (eds.). *Utilitarian Logic and Politics: James Mill's 'Essay on Government', Macaulay's Critique and the Ensuing Debate*. Oxford: Oxford University Press, 1978.

Llewellyn-Jones, Rosie. *A Fatal Friendship: The Nawabs, The British and the City of Lucknow*. New Delhi: Oxford University Press, 1985.

Low, D. A. *The Lion Rampant: Essays in the Study of British Imperlialism*. London: Frank Cass, 1973.

Lucas, Samuel. *Dacoitee in Excelsis: or, The Spoilation of Oude by the East India Company* (*c.* 1857). Lucknow: Pustak Kendra, 1971.

Lyall, Alfred C. *Asiatic Studies, Religious and Social.* London: John Murray, 1882.
Rise and Expansion of British Dominion in India. London: John Murray, 1894.

Macaulay, T. B. 'Lord Clive' (1840), in T. B. Macaulay, *Critical and Historical Essays.* 2 vols. London: Dent, 1961, vol. II, 479–549.
'Hallam's Constitutional History,' in *Lord Macaulay's Essays and the Lays of Ancient Rome.* London: Longmans, Green, 1891, 51–99.

Maclagan, Michael. *'Clemency' Canning: Charles John, 1st Earl Canning, Governor-General and Viceroy of India, 1856–1862.* London: Macmillan, 1962.

MacMunn, George. *The Underworld of India.* London: Jarrolds, 1933.
Living India: Its Romance and Realities. London: C. Bell, 1934.

Mahajan, Jagmohan. *The Raj Landscape: British Views on Indian Cities.* New Delhi: Spantech, 1988.

Maine, Henry Sumner. *Village-Communities in the East and the West.* London: John Murray, 1871.

Majumdar, R. C. (ed.). *British Paramountcy and Indian Renaissance.* Bombay: Bharatiya Vidya Bhavan, 1963.

Marshall, P. J. *The Impeachment of Warren Hastings.* Oxford: Oxford University Press, 1965.
'British Emigration into India in the Nineteenth Century', in P. C. Emmer and M. Mörner (ed.), *European Expansion and Migration Essays on the Inter-continental Migration from Africa, Asia, and Europe.* New York: Berg, 1992, 179–96.

Marshall, P. J. (ed.). *The Writings and Speeches of Edmund Burke. Vol. v. India: Madras and Bengal, 1774–1785.* Oxford: Clarendon, 1981.

McLaren, Martha. 'From Analysis to Prescription: Scottish Concepts of Asian Despotism in Early Nineteenth-Century British India', *International History Review*, 15 (1993), 469–501.

Mehta, Uday Singh. *Liberalism and Empire: A Study in Nineteenth-century British Liberal Thought.* Chicago: University of Chicago Press, 1999.

Metcalf, Thomas R. *An Imperial Vision: Indian Architecture and Britain's Raj.* London: Faber, 1989.
Ideologies of the Raj. Cambridge: Cambridge University Press, 1997.

Mill, James. *History of British India* (1817). (5th edn). 10 vols. H. H. Wilson (ed.). London: James Madden: 1858; rpt. London: Routledge, 1997.

Mill, John Stuart. *On Liberty and other Essays.* John Gray (ed.). Oxford: Oxford University Press, 1998.

Mishra, B. B. *The Indian Middle Classes: Their Growth in Modern Times.* London: Oxford University Press, 1961.

Moore, R. J. *Liberalism and Indian Politics: 1872–1922.* London: Edward Arnold, 1966.

Morris, Henry. *Heroes of our Indian Empire.* 2 vols. London: Christian Literature Society for India, 1908.

Neill, Stephen. *A History of Christianity in India.* 2 vols. Cambridge: Cambridge University Press, 1984.

O'Malley, L. S. S. *The Indian Civil Service, 1601–1930.* London: Frank Cass, 1965.

Omissi, David. *The Sepoy and the Raj: The Indian Army, 1860–1940.* London: Macmillan, 1994.

Pearson, Charles H. *National Life and Character: A Forecast.* London: Macmillan, 1893.

Peers, Douglas M. *Between Mars and Mammon: Colonial Armies and the Garrison State in India, 1819–1835.* London: Tauris, 1995.

'"Those Noble Exemplars of True Military Tradition": Constructions of the Indian Army in the Mid-Victorian Press', *Modern Asian Studies,* 31.1 (1997), 109–42.

Pemble, John. *The Raj, The Indian Mutiny, and the Kingdom of Oudh, 1810–1859.* New Jersey: Harvester, 1977.

Penner, Peter. *The Patronage Bureaucracy in North India: The Robert M. Bird and James Thomason School, 1820–70.* Delhi: Chanakya, 1986.

Philips, C. H. *The East India Company, 1784–1834.* Manchester: Manchester University Press, 1940.

Popplewell, Richard. *Intelligence and Imperial Defence: British Intelligence and the Defence of the Indian Empire, 1904–1924.* London: Frank Cass, 1995.

Porter, Andrew. 'Gentlemanly Capitalism and Empire: The British Experience since 1750', *Journal of Commonwealth and International History,* 18.3 (October 1990), 265–95.

Potts, E. D. *British Baptist Missionaries in India, 1793–1837.* Cambridge: Cambridge University Press, 1967.

Prescott, William Hickling. *History of the Conquest of Mexico and History of the Conquest of Peru* (1843–4). New York: Modern Library, 1961.

Raikes, Charles. *Notes on the North-Western Provinces of India.* London: Chapman and Hall, 1852.

Reeves, P. D. (ed.). *Sleeman in Oude: An Abridgement of W.H. Sleeman's 'A Journey Through the Kingdom of Oudh in 1849–50'.* Cambridge: Cambridge University Press, 1971.

Rendall, Jane. 'Scottish Orientalism: From Robertson to James Mill', *The Historical Journal,* 25.1 (1982), 43–69.

Renford, R. K. *The Non-Official British in India to 1920.* New Delhi: Oxford University Press, 1987.

Robertson, William. *A Historical Disquisition concerning the Knowledge the Ancients had of India.* Dublin: J. J. Tourneisen, 1791.

Robinson, Ronald and John Gallagher. *Africa and the Victorians: The Official Mind of Imperialism.* London: Macmillan, 1961.

Robson, John M., Martin Moir and Zawahir Moir (eds.). *The Indian Writings of John Stuart Mill.* Toronto: University of Toronto Press, 1990.

Rosselli, John. *Lord William Bentinck: The Making of a Liberal Imperialist, 1774–1839.* London: Chatto and Windus, 1974.

Ruskin, John. *A Knight's Faith: Passages in the Life of Sir Herbert Edwardes*, in John Ruskin (ed.), *Bibliotheca Pastorum*, vol. IV. London: n.p., 1875–85.

Ryan, Alan (ed.). *Utilitarianism and other Essays: J. S. Mill and Jeremy Bentham.* London: Penguin, 1987.

Sarkar, Sumit. *The Swadeshi Movement in Bengal, 1903–1908.* New Delhi: People's Publishing House, 1973.

Seeley, John. *The Expansion of England.* London: Bernhard Tauchnitz, 1883.

Semmel, B. *The Governor Eyre Controversy.* London: McGibbon, 1962.

Sen, S. P. (ed.). *Historians and Historiography in Modern India.* Calcutta: Institute of Historical Studies, 1973.

Singh, Nihar Nandan. *British Historiography on British Rule in India. The Life and Writings of Sir John William Kaye, 1814–76.* Patna: Janki, 1986.

Sleeman, William. *A Journey Through the Kingdom of Oude in 1849–50.* 2 vols. London: Bentley, 1858.

  Report on the Depredations Committed by the Thug Gangs of Upper and Central India, from the Cold Season of 1836–37, Down to their Gradual Suppression in the Year 1839. Calcutta: Military Orphan Press, 1840.

Smith, Goldwin. *The Empire: A series of letters printed in the 'Daily News', 1862, 1863.* Oxford: n.p., 1863.

Southey, Robert. *History of Brazil.* 3 vols. London: Longman, Hurst, 1810–19.

Spear, Percival. *A History of Delhi under the Later Mughals.* New Delhi: D. K. Publishers, 1995.

  The Nabobs: A Study of the Social Life of the English in Eighteenth-Century India (1932). London: Oxford University Press, 1963.

Stephen, James Fitzjames. *Liberty, Equality, Fraternity.* R. J. White (ed.). Cambridge: Cambridge University Press, 1967.

Stocking, George W. Jr. (ed.). *Colonial Situations: Essays on the Contextualisation of Ethnographic Knowledge.* Madison: University of Wisconsin Press, 1991.

  Victorian Anthropology. New York: The Free Press, 1987.

Stokes, Eric. *The English Utilitarians and India.* Oxford: Clarendon, 1959.

Stone, Lawrence (ed.). *An Imperial State at War: Britain from 1689 to 1815.* London: Routledge, 1994.

Taylor, Miles. 'Imperium et Libertas? Rethinking the Radical Critique of Imperialism during the Nineteenth Century', *Journal of Commonwealth and Imperial History*, 19.1 (January 1991), 1–23.

Thomas, William. *The Philosophic Radicals: Nine Studies in Theory and Practice, 1817–1841.* Oxford: Clarendon, 1979.

Tidrick, Katherine. *Empire and the English Character.* London: Tauris, 1990.

Tod, Lt. Col. James. *Annals and Antiquities of Rajast'han: or, the Central and Western Rajpoot States of India* (1829–32). London: Smith, Elder, 1914.

Trevelyan, Charles. *On the Education of the People of India.* London: n.p., 1838.

Trotter, Lionel James. *The Bayard of India: A Life of General Sir James Outram.* Edinburgh: Blackwood, 1903.

  The Life of John Nicholson: Soldier and Administrator. London: John Murray, 1897.

Wesseling, H. L. *Imperialism and Colonialism: Essays on the History of European Expansion*. Westport, CT: Greenwood Press, 1997.

Whelen, Frederick G. *Edmund Burke and India: Political Morality and Empire*. Pittsburg: University of Pittsburg Press, 1996.

White, Arnold. *Efficiency and Empire*. London: Methuen, 1901.

Wickmire, Franklin B. and Mary Wickmire. *Cornwallis, The Imperial Years*. Chapel Hill: University of North Carolina Press, 1980.

Wilks, Mark. *Historical Sketches of South India in an Attempt to trace the History of Mysoor from the origins of the Hindoo Government of the State to the extinction of the Mohammedan Dynasty in 1799*. 3 vols. London: n.p., 1810–17.

Yalland, Zöe. *Boxwallahs: The British in Cawnpore, 1857–1901*. Wilby: M. Russell, 1994.

    Traders and Nabobs: The British in Cawnpore, 1765–1857. Salisbury: M. Russell, 1987.

Young, G. M. (ed.). *Macaulay: Prose and Poetry*. Cambridge: Cambridge University Press, 1970.

Zastoupil, Lynn. *John Stuart Mill and India*. Stanford, CA: Stanford University Press, 1994.

Zavos, John. *The Emergence of Hindu Nationalism in India*. New Delhi: Oxford University Press, 2000.

LITERARY AND CULTURAL STUDIES, NINETEENTH AND TWENTIETH CENTURIES

Adams, Percy. *Travel Literature and the Evolution of the Novel*. Lexington: University of Kentucky Press, 1983.

Ahmad, Leila. 'Western Ethnocentrism and Perceptions of the Harem', *Feminist Studies*, 8.3 (1982), 521–34.

Arnold, Guy. *Held Fast for England: G. A. Henty, Imperialist Boys' Writer*. London: Hamish Hamlinton, 1980.

Asad, Talal (ed.). *Anthopology and the Colonial Encounter*. London: Ithaca Press, 1973.

Bann, Stephen. *The Inventions of History: Essays on the Representation of the Past*. Manchester: Manchester University Press, 1990.

    The Clothing of Clio: A Study of the Representation of History in Nineteenth-Century Britain and France. Cambridge: Cambridge University Press, 1984.

Barker, Francis *et al.* (eds.). *Europe and its Others*. 2 vols. Colchester: University of Essex Press, 1985.

Barrell, John. *The Infection of De Quincey: A Psychopathology of Imperialism*. New Haven: Yale University Press, 1991.

Bassinger, Tim and Tom Flynn. *Colonialism and the Object: Empire, Material Culture and the Museum*. London: Routledge, 1998.

Bhabha, Homi K. *The Location of Culture*. London: Routledge, 1994.

Brantlinger, Patrick. *Rule of Darkness: British Literature and Imperialism, 1830–1914*. Ithaca: Cornell University Press, 1988.

Breckenridge, C. and P. Van der Veer (ed.). *Orientalism and the Post-Colonial Predicament*. Philadelphia: University of Pennsylvania Press, 1993.

Bristow, Joseph. *Empire Boys: Adventures in a Man's World*. Manchester: Manchester University Press, 1991.

Cannon, Garland. 'The Literary Place of Sir William Jones', *Journal of the Asiatic Society*, 2.1 (1960), 47–61.

The *Life and Mind of Oriental Jones: Sir William Jones, the Father of Modern Linguistics*. Cambridge: Cambridge University Press, 1990.

Clark, Gail S. 'Imperial Stereotypes: G. A Henty and the Boys' Own Empire', *Journal of Popular Culture*, 18.4 (Spring 1985), 43–51.

Colley, Linda. *Britons: Forging the Nation, 1707–1837*. London: Pimlico, 1992.

Conant, Martha Pike. *The Oriental Tale in England in the Eighteenth Century*. New York: Columbia University Press, 1908.

Crane, Ralph J. *Inventing India: A History of India in English-Language Fiction*. Basingstoke: Macmillan, 1992.

Das, Sisir Kumar. *A History of Indian Literature: 1800–1910, Western Impact: Indian Response*. New Delhi: Sahitya Akademi, 1991.

David, Deirdre. *Rule Britannia: Women, Empire and Victorian Writing*. Ithaca: Cornell University Press, 1995.

Dawson, Graham. *Soldier Heroes: British Adventure, Empire and the Imagining of Masculinities*. London: Routledge, 1991.

Dirks, Nicholas (ed.). *Colonialism and Culture*. Ann Arbor: University of Michigan Press, 1992.

Dixon, Robert. *Writing the Colonial Adventure. Race, Gender and Nation in Anglo-Australian Popular Fiction, 1875–1914*. Cambridge: Cambridge University Press, 1995.

Dixon, W. Hepworth (ed.). *Lady Morgan's Memoirs: Autobiography, Diaries and Correspondence*. 2 vols. London: W. H. Allen, 1863.

Drew, John. *India and the Romantic Imagination*. New Delhi: Oxford University Press, 1987.

Druce, Robert. '"And to think that Henrietta Guise was in the hands of such human demons": Ideologies of Anglo-Indian Novels from 1859 to 1947', in C. C. Barfoot and Theo D'haen (ed.), *Shades of Empire in Colonial and Post-Colonial Literatures*. Amsterdam: Rodolphi, 1993, 17–34.

Duane, Patrick A. 'Boy's Literature and the Idea of Empire, 1870–1914', *Victorian Studies*, 24.1 (Autumn 1980), 105–21.

Ellis, S. M. *The Solitary Horseman; or, the Life and Adventures of G. P. R. James*. London: Cayne, 1927.

Fanon, Franz. *The Wretched of the Earth* (1961). Tr. Constance Farrington. London: Penguin, 1990.

Fenn, G. M. *George Alfred Henty: The Story of an Active Life*. London: Blackie, 1907.

Finkelstein, David and Douglas Peers (ed.). *Negotiating India in the Nineteenth-Century Media*. Basingstoke: Macmillan, 2000.

Fitzpatrick, W. J. *Lady Morgan: Her Career, Literary and Personal*. London: Charles J. Skeet, 1860.

Frye, Northrop. 'New Directions for Old,' in Henry A. Murray (ed.), *Myth and Mythmaking*. Boston: Beacon, 1960, 115–31.

Gates, Henry Louis Jr. (ed.). *'Race', Writing, Difference*. Chicago: University of Chicago Press, 1986.

Ghosh, Indira. *Women Travellers in Colonial India*. Delhi: Oxford University Press, 1997.

Girouard, Mark. *The Return to Camelot: Chivalry and the English Gentleman*. New Haven: Yale University Press, 1981.

Graham, Sarah. *An Introduction to William Gordon Stables*. Twyford: Twyford and Ruscombe Local History Society, 1982.

Green, Martin. *Dreams of Adventure and Deeds of Empire*. London: Routledge, 1980.

Green, Roger Lancelyn. *Teller of Tales: British Authors of Children's Books from 1800–1964*. New York: Watts, 1965.

Greenberger, Allen J. *The British Image of India: A Study in the Literature of Imperialism: 1880–1960*. Oxford: Oxford University Press, 1969.

Gregg, Hilda. 'The Indian Mutiny in Fiction', *Blackwood's Edinburgh Magazine* (February 1897), 218–31.

Gupta, Brijen Kishore. *India in English Fiction: 1800–1970; Annotated Bibliography*. Metuchen: The Scarecrow Press, 1973.

Helgerson, Richard. 'Camoes, Hakluyt, and the Voyages of Two Nations', in Nicholas Dirks (ed.). *Colonialism and Culture*. Ann Arbor: University of Michigan Press, 1992, 27–63.

Hyam, R. *Empire and Sexuality: The British Experience*. Manchester: Manchester University Press, 1990.

Jameson, Frederic. *The Political Unconscious: Narrative as a Socially Symbolic Act*. London: Methuen, 1981.

Katz, Wendy R. *Rider Haggard and the Fiction of Empire*. Cambridge: Cambridge University Press, 1987.

Kaul, Chandrika. 'Imperial Communications, Fleet Street and the Indian Empire: c. 1850–1920', in Michael Bromley and Tom O'Malley (eds.), *A Journalism Reader*. London: Routledge, 1997.

Kaye, J. W. 'English Literature in India', *Calcutta Review*, 5 (1846), 202–20.
'Military Life and Adventure in the East', *Calcutta Review*, 8 (1847), 195–230.
'Poetry of Recent Indian Warfare', *Calcutta Review*, 11 (1848), 220–56.
'The Romance of Indian Warfare', *North British Review*, 12 (1849), 193–224.

Kejariwal, O. P. *The Asiatic Society of Bengal and the Discovery of India's Past, 1784–1838*. New Delhi: Oxford University Press, 1988.

Kopf, D. *British Orientalism and the Bengal Renaissance, 1773–1835*. Berkeley: University of California Press, 1969.

Leask, Nigel. *British Romantic Writers and the East: Anxieties of Empire*. Cambridge: Cambridge University Press, 1992.
'Towards an Anglo-Indian poetry? The Colonial Muse in the writings of John Leyden, Thomas Medwin, and Charles D'Oyly', in Bart Moore-Gilbert (ed.). *Writing India, 1757–1990: The Literature of British India*. Manchester: Manchester University Press, 1996, 52–85.

Levin, David. *History as Romantic Art: Bancroft, Prescott, Motley, and Parkman.* Stanford, CA: Stanford University Press, 1959.

Lyall, Alfred C. *Studies in Literature and History.* London: John Murray, 1915.

MacDonald, R. H. *The Language of Empire: Myths and Metaphors of Popular Imperialism, 1880–1918.* Manchester: Manchester University Press, 1994.

Sons of Empire: The Frontier and the Boy Scouts' Movement, 1890–1918. Toronto: University of Toronto Press, 1993.

Mackenzie, J. *Orientalism, History, Theory, and the Arts.* Manchester: Manchester University Press, 1995.

Mackenzie, J. (ed.). *Imperialism and Popular Culture.* Manchester: Manchester University Press, 1986.

Imperialism and the Natural World. Manchester: Manchester University Press, 1990.

Popular Imperialism and the Military: 1850–1950. Manchester: Manchester University Press, 1992.

MacMillan, Margaret. *Women of the Raj.* London: Thames and Hudson, 1988.

Majeed, J. *'Ungoverned Imaginings': James Mill's History of British India and Orientalism.* Oxford: Clarendon, 1992.

Mangan, J. A. (ed.). *'Benefits Bestowed'? Education and British Imperialism.* Manchester: Manchester University Press, 1988.

Making Imperial Mentalities: Socialisation and British Imperialism. Manchester: Manchester University Press, 1990.

Mishra, Udayon. *The Raj in Fiction: A Study of Nineteenth-century British Attitudes towards India.* Delhi: B. R. Publication, 1987.

Mitter, Partha. *Much-Maligned Monsters: History of European Reaction to Indian Art.* Oxford: Clarendon, 1977.

Art and Nationalism in Colonial India, 1850–1922: Occidental Orientations. Cambridge: Cambridge University Press, 1994.

Moore-Gilbert, Bart (ed.). *Writing India, 1757–1990: The Literature of British India.* Manchester: Manchester University Press, 1996.

Oaten, E. F. *A Sketch of Anglo-Indian Literature.* London: Kegan Paul, 1908.

Odie, William. 'Dickens and the Indian Mutiny', *The Dickensian*, 68.366 (1972), 3–15.

Park, Hyunji. '"The Story of our Lives": *The Moonstone* and the Indian Mutiny in *All the Year Round*', in David Finkelstein and Douglas Peers (eds.), *Negotiating India in the Nineteenth-Century Media*, Basingstoke: Macmillan, 2000, 84–109.

Parry, Benita. *Delusions and Discoveries: Studies on India in the British Imagination, 1880–1930* (1972). London: Verso, 1998.

Paxton, Nancy. 'Mobilizing Chivalry: Rape in British Indian Novels about the Indian Uprising of 1857', *Victorian Studies*, 36 (Fall 1992), 5–30.

Peters, Laura. '"Double-dyed Traitors and Infernal Villains": *Illustrated London News, Household Words*, Charles Dickens and the Indian Rebellion', in David Finkelstein and Douglas Peers (eds.), *Negotiating India in the Nineteenth-Century Media*, Basingstoke: Macmillan, 2000, 110–34.

Pinney, Christopher. 'Colonial Anthropology in the "Laboratory of Mankind"', in C. A. Bayly (ed.), *The Raj: India and the British, 1600–1947*. London: National Portrait Gallery, 1991, 252–9.

Pratt, Marie Louise. *Imperial Eyes: Travel Writing and Transculturalism*. London: Routledge, 1992.

Richards, Jeffrey (ed.). *Imperialism and Juvenile Literature*. Manchester: Manchester University Press, 1989.

Richards, Thomas. *The Imperial Archive: Knowledge and the Fantasy of Empire*. London: Verso, 1993.

Rousseau, G. S. and Roy Porter (eds.). *Exoticism in the Enlightenment*. Manchester: Manchester University Press, 1990.

Rubin, David. *After the Raj: British Novels of India since 1947*. Hanover: New England University Press, 1986.

Russell, Ralph (ed.). *Ghalib: The Poet and his Age*. London: Allen and Unwin, 1972.

Said, Edward. *Orientalism: Western Conceptions of the Orient*. New York: Pantheon, 1978.

Schwab, Raymond. *The Oriental Renaissance: Europe's Rediscovery of India and the East, 1680–1880*. Tr. Gene Patterson-Black and Victor Reinking. New York: Columbia University Press, 1984.

Sencourt, Robert. *India in English Literature*. London: Simpkin, Marshall and Co., 1925.

Sharpe, Jenny. *The Allegories of Empire: Figure of the Woman in the Colonial Text*. Minneapolis: Minnesota University Press, 1993.

Shattock, Joanne and Michael Wolff (eds.). *The Victorian Periodical Press: Samplings and Soundings*. Leicester: Leicester University Press, 1982.

Singh, Bhupal. *A Survey of Anglo-Indian Fiction* (1934). London: Curzon Press, 1975.

Steig, Margaret F. 'Indian Romances: Tracts for the Times', *Journal of Popular Culture*, 18.4 (Spring 1985), 2–15.

Sutherland, John. *The Longman Companion to Victorian Fiction*. Harlow: Longman, 1988.

Teltscher, Kate. *India Inscribed: European and British Writing on India, 1600–1800*. New Delhi: Oxford University Press, 1995.

Thomas, Nicholas. *Colonialism's Culture: Anthropology, Travel and Government*. Cambridge: Polity, 1994.

Tillotson, G. H. R. 'The Indian Picturesque: Images of India in British Painting, 1780–1880', in C. A. Bayly (ed.). *The Raj: India and the British*. London: National Portrait Gallery, 1990, 131–51.

White, Hayden. *Tropics of Discourse: Essays in Cultural Criticism*. Baltimore: Johns Hopkins University Press, 1978.

Wurgraft, Lewis, D. *The Imperial Imagination: Magic and Myth in Kipling's India*. Middletown, DE: Wesleyan University Press, 1983.

Index list